# GOOD *enough* PARENTING

"In a world of too much information, Good Enough Parenting teaches parents how to *meet core emotional needs*, and, at the same time, how to avoid passing down their own dysfunctional behaviors. Schema Therapy has been successful with adults, but I have always wanted to see someone do something on preventing schemas, or Lifetraps, in children, and here it is!"

— **Dr. Jeffrey Young**, *Dept. of Psychiatry,*
*Columbia University, New York Founder, Schema Therapy*

"This ground-breaking book will help parents raise healthier children, and when they grow up, healthier and more successful adults. I highly recommend it."

— **Charles L Whitfield**, M.D.
*International bestselling author, "Healing the Child Within";*
*"Wisdom to Know the Difference: Core Issues in Relationships, Recovery and Living"*

"Some experts propose that the best gift we can give to our children is a healthy parent. *Good Enough Parenting* offers us the opportunity to peer into the complexities of our own personalities, life traps, and coping styles, to discover those unique challenging moments in parenting…the ones that can activate longstanding personal struggles as well as amazing strengths. In addition to providing clear and accessible information, along with powerful tools for effective parenting, John and Karen Louis invite the reader to experience an investigative journey into the "personal" trappings and triggers that occur under the condition of being a parent. You will find step-by-step strategies for overcoming some of the most difficult obstacles, not the least of which is learning how to eliminate the unhealthy distraction of critical self-judgments in favor of harnessed responsibility and joyfulness, and managed expectations. Grounded in the robust foundational work of the evidenced-based Schema Therapy approach, *Good Enough Parenting* will be a valuable asset to your library."

— **Wendy Behary**
*Author, "Disarming the Narcissist…Surviving and Thriving with the Self-Absorbed"*
*President, International Society of Schema Therapy (ISST)*

"In *Good Enough Parenting*, John and Karen Louis put powerful new understandings and tools into parents' hands and show them, with an engaging blend of clarity, authority, warmth, openness and humility, exactly how to use these to transform the quiet day to day moments, common challenges and emotional crises of parenthood into opportunities to set their children on the path to flourishing as adults. In this first of its kind guide, John and Karen integrate the insights and strategies of an important new approach to meeting core emotional needs, Schema Therapy, with the latest research related to parenting. They do so in a way that makes clear their extensive experience in helping parents, as church leaders and as parents; doing full justice to the complexity and challenges of parenting and yet keeping it simple and clear enough to be of immediate and practical relevance. Parents and professionals helping parents should read this book."

— **George Lockwood**, Ph.D., *Director, Schema Therapy Institute Midwest Representative for Public Affairs, International Society of Schema Therapy (ISST)*

"This handbook presents a detailed and scientifically based schema perspective on parenting, linking theoretical knowledge with expressive examples from everyday life (including from the authors' own family) plus vivid cartoons. The tone of the book is non-judgmental, warm and encouraging, while the title 'good enough parenting' cautions us against unrelenting standards."

— **Eckhard Roediger**, M.D., *Secretary, International Society of Schema Therapy (ISST) Frankfurt*

"The heart of practicing Schema Therapy is healing the wounds and trauma created in childhood as parents fail to meet the core emotional needs of their children. With characteristic humor, insight and commitment to an inner life, John and Karen Louis address a need of Schema Therapy in offering a practical guide for raising children with an understanding of core emotional needs and what is required to meet them. They combine experience as parents, therapists and church leaders to offer a valuable perspective on raising happy and emotionally healthy children."

— **Catherine Amon**, MSW, M.Div., *Cognitive Therapy Center of New York*

"A very insightful and practical parenting book that transcends race and culture! A must read for all parents with kids of any age. It has opened our eyes to a healthier way of communicating with our children to make sure we meet their needs and stay connected to them. The changes in them and us have been dramatic. Thank you so much!"

— **Dr. Mark Timlin**, MBChB, MPH, MBE, and **Vicki Timlin**, *Melbourne*

# GOOD
## PARENTING
### enough

*An In-Depth Perspective on*
*Meeting Core Emotional Needs*
*and Avoiding Exasperation*

## John Philip Louis
*and*
## Karen McDonald Louis

NEW YORK

GOOD **enough** PARENTING

*An In-Depth Perspective on Meeting Core Emotional Needs and Avoiding Exasperation*

© 2015 John Philip Louis *and* Karen McDonald Louis.

Published in New York, New York, by Morgan James Publishing. Morgan James and The Entrepreneurial Publisher are trademarks of Morgan James, LLC.
www.MorganJamesPublishing.com

The Morgan James Speakers Group can bring authors to your live event. For more information or to book an event visit The Morgan James Speakers Group at www.TheMorganJamesSpeakersGroup.com.

A **free** eBook edition is available
with the purchase of this print book.

ISBN 978-1-63047-406-5  paperback
ISBN 978-1-63047-407-2  eBook
ISBN 978-1-63047-408-9  hardcover
Library of Congress Control Number:
2014948857

CLEARLY PRINT YOUR NAME ABOVE IN UPPER CASE

**Instructions to claim your free eBook edition:**
1. Download the BitLit app for Android or iOS
2. Write your name in **UPPER CASE** on the line
3. Use the BitLit app to submit a photo
4. Download your eBook to any device

**Cover Design by:**
Rachel Lopez
www.r2cdesign.com

**Interior Design by:**
Bonnie Bushman
bonnie@caboodlegraphics.com

In an effort to support local communities, raise awareness and funds, Morgan James Publishing donates a percentage of all book sales for the life of each book to Habitat for Humanity Peninsula and Greater Williamsburg.

Get involved today, visit
www.MorganJamesBuilds.com

Habitat
for Humanity®
Peninsula and
Greater Williamsburg
Building Partner

# TABLE OF CONTENTS

......................................................

# ACKNOWLEDGEMENTS
# AND DEDICATIONS

First and foremost, **thanks to God**, who is the ultimate parent: *Thank You, for giving us all things, and for meeting our core emotional needs.*

Thank you to **Dr. Jeffrey Young**, founder of schema therapy, whose influence is on every page: *Meeting you set us on a new path of preventing schemas before they begin. We appreciate the time you set aside for us are grateful that you encouraged us to follow our dream.* Thank you to **Pat Sim**, our assistant and Movie Therapy partner. *We appreciate our friendship and partnership over the last two decades. We definitely could not have pulled this off without you!*

## THANKS TO OUR DEDICATED RESEARCH TEAM
**Dr. George Lockwood, Dr. Harold Sexton, Dr. Asle Hoffart and Teo Yig Zern (Yiren)** used their expertise and diligence to refine our data and spent many hours pouring over what must have seemed like endless statistics. The **Singapore National Council of Social Services (NCSS)** helped to finance our research.

THANKS TO OUR TALENTED EDITING/ARTWORK/FORMATTING TEAM

**Our deepest gratitude goes to a special editor, Catherine Amon, a friend and mentor who understood the connection between schema therapy and spirituality as few others do:** *Catherine, your passing was sudden and you will be missed. You will always be with us in our work, and your contribution lives on in the pages of this book.* **Dr. Shirlena Huang, Dr. Randy Janka, and Lisa Laoye** helped us when they had no time to do so; they deserve the utmost thanks for their respective painstakingly detailed input. **Dr. Mark Timlin and his wife, Vicki** gave intelligent and energetic feedback. **Paul Ramsey, Mark Templer, and Anna O'Brien** each did a read through; their critiques were meaningful and made a difference. **Sher Lee Wee** made herself available and used her gifts as an artist to draw the cartoons—a huge addition to this work and to our workshops. **Tan Beng Hwa** patiently worked on the graphics and **Abraham Augustin** formatted the really monotonous bits.

## FINAL THOUGHTS

**Thanks to our parents, Mrs. Philip Eastus Louis (aka Mama Louis) and Craig & Ann McDonald (aka PawPaw & MeeMaw),** who are incredibly supportive of the work we do: *We are grateful for the ways you met our core emotional needs. You are awesome grandparents, as well!* **And finally, thank you to our wonderful children, Sonia and David; this book is dedicated to you.** *We cannot imagine life without you; a large part of the joy in our lives is because of you! We respect you for who you are, and are becoming. Spending time with you is one of our favorite things to do on the planet! Thank you for your friendship, honesty, and partnership and for showing us so much forgiveness in our journey to become Good Enough Parents.*

# PREFACE

· · · · · · · · · · · · · · · · · · ·

We approached the writing of a parenting book with fear and trembling, so we feel a little compelled to explain what brought us here, as a justification for what may seem like the hubris of such an undertaking—why the need for yet another parenting book? What makes this book unique is that it is the first book that we know of that tries to explain how schema therapy relates to parenting, how to prevent schemas in children (or at least how to keep them from causing harm), and how to meet children's core emotional needs. The short version of how our Good Enough Parenting workshop and ultimately this book came to be is that in October 2007, we attended a seminar called "An Introduction to Schema Therapy" by Dr. Jeffrey Young, the therapy's founder. During a Q & A session, one of the participants asked Dr. Young, "Your theory states that "schemas" (automatic negative thoughts/memories/ beliefs) are developed in childhood—has anyone come up with a schema prevention program for parents?" Half in jest, Dr. Young replied that his life's work had been coming up with the therapy, so he had never had the time to work on prevention, but please feel free to do so. We took him seriously, and privately expressed interest, telling Dr. Young about the parenting presentations we had been doing that used movie scenes to give parents awareness, since our lessons seemed to align with what Dr. Young said would prevent the development of schemas. He encouraged John to train with him in Manhattan, and by May 2008, Dr. Young gave our schema prevention prototype the green light. In the autumn, we conducted the first run of our new workshop, "Good Enough Parenting", to a crowd of 600 in Singapore. As we began to train facilitators, we were asked, "When are you going to write a parenting book to go with the workshop?" Because we feel strongly that the best gift parents can give their children is to love each other, we had already developed a marriage workshop with an accompanying book, *I Choose Us*, as a kind of prequel to this book—*Good Enough Parenting* is really Volume II. We set aside a year to work on the Christian version, since our primary audience was church parenting groups. Later, the schema therapy community, several educational institutions, and even some government agencies became interested, hence the need for a secular version. So, now you know how this book came about. Please receive it in the spirit with which it was written, from two parents who understand only too well that we are not perfect! We hope you will be able to use it throughout your parenting journey as a guide to being "good enough".

*John and Karen Louis, Singapore*

SECTION ONE

# INTRODUCING GOOD ENOUGH PARENTING

# Chapter One

## PARENTING MATTERS

......................................................

While putting together a workshop for Singapore's Health Promotion Board on the topic of building self-esteem in children, I solicited help from our then 11-year old son, who had (and still has) a good sense of self-worth.

Karen: (*sitting next to David on the sofa*) Hey, sweetie, I need some help for a presentation I am working on. May I ask you a question?

David: Sure, Mom.

Karen: Ok, just out of curiosity, what would you do if a kid in your school told you that you were stupid?

David: (confidently) I'd tell him that he was stupid!

Karen: Ok... and just out of curiosity, what would you do if one of your *teachers* told you that you were stupid?

David: (thoughtfully and with a smile) Well, I probably wouldn't *tell* them they were stupid, but I would *think* it!

Karen: One more question...what would you do if I told you that you were stupid?

David: (slowly, with a bit of sadness) Well, I would probably get angry—but I might believe *you*.

Parenting matters. Don't let anyone tell you that parenting is not important. It is the most significant job that you will ever do, with far-reaching consequences.

We distilled a painstakingly long and detailed study summarizing over 1000 parenting articles into two sentences:

- Teens whose parents are supportive and caring, but who also consistently monitor and enforce family rules, are more likely to be motivated and successful at school, as well as psychologically and physically healthy.
- In contrast, adolescents whose parents are overly strict and give them little independence, as well as those whose parents are warm but permissive, are more likely to be impulsive and engage in risky behavior.[1] (RR1.1)

These findings are not really surprising; they sound like common sense. Parents should be close to their teens, practice what they preach, and avoid being both too controlling and too permissive. However, the following bit of research is a bit more startling: A study of almost 600 families in New York over 18 years found that unhealthy parenting was more of a predictor of children's mental illness than the mental health of the parents themselves! The more frequent occurrence of unhealthy parenting, the more likely the occurrence of mental illness in children (RR1.2).[2] Parenting matters.

We recognize that most parents are trying their best to love their children, and that their mistakes are usually *unintentional* and *subtle*. And while there is no such thing as a perfect mom or dad, parents can learn to be "good enough". (We didn't make up that phrase—English pediatrician and psychoanalyst Donald Winnicott wrote about the "good enough mother" over a half-century ago.[3]) Good Enough Parenting takes being intentional, and it takes training.

Allow us to illustrate this principle with a story from Karen's extended family in Texas. The McDonalds play a card game called Liverpool Rummy. They see every holiday as an excuse for a tournament; three tables or more of six players is not an uncommon sight at any gathering. While new family members struggle to learn the intricacies of the game with its idiosyncratic rules, after a few Thanksgivings and Christmases they begin to pick up the skills needed and pretty soon they start winning, or at least not coming in last. They learn not to sit behind the uncle who buys *everything*, to beware the aunt who always plays low, and to not be surprised when a certain cousin breaks into song if he loses! The outcome of the game is determined partly by the cards one is dealt, but also very much by how one plays the game. Some players moan about their bad luck, and eventually make excuses about why Liverpool is not their thing. Others hone their skills, year after year, and get better and better.

Parenting is very similar. When prospective parents combine their gene pools, part of the excitement of having a child is to discover what characteristics have been "dealt," if you will. Children's temperaments are inborn; parents do not get to choose which temperament they prefer—this is the "nature" side of things. But there is also the "nurture" side, and that is where our part comes in. We can be trained. We can learn strategies. We can study our children and know which one "plays low", and which one is likely to "break into song". We may not win every hand, but we can improve with time, and get better and better. *That* is Good Enough Parenting.

Why is Good Enough Parenting effective? Good Enough Parenting helps parents meet what we call "the core emotional needs" and will:

- Equip parents to raise emotionally healthy and autonomous children who will make a positive contribution to their world
- Prevent parents (as much as possible) from passing down dysfunctional attitudes and behaviors
- Give step-by-step advice, in the case of teenagers or adult children, on how to repair and reconnect after a conflict.

In *Good Enough Parenting*, we have explained the importance of "core emotional needs", defined and described them, and have discussed the long-term problems that come from *not* meeting them. We have used cartoons to illustrate how lifetraps get passed, and have included a "Basic Safety Zone" in each section, warning parents about steering clear of specific dangers associated with each core emotional need. We have given parents practical instruction about how to meet the different needs, and suggested exercises and activities. We have sprinkled the book with stories from our family (with our children's permission) and called those bits "Louis Lowdown". We have also included real life stories of parents and/or children who we have counseled personally or whose counseling we have supervised. We changed names and some details to protect confidentiality; in the case of stories made up for the sake of illustration, we have labeled them "vignettes". On top of all this, we have filled the book with bite-sized nuggets of research; for those of you desiring to dine on more substantial data, look for the symbol "RR"(Research Reveals). Whenever you see an RR followed by a chapter and series number, you will be able to match it with more detailed research in our website, www.gep.sg. Look there also for information on our "Good Enough

Parenting" Workshops, which combine movies, instruction and interaction to help moms and dads in their parenting journey.

We wish we could give you a formula, but even though we use scientific research and methods, children are not science projects—there is no equation that works with every child. Dear friends of ours who are also great parents once told us they put so much time into "studying" each of their four very different offspring that they had the equivalent of a Ph.D. in each child! That attitude is necessary if we want to be Good Enough Parents, because parenting is as much an art as it is a science, with each child his own priceless masterpiece.

Warning: *Good Enough Parenting* is not for the faint-hearted. This is not a "feel-good" book. Practicing the principles of Good Enough Parenting take courage, passion, and perseverance and blood, sweat, and tears. But the joy and satisfaction that come when you are emotionally connected with your child, when you share many of the same values, when he is functioning at a healthy level in his world, when she loves being with you and is successful when apart, when you see them thriving in relationships, make Good Enough Parenting worth every minute.

# Chapter Two

# THE CASE FOR
# CORE EMOTIONAL NEEDS

········································································

Water, sunlight, air and nutrients are the core needs for plant life. In the same way, human beings must have their core emotional needs met in order for them to be mentally and emotionally healthy. And just as wilted leaves are the first signs that a plant is not thriving, so, too, there are signs when core emotional needs are not being met adequately in children, leading to a broad range of dysfunctional patterns later in life.

Meeting the core emotional needs is not a nice tip for parenting, or a quaint suggestion to improve behavior, but an absolute necessity for raising healthy and happy children. After two and a half decades of working among different cultures, and being parents ourselves, we are

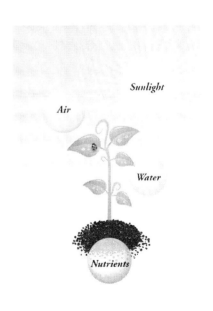

Figure 2.1: Needs of a Plant

7

convinced that helping children to be able to function and thrive in an adult world comes down to the parents meeting their core emotional needs. If these are not met, children will internalize these frustrating and painful experiences and struggle to cope, which then leads to the development of what Dr. Jeffrey Young calls early maladaptive schemas or "lifetraps". Young's theory has led to the discovery of 18 lifetraps/schemas. He developed Schema Therapy to help adults change these patterns which otherwise repeatedly play themselves out throughout one's life.[1] One of the exciting purposes of *this* book is to prevent active harm-causing lifetraps from forming in the first place!

## Lifetraps, Coping Styles and Domains

Think of lifetraps like this: during childhood, we develop certain thinking patterns. For example, the first born child in a family where the breadwinner is struggling to make ends meet might develop a greater sense of responsibility than the last born in a family of four with an upper middle class income. In the same way, a child who has been brought up in a neighborhood which values athletic achievement might develop differently if he moves to a city that places a premium on academic performance.

Unfortunately, influences on a child are not always so benign. A child who is sexually molested by a relative might think that he cannot trust any authority figure. A child who is bullied at school might begin to think she is unlovable. A child who is berated by his parents might begin to think he is worthless or that he will never measure up. These toxic experiences lead to the development of negative patterns of thinking, feeling and behaving; conscious and non-conscious painful memories; and beliefs about ourselves and others that carry over into our adulthood, into our marriage and into our parenting! These thoughts and beliefs are *distorted*. The *stronger* our lifetraps, the more *distorted* our view (see Figure 2.2).

We all develop lifetraps in childhood, partly due to inborn temperament, and partly due to environment. *However, the number and strength of our lifetraps increases to the extent that our core emotional needs are not met.* Perhaps we tried gaining attention or love from our caregivers. Perhaps our number one goal was to avoid being shamed. Perhaps we had an early sexual experience or were held to a very high standard. If we were abused, abandoned, shamed, or deprived of love by our parents, siblings, or peers, we almost certainly would have developed some corresponding active lifetraps.

Incidentally, these lifetraps are kind of related to each other—they tend to come in groups or clusters. If an individual has one lifetrap, he is likely to have a related lifetrap. In research, these clusters are called "domains". Research has found that Young's schemas cluster into four domains; these four domains correspond to our four core emotional needs.

Part of the dysfunction is the lifetrap. The other part of the dysfunction is the way we cope when these lifetraps are triggered. When our core emotional needs are not met as children, we get exasperated and subconsciously develop a way to cope with the pain of the unmet need. The way that we cope (e.g. to run away or fight back) has a lot to do with our temperament. We bring these coping styles into our adult life; they may appear to lessen the pain in the moment, but invariably they perpetuate or intensify the lifetrap in the long run and leave our deeper needs unmet. There are three ways people cope when their lifetraps are triggered: surrender, avoidance, or overcompensation, sometimes referred to as counterattacking. (Eighty years ago, Walter Cannon first identified fight and flight as common responses to stress; combined with fright, these correlate to the three coping styles.[2])

Figure 2.2: Lifetraps (Schemas) Distort Views about Ourselves and Others

## Surrender

The surrender coping style is based on a fear of what we believe is the truth the lifetrap tells about us. We react from a negative and fearful place where the lifetrap is in control of what happens to us. The message of this coping style is: *"What my lifetrap is telling me about myself is true and I am powerless to change it."*

Children with the surrender coping style believe in their own distorted diminished view of themselves. They then act in ways to confirm this distorted view. If a father says something rude, for example, that the child is ugly or stupid, the child agrees with him in her heart—she really believes that she is stupid. Children who surrender to these kinds of critical messages will have a low opinion of themselves. This causes them to have a distorted view of others, and a distorted notion of how others view them. They tend to blame themselves, comply and give in when something goes wrong. The voice in their heads says, "It is my fault." Surrendering types (see Figure 2.3) who face criticism and blame usually:

- Feel inferior to others
- Accept all criticism
- Look for events to confirm "it is their fault"
- Put the needs of others before their own.

Examples of "surrender behavior" associated with criticism and blame:

- Giving in to others during arguments
- Being overly apologetic
- Keeping rules compliantly
- Being drawn to others who are more confident.

Figure 2.3: Surrender Coping Style

There are many other types of toxic experiences to which children surrender (e.g. deprivation and neglect, being excluded from a group, physical abuse) and each leads to its own pattern of beliefs, feelings and behaviors.

## Avoidance

The avoidance coping style is based on flight from the pain associated with the lifetrap. We react by avoiding situations and interactions that lead to the lifetrap being triggered. The message of (or underlying belief associated with) this coping style is, "*It is too painful and uncomfortable to hear or feel my lifetrap. I must keep myself separate and distracted so I am not aware of this painful truth about myself.*"

When their needs are not met or when their lifetraps get triggered, children with this coping style will do anything to escape feeling disappointment and pain. They bypass situations that could be painful and trigger their lifetrap. Sometimes they feel powerless; they come up with ways to delay thinking about the situation. They circumvent conflict and intimacy by distracting themselves. Avoiders are prone to addiction, and often try to forget their pain by drinking excessively, taking drugs, being involved in promiscuous sex, overeating, or other self-destructive behavior. Some will choose instead to immerse themselves in schoolwork or a hobby. They usually do not want to talk about their issues and will make excuses for not doing so. The voice in their head is "I will avoid emotional pain at all costs." Sometimes they are not able to remember much from the past, and draw a blank when the past is questioned or explored because it hurts too much to remember. Children with the avoidance coping style often struggle with being deceitful, and are sometimes uncomfortable with eye contact. Avoiding types (see Figure 2.4) tend to:

- Be out of touch with their own feelings
- Dampen their feelings with substances (food, alcohol, drugs) or activities (gambling, sex, workaholism)
- Act like they do not have a problem
- Avoid intimate relationships
- Walk around numb
- Avoid confronting problems.

Those who cope by avoiding often spend an inordinate amount of time engaged in the following activities:

- Reading newspapers and magazines
- Surfing the net, shopping online
- Cleaning their room
- Checking social network sites
- Monitoring their favorite sport or team
- Running or playing a team sport
- Watching television
- Drinking alcohol, smoking, or overeating
- Talking on the phone or texting.

## Overcompensation

The overcompensation coping style stems from the desire or need to fight what we believe is the

Figure 2.4: Avoidance Coping Style

underlying truth the lifetrap holds about us. We react by behaving in a way designed to create the opposite effect of the lifetrap. The message, or underlying belief associated with this coping style is, *"I must fight as hard as I can to think and act as though what my lifetrap says about me is not true."*

When their lifetraps get triggered, children with this coping style who have been treated harshly and criticized, for example, will feel attacked, and they will attack back in order to prove that the negative feeling they have about themselves is not true. They will lash out in anger and attack the source of the negative message. Those who have been abused will abuse others or fight for justice when they feel unsafe; those who have been deprived of love and affection will convince themselves and others they are tough and do not need others in this way.

Overcompensation can take many forms, depending upon what painful message and/or experience the individual is fighting against. Those with this coping style often overreact to small slights or disappointments and can come across as, for example, rude, insensitive, and demanding or aloof and above it all. Someone who is overcompensating (see Figure 2.5) may:

- View disagreements as a threat, going out of their way to prove that others are wrong
- View feedback as criticism, going out of their way to prove that the opposite is true
- Appear strong, but actually be fragile
- Not care who gets hurt in the process of proving themselves right
- Prioritize protecting their image over intimacy
- Put their own needs first over the needs of others
- Constantly bring up their unhappiness about others' annoying traits while acting as if they themselves are perfect
- Not wait for a suitable time to talk; wanting it done there and then
- Throw tantrums and abuse others with name-calling
- Make unhealthy comparisons with others during quarrels
- Criticize and have no qualms about getting involved in long, drawn-out fights
- Be an overachiever—unusually driven at work or with projects outside normal working hours.

Understanding our coping style leads to self-awareness, which in turn helps us to have more empathy on our children and be better equipped to meet their core emotional needs. Understanding ourselves better leads to understanding our children better.

Figuro 2·5· Overcompensation Coping Style

•••••••••••••••••••••••••••••••••••••••••••

### *Louis Lowdown*

Anyone who knows us knows that John is an overcompensator, while Karen is an avoider. Our first-born tends toward an overcompensation coping style in keeping with her temperament; our son tends toward avoidance. The four of us understand that we all cope with conflict and stress differently and we work hard to be sensitive to and navigate our various styles.

•••••••••••••••••••••••••••••••••••••••••••

## The Foundation of Core Emotional Needs

Abraham Maslow was the first to write prominently about our needs as humans. He taught about five sets of needs: physiological essentials, safety, belongingness, esteem, and self-actualization. Maslow arranged them into a hierarchy—once the most basic need is satisfied, another emerges, and so forth. He qualified that this does not mean that each need has to be satisfied 100% before moving on to the next need, since most people feel satisfied even when their needs are being partially met—some needs are more unconscious than conscious.[3] Physiological and safety needs are more likely to be conscious, identifiable and more easily measured than psychological needs. Physiological needs include, among other things, the body's effort to remain a constant normal state, such as water content of the blood, salt content, oxygen content, constant temperature of the body, etc. Safety needs include the need for security, stability, dependency, protection and freedom from fear, anxiety, and chaos, as well as the need for structure, order, law, and limits.

Maslow posited that when people live in environments where their conscious needs were satisfied, those conscious needs would no longer act as a primary motivator. However, in the case of an outbreak of war or a natural disaster, people would involuntarily revert back to the conscious needs in the hierarchy, such as physiological essentials and safety, which would again become their primary motivators.[4] Maslow said that as long as people live in an environment where these basic levels of needs are being met, humans would move up his "hierarchy" and be motivated by the next level of needs, involving love, affection and belonging. These higher needs are neither tangible nor easily measured. When we are hungry, we physically experience the gnawing at our insides and are driven to eat. When we are thirsty, we crave a drink. When subjected to extreme temperatures, we seek relief instantly. But even though the needs higher up in the hierarchy are not as tangible and identifiable, they are every bit as real. For example, if a child in primary school was left out of games during recess and not allowed to be part of a group, the child would probably feel hurt, but she might not be able to identify that she felt pain because her need for acceptance and connection was not getting met. However, that would not make the pain any less real. We have as much of an insatiable thirst and hunger for the core emotional needs to be met as we do for food, clothing and shelter. Core emotional needs are as real as our physical needs. They may have been identified in the twentieth century by therapists and psychologists, but they have existed as long as man has; when deprived of such needs, humans are less healthy. In the words of Maslow, "Who will say that a lack of love is less important than a lack of vitamins?"[5]

## Definition of a "Core Emotional Need"

We adapted the work of fellow schema therapists George Lockwood and Paul Perris and put forward the following as to what constitutes a core emotional need:

- Meeting or not meeting this need should lead to an increase or decrease in well-being, and it should affect not only psychological functioning alone, but also result in an impact on such things as brain function, bodily functions, and family functionality.
- Each proposed core need should make its own contribution to well-being and not be derived from or overlap with any other core need.
- The core need must be evident universally across cultures.[6]

This desire to have our core emotional needs met began when we came out of the womb. As we grew, we learned to cope in different ways when our needs were not adequately met. As children, we were not able to look at our parents (or others in authority) and think, "Oh, they had a rotten childhood, so I am sure they don't really mean what they say." We could not help but take their words (or lack of words) personally. We internalized their messages, so much so that those messages became part of our makeup. We formed distorted views about ourselves and others (lifetraps), and we acted on them. We heard a distorted voice in our head, though there may have been little or no truth in it. This voice may have tried to convince us that:

*People I love will eventually leave me.*
*If they really knew me, they would know that I am worthless.*
*People cannot be trusted.*
*Something bad is bound to happen.*
*I just can't get close to other people.*
*Dad was right—I'll never amount to anything.*
*Showing emotions is weak.*
*I should be punished.*

This voice sometimes stays with us into adulthood. For many of us, this distorted voice is so strong that it still has power over our behavior and decision-making process. The more we counsel people, the more we have come to realize the power of not having our core emotional needs met in childhood. Both of us have seen the strong correlation between early experiences and current unhealthy behavior and thinking. For some of us, our lifetraps are so prevalent and strong that they become a roadblock to us becoming healthy adults. They also become a barrier in our relationships with others, including our spouses.

Jeffrey Young's theory is that when core emotional needs are not met on a consistent basis, children experience *frustration* and will develop lifetraps plus a coping style that complements their inborn temperament.[7] Children become exasperated and experience frustration when these needs are repeatedly not met, and when they experience trauma. One of the main purposes of this book is to help parents gain awareness about ways in which they discourage their children by not meeting their core emotional needs. Drawing from our own research and that of others, we have identified four core emotional needs, and then added what we called a "plus one" core emotional need. They are Connection and Acceptance, Healthy Autonomy and Performance, Reasonable Limits, Realistic Expectations, and *Spiritual Values and Community*. At the other end of the spectrum are the Schema Domains, i.e., the larger groups into which the schemas or lifetraps cluster; these four domains correspond to our four core emotional needs.

| Core Emotional Needs | Schema Domains |
|---|---|
| Connection and Acceptance | Disconnection and Rejection |
| Healthy Autonomy and Performance | Impaired Autonomy and Performance |
| Reasonable Limits | Impaired Limits |
| Realistic Expectations | Exaggerated Expectations |
| *Plus one: Spiritual Values and Community* | |

Understanding needs makes a huge difference in our parenting. Think about young children—they may not know what to say when they are needy emotionally or psychologically. They are aware when they are hungry or thirsty, but what about their unseen needs? Unconsciously, in order to get those invisible needs met, they will act out, and they will not even know it.

We sometimes do the same as adults. We have unconscious feelings and thoughts, unconscious reactions and unconscious behavior. There are times when our automatic reactions take control and moments later we wonder why we acted in a certain manner; we shout or cry, and do not know why.

If parents are educated about children's core emotional needs, they will be in a better position to respond to their children, rather than react to their child's misbehavior, end up in conflict, or worse still, deprive them further of having these needs met. If parents do not meet their children's core emotional needs, their children will be frustrated and traumatized, becoming exasperated and discouraged, and will develop harm-causing lifetraps, plus coping styles in accordance with their temperament.

Throughout this book we will follow the steps listed below:

- Parents need to be attuned to what core emotional needs are not being met when there is a pattern of misbehavior.
- Parents need to see how their children are getting exasperated or discouraged and how this is being acted out.

- Parents need to take steps to meet these core emotional needs as well as they are able.
- Parents need to come up with a routine and lifestyle where these needs are being met consistently.

One caveat—when rushing to meet the core emotional needs, we must avoid extremes. While we need to connect, we should avoid being enmeshed. While we need to avoid exaggerated expectations and unreasonable limits, we cannot go to the other extreme and be neglectful and permissive. Good Enough Parenting is about not giving too much and not giving too little—it's about meeting these needs in a balanced and satisfactory way.

Many of us grew up on the receiving end of at least one of these extremes. Some of us have been under-parented: our parents were not there for us emotionally or even physically, we were emotionally-deprived, we missed out on the love and guidance we needed and we needed to be stoic to fend for ourselves emotionally. Others of us had parents who were overly critical: we were left with a sense of shame, rejection and defectiveness, and these bad feelings often contributed to a complicated mix of hate, love, gratitude and resentment. On the other hand, some of us were so enmeshed with our parents that we did not know where they ended and we began; this left us feeling, even as adults, that we were not free to go out into the world to pursue our own path and dreams, separate from our parents. All of these extremes cause dysfunction of some kind or another.

The main premise of *Good Enough Parenting* is if parents meet their children's core emotional needs adequately, the chance of a healthier outcome is greatly increased;

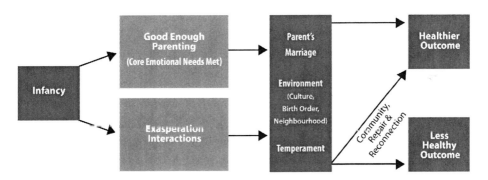

Figure 2.6: Good Enough Parenting Model - The Interplay of the Different Factors on the Outcome of Parenting

if children experience repeated exasperation interactions, the chance of a healthier outcome is greatly decreased, but even then, if parents make amends, repair and tap into the power of a community, a healthier outcome is still possible (see Figure 2.6).

## How Marriage Affects Parenting

Many parents believe, "It does not matter if my spouse and I do not get along, as long as we are there for the children." Parents who have this philosophy often forget what it was like for them when they were growing up with the two people that they love the most in the world not getting along, their Dad and Mom. They have forgotten how it hurt them emotionally, and how much insecurity was bred into them by the lack of stability and the level of conflict in their parents' marriage. Or they grew up in a harmonious home and rarely witnessed their parent's quarrel—and did not experience the effects firsthand.

An overwhelming amount of research over the last 20 years has surfaced showing a correlation between the quality of one's marriage and the quality of one's parenting. Cummings and Davies have arguably done the most work on the effects of marital conflict on the child's development process. They define marital conflict as "any major or minor inter-parental interaction that involved a difference of opinion, whether it was mostly negative or even mostly positive."[8] Based on this definition they wrote about conflicts being either constructive or destructive. How it is handled makes a huge difference to its effect on children. They concluded that conflict which gets resolved "may have relatively benign effects on children."[9]

••••••••••••••••••••••••••••••••••••••••••••••••••••••••••••••

### *Louis Lowdown*

We have been married for over 25 years and while we can't boast of having less conflicts than most, but we can say we have tried to resolve issues quickly—this has really helped us stay connected as a couple.

One evening after dinner, when our children were about eleven and nine years old, they took me (Karen) aside for a chat. Soon their mission became clear—they suspected all was not well between Mom and Dad and wanted to gather information. I said we were fine, but they would not relent. Finally I admitted we had just "had words" before dinner, but we would solve it easily as soon as we had a chance to speak. I also asked how they knew, since the atmosphere at dinner had been as upbeat as usual. The little detectives explained they noticed we had been speaking only to them, not to each other—I was shocked at how attuned their antennae had been! The conversation continued...

Kids: What were you fighting about anyway?

Mom: Well, the short version is that Dad did something helpful but instead of saying thank you, I blurted out how he might have done it a bit better, so Dad felt disrespected and unappreciated.

Kids: Mom! That's terrible! You shouldn't have done that!

Mom: I know, I regretted saying it as soon as it left my mouth...

Kids: Well, didn't you apologize???

Mom: Well, yes, but–

Kids: What?! You apologized and he didn't forgive you? He's a preacher and he tells everyone else to forgive! What a hypocrite!

Mom: Guys, hold on here, your Dad didn't have time to do anything. I said it right after I put the dinner on the table, so there wasn't time to discuss anything.

Kids: Don't worry Mom, we will talk to Dad first.

Mom: That's really not necessary.

Kids: It's okay, we got this...

The kids walked into the office area where I (John) was doing some paper work.

Kids: Dad, Mom said she was disrespectful to you.

Dad: Yes, but don't worry about it—we will have a talk in just a minute.

Kids: But Dad, didn't she already apologize to you?

Dad: Well, erm, yes, but...

Kids: So shouldn't you forgive her? You always say "if someone says 'sorry'"...

Dad: You're right. Thanks for speaking up. I'll talk with Mom now. I love you.

Kids: We love you, too, Dad.

The kids left with huge smiles on their faces, knowing that we would be reconciled. I (John) was full of remorse for not having forgiven my wife immediately. And I (Karen) was full of remorse for having been a know-it-all.

After we made up, we all had a nice laugh, and we marveled at our two kids who would never let us get away with anything!

...........................................................................

While this is a rather simple and light-hearted example, it does show how sensitive children are when their parents are at odds with each other. They internalize our silent messages to our spouse, and then slowly over a period of time if the tension is repeated and not resolved satisfactorily, their well-being is affected. Mistakes made by one spouse or the other, if repaired quickly will not have much of a negative effect on the children, but a lifestyle of unresolved conflicts between the parents will eventually take its toll on them.

Cummings and Davies also found that extended marital conflicts affect children over a period of time. They wrote:

...However, the risk factor operates over time and insidiously, by altering family and child functioning over time.[10]

The types of arguments that have a more negative impact on the children are those left unresolved over long periods of time, repeated heated conflicts, and conflicts where one parent is being subjugated by the other. These are called destructive conflicts and they include physical aggression, verbal hostility and non-verbal hostility (RR2.1).

There are many ways a poor marriage can influence a child's well-being, and it begins with destructive conflict. Some might ask, just how does destructive conflict interfere with our parenting? Destructive conflict directly affects the child's emotional security, which is linked to the child's confidence in the parents' ability to handle the conflict and to maintain family stability. In the case of destructive conflict, children become concerned about preserving emotional security, even getting involved in the conflict, as well as becoming emotionally distressed, and almost always interpret their parents' interaction negatively.[11]

Destructive conflict also *indirectly* affects the quality of the parent-child relationship. It is very common for parents who are in conflict to become depressed, which over time affects the attachment quality of their relationship.[12] Marital conflict discourages the parents, so that the parents then have less energy to manage their children with adequate supervision, open communication, and enforcement of rules for appropriate child conduct. Marital conflict also negatively affects the teamwork needed for parenting.[13]

It is true that some destructive conflicts may have a benign effect on children. There are children whose temperaments are able to block out these negative effects. The poor quality of their parent's marriage may have minimal impact on them. Some children have resilient temperaments that also cushion the blow.[14]

However, this is more the exception than the norm. When the quality of our marriage is poor, with patterns of destructive conflict, we are putting our children at risk of being negatively affected. Many parents erroneously assume since they were not affected by their parents' quarrels, their children will not be impacted by theirs. This view does not take into account that their children might have a more sensitive temperament and, therefore, be more susceptible to damage by the same type of conflict. Parents need to realize that the way they conduct themselves during a conflict is important and that reaching a satisfactory resolution will go a long way to reducing the child's level of distress.

So what do we do when there is tension between parents? Cummings and Davies point us toward forgiveness and reconciliation (see Chapters Nineteen and Twenty), because children's anxiety levels will be reduced to the extent that the parents' conflicts are resolved satisfactorily. This means that conflicts between moms and dads need to be genuinely resolved at an emotional level, not just at a rational level. Children need to know that their parents resolve issues in a healthy way—this has obvious benefits to both children and parents! However, if one parent is subjugated to the other during the "make-up" session and the kids notice a "forced-submissive" kind of resolution, they will feel that one parent is "winning"; this will not sit well with the kids.[15] The resolution between parents has to be genuine and complete at an emotional level, not white-washed or faked, or with one parent always capitulating and the other always getting their way. Children can tell the difference between genuine and superficial reconciliation. (We feel that teens can 'smell' hypocrisy and insincerity!)

When parents resolve their conflicts constructively, they are modeling healthy conflict resolution skills for their children, who will hopefully learn how to handle such conflicts themselves.[16] On the other hand, parents who do not get along are sending the message that using hostility, aggression and withdrawal are valid solutions for overcoming problems.

But we've only begun to scratch the surface—the latest findings show that marital conflicts cause all sorts of other problems for children. They diminish children's school performance, and affect their emotional security and the quality of their peer relationships.[17] Marital conflicts also cause disruption to children's sleep, physical ailments, depression, anxiety, "introvertedness" and acting out.[18] Difficulty controlling and monitoring children's behavior is the most sustained parenting problem faced by divorced mothers.[19] (RR2.2)

We end this portion on marriage with an analogy by Cummings and Davies, who compare a healthy marriage to a strong bridge:

> When the marital relationship is high-functioning, a secure base is provided for the child. Like a structurally sound bridge, a positive marital relationship supports the child's optimal functioning in the context of potentially threatening conditions, fostering explorations and confident relationships with others. When destructive marital conflict damages the bridge, the child may become hesitant to move forward and lack confidence, or may move forward in a dysfunctional way, failing to find the best footing in relations with others or within the self.[20]

So far we've been introduced to the new concepts of core emotional needs, coping styles, and schemas/lifetraps, and domains. We've learned how important a healthy marriage is to parenting, and we have only finished the second chapter. At this point, we would encourage you to take a time-out for some self-reflection. Dr. Jeffrey Young and his team were able to identify a total of 18 lifetraps, in other words, 18 different kinds of unhealthy thinking patterns and beliefs. It would probably be helpful for you to investigate which unhealthy thinking patterns are affecting you negatively, and what your predominant coping style may be, and how these all developed in the first place. If you learn how to attack lifetraps with the goal to weaken them, and if you can lessen the intensity of your coping style, you will be happier and healthier as an individual and as a parent. If you wish to fill out a schema inventory, visit www.schematherapy.com for more information. We would also encourage you to go through our marriage book, *I Choose Us* [21]. As a companion to this book, *I Choose Us* contains exercises and journaling tools that will help you to identify and begin working on your own harm-causing lifetraps, weaken your coping style, and, if you're married, move toward Love Connection with your spouse.

As you journey through this book, you will be better equipped to break unhealthy cycles, prevent your dysfunction from passing down, and meet your children's core emotional needs, with the goal of raising a healthier generation. And hopefully, in just the same way that computers and phones are always being "upgraded", your children will be, for the most part, the new and improved version of you!

# Chapter Three

# THE FRUSTRATION OF
# CORE EMOTIONAL NEEDS

······································

This concept is so central to *Good Enough Parenting* that we wanted to give it its own chapter. As we said, the basic premise of *Good Enough Parenting* is that as parents we must adequately meet the core emotional needs of our children. If we do not, they will be at risk of facing frustrative and traumatic experiences, or becoming exasperated, which will lead to the development of active schemas or lifetraps.

When we speak about exasperation and frustration, we mean the frustration that comes as a result of not having core emotional needs met, not the frustration that happens in life from time to time. All children will face little frustrations in different shapes and forms throughout life—losing a favorite toy, not winning in a sport, being disappointed by a friend, not receiving the gifts they had their heart set on, even getting upset by the occasional mistakes we make as parents. These kinds of frustrations are normal; if children never experience frustration, that causes a different kind of exasperation, because they will become entitled! (We digress!)

Normal frustration in life is different than *a lifestyle* of repeated frustration, trauma, and exasperation that takes place when core emotional needs are not met. This state of repeated exasperation eventually shapes a child's worldview and affects his way of thinking. The child's thoughts about himself and others become distorted, he develops harm-causing lifetraps, and his coping style gets more pronounced.

## Unintentional and Subtle

We know most parents love their children and want to be the best parents they can be. They are not trying to deprive their children of anything; the mistakes they make are usually *unintentional* and *subtle*. While some harmful wrong-doings by parents are overt and obvious, such as yelling in anger, name-calling, and physical violence, there are many more times when the mistakes are just not that straightforward. Even when they stem from well-meaning intentions, if they are a regular part of a family's lifestyle, there will be consequences.

We will illustrate how parents may be unconsciously and subtly (or not so subtly) exasperating their children with the following vignettes: (from here we will use the term "exasperation interaction" interchangeably with the idea of "frustrative and traumatic experiences".)

One-year-old Alan is not around his parents much during the day. His mother's house cleaner brings him to a day care center in the morning, leaves him at his grandparents' house in the afternoon, and feeds him his dinner in the early evening. Alan's parents work, and come home late because of the demanding nature of their jobs. It is not unusual for Alan to cry and be grumpy and distracted.

What is the underlying reason? Alan is experiencing a lifestyle of not having his core emotional need for **Connection and Acceptance** adequately met. If Alan were experiencing physical discomfort such as an earache or a sore throat, he would be difficult to soothe until someone tended to that need. The same goes for emotional needs—it's just that they are not as apparent. Whenever Alan reacts from the deprivation of connection, his parents put it down to something else, such as him being difficult, hungry, thirsty, sleepy, or catching a cold, not realizing that Alan is mostly reacting from not having a need met.

Children do not have the words to express these needs but will react when there is deprivation nonetheless. How can we expect children to make known these emotional needs when even adults are largely ignorant? If Alan's parents were to be asked, they would probably say that they have to focus on their careers because they want their child to be taken care of financially. These are good and well-meaning parents and the harm they are causing is unintentional and subtle; this lifestyle prevents them from meeting their son's core emotional needs. The consequences of not doing so can be grave, *especially to children with very sensitive temperaments.*

Sarah's mother, a highly-controlling woman, decides what clothes her five-year-old daughter should wear, what books she should read, and when and where she will play with her friends, without giving Sarah any choice in the matter. Sarah is not allowed to play in others' homes or have sleepovers like her other friends. Her mother dictates all matters and this has become very much a part of her lifestyle. Sarah depends on her mother for everything. She is not comfortable being on her own and making choices that others her age are making. She gets frustrated easily, cries and becomes angry, so her mother disciplines her for not being good-mannered, which then frustrates her even more. Sarah becomes angry because her core emotional need for *Healthy Autonomy and Performance* is not being adequately met. Her mother is completely oblivious to this and focuses on Sarah's outward behavior. She thinks her highly-controlling nature will help steer her daughter in the right direction while in reality, Sarah's frustration will continue and she will develop an unhealthy way of coping. If Sarah's mother were to be asked why she is so controlling of her daughter, she probably would say that she is trying to be thorough. It could be that Sarah's dependence makes her feel useful as a mother—she certainly would not want to cause harm to her daughter, but is doing so, subtly and unintentionally.

Simon, a first grader, is energetic, highly curious, and wants to explore every new object he comes across. His parents are around but they do not know how to set proper limits to his behavior. At school, Simon does not obey rules and is bossy around other children. When he does not get his way, he displays anger by hitting. His aggressive behavior has caused him to be disliked by many and as a result he does not have many friends. Adults often stare disapprovingly when he misbehaves in public places. As he realizes that he is not well-liked, he will develop a poor sense of self, which will cause frustration to develop, and over time, this may cause him to become *more* aggressive. If his parents continue to fail in providing adequate guidance and do not expect him to obey some *Reasonable Limits*, his frustration will continue as others give signals that he is not pleasant to be around. He will also feel frustrated at the lack of guidance from his parents. If we were to ask the parents why they are not more involved, they would chalk it up to not wanting to be too controlling or maybe just being too busy: "He'll shape up soon enough"—an example of how overly permissive parenting yields costly results.

Maria is only four years old and is already being sent to a kindergarten that prepares children to excel in math and science. Her mother, who directs her to do extra work so that she can score well in these subjects, often interrupts Maria's playtime. She also limits her daughter's time with friends, and constantly nags Maria about doing better at school. Maria gets frustrated, though she does not know the word for that feeling. She looks unhappy and sullen much of the time. She daydreams a lot and does not concentrate on her schoolwork, which is already excessive. Her mother puts this down to laziness and lack of focus. Her demands are extreme—she is definitely not meeting the core emotional need for *Realistic Expectations*. Maria feels exasperated and frustrated most of the time. She is rude to her mother and has started angrily lashing out at her friends in kindergarten. Her mother feels that she is a good Mom, looking out for her daughter. Again, the mother would probably say that her expectations are for Maria's own good, but she has little idea of the unintentional harm and exasperation that she had caused her daughter to experience through her repeated unrealistic expectations.

Ben is a fourteen-year old boy who finds it difficult to fit in. He is not into sports like the other boys his age. He feels ashamed of his acne, his oily hair, and his looks in general. Ben avoids interacting with other boys and often feels left out. He spends most of his time in his room alone. His parents are pleased with this behavior since they feel that he is a "good boy" who does not mix with the "wrong" crowd. Further, since he is good student, they are proud of his progress at school and boast about him incessantly, thinking that will build up his self-esteem, but it makes him feel guilty instead. Ben appears to get along well with others, but does not actually connect well and feels lonely. He often goes to bed crying, longing to have a best friend. He does not feel like he fits in anywhere. As his loneliness increases, he starts to surf the web to soothe his pain, and becomes addicted to Internet pornography. His parents are completely unaware—all they seem to be concerned with is how well he is doing at school. Ben's loneliness is causing him frustration. He feels lousy about himself and knows deep down that he is headed in the wrong direction. He resents his parents for not understanding his challenges, but he is also afraid to tell them. His parents continue to be oblivious to his needs. They have no idea what he is feeling. They mean absolutely no harm, but as unintentional as it is, harm is still being caused. Imagine if Ben were part of a functional community, where he felt accepted, loved, guided and challenged? His feelings of loneliness might be reduced, at least to a degree. His close relationships with peers and adult friends might help him deal with his porn addiction. If his parents could have helped Ben to have his need for *Spiritual Values and Community* met, it could have made such a difference.

Back to exasperation—since it usually takes place *subtly* and *unintentionally*, parents must examine if something in their lifestyle might be accidentally sabotaging their own parenting. Sometimes this happens when moms and dads imitate behaviors from their own parents that they observed and experienced growing up. Sometimes it can be the exact opposite—an overreaction to what they experienced. And sometimes it stems from fear of what their children may become if they keep heading in a certain direction; perhaps "Junior" reminds them of Uncle Ned, the bankrupt womanizer who could not hold a job. It could even be caving in to parental peer-pressure, worrying about what other parents might be thinking. Or it can occur because of a reaction to something they have read or heard in the media.

## Moral, Conventional, Personal, Prudential

We cannot end this introduction to exasperation interactions without pointing out that many of the issues about which parents and children argue are matters of opinion and preference. Parents who refuse to be dragged into "disputable matters" and focus their energies on truly important issues have a greater chance of helping their children to be morally and emotionally healthy and avoiding exasperation interactions.

We believe that the research of Dr. Larry Nucci,[1] (a professor at the University of California at Berkeley and an expert in children's social and moral development) sheds light on what kind of issues should carry more weight than others. He put different ways of looking at right and wrong into "domains", (not to be confused with Schema Domains) and found that all cultures have common ideas of "right and wrong", encompassing concepts such as fairness, justice, and honesty. According to Nucci, a five-year-old boy, regardless of where he is raised, knows it is never right to hit a smaller child or to keep all the candy for himself. He calls this the **Moral Domain**, and says it is pretty much the same across the world, whether you are talking about Singapore, South Africa or Scandinavia.

The **Conventional Domain** deals with issues that tend to be arbitrary, it exists through the social agreement of people who are part of a social system. For example, in some cultures it is perfectly fine to address another person by their given name, but in other cultures this would seem very informal, and in some places, downright rude. Burping aloud at the table is condemned in some places but seen as a compliment to the chef in others. A third domain he labels as the **Personal Domain**, which deals with matters of privacy and personal preference, such as a person's style of dress or hairstyle. As a child grows this domain will also increase with their autonomy. Finally, there is the **Prudential Domain** involving safety and well-being and pertaining to rules associated with things like the consumption of alcohol, using drugs, smoking and driving.

Of all the above domains, which should be the main focus—Moral, Conventional, Personal or Prudential? When discipline is being administered, should one domain take precedence over another? Disciplining and training children about issues within the

Moral Domain, which are truly about right and wrong, is central to their development. However, when parents argue with and discipline their children for "offenses" within the conventional and personal domains, children, especially adolescents, will often infer hypocrisy and rebel. As parents fight with their children about the arbitrary and personal choice issues that are not truly a matter of right and wrong, their children will become exasperated and will experience frustration of their core emotional needs.

With this understanding, as parents we will be able to know where our focus primarily should be, when we should make something a big deal, when it is acceptable to be indignant—and over what issues.

**Important Qualifier:** Repeated frustrative and traumatic experiences are *not* the same as occasional mistakes by parents who generally do a great job meeting these core emotional needs. It has been said that having children changes parents. Most of us, if we persevere and continue to grow as individuals, and are willing to be humble and learn, will change for the better. However, during this journey we will all make mistakes, whether it is losing our cool, being forgetful, getting frustrated, and perhaps even at times being overly intrusive, demanding, or permissive. Such mistakes can be repaired easily and not repeated frequently if we gain awareness through feedback from our spouse and from our children. What we are warning against are the kind of harmful dynamics that become a part of the normal interactions that make up a family's lifestyle and culture. These repeated frustrative and traumatic experiences facilitate the development of harm-causing lifetraps and unhealthy coping styles.

# Chapter Four

# EXASPERATION INTERACTIONS

ave you ever said, "That really pushes my buttons"? We all have trigger points, situations that cause us to feel exasperated. As counselors, and as parents, we have observed that there are specific interactions that always seem to cause exasperation in children. This exasperation eventually leads to children experiencing a frustration of their core emotional needs repeatedly not being met—and later in adulthood may be remembered as trauma. The individual interactions we are identifying in this chapter were confirmed during our research using the Young Parenting Inventory (YPI)[1] from the schema therapy model. They are Belittling, Perfectionistic & Conditional, Controlling, Punitive, Emotionally Depriving & Inhibiting, Dependent & Selfish, Overprotective, Pessimistic, and Overly Permissive. Being on the receiving end of any of these interactions blocks children's core emotional needs from being met.

Let us now go through each research proven frustration and trauma-causing interaction specifically:

## Belittling

Children feel belittled when their parents make fun of them, call them names, make derogatory remarks about things that are important to them, disparage their looks, or humiliate them in any way. When belittling takes place, children will feel put down, flawed and/or rejected, and will experience a range of other emotions depending on their temperament, and ultimately will develop a negative view of themselves. Why would parents belittle their children? Some parents' philosophy is that humiliating their children will induce them to change their "inappropriate" behaviour. Sometimes parents are trying to prevent their children from having "a big head". Sometimes they are embarrassed about their children's emotions, particularly for boys. Children in such environments quickly shut down. They are afraid to voice their preferences and feelings. These parents usually have deep pain or hurts themselves that have not been dealt with properly. Perhaps they are angry most of the time, and have little or no positive outlook on life. They think that humiliation is the best way to bring about change in their children. They put their children down around issues that trigger their own feelings of inadequacy or defectiveness. The overall effect is that children who feel belittled and rejected become exasperated and are eventually traumatized. Years ago, children on the playground said, *"Sticks and stones may break my bones but words will never hurt me."* Nothing could be further from the truth. Words have the power to divide nations, end friendships, wreck marriages, and do untold harm to children.

*Examples:*
(from parents to a son)
*If you were not such a sissy you would take up a real sport instead of ballet.
    Maybe we should call you by a girl's name.*
*Stop being a wimp and learn to take it like a man.*
*Hey, butterfingers, no coach in his right mind would let you be on his team.*
(from parents to a daughter)
*We were expecting a boy, not a girl!*
*Here we go again, is this your monthly woman thing? Why can't you think
    straight?*
*If you would lose some weight, maybe you could get a boyfriend.*
(from parents to either sons or daughters)
*If you don't get into a good school, you will bring shame to the family name.*
*I wish I never had you.*
*What's wrong with you?*

Children who regularly hear such comments are not likely to feel accepted and connected with their parents, nor will they readily be in a position to get their other core emotional needs met.

A study done jointly by Harvard Medical School and McLean Hospital in Boston, USA, published in 2006, highlighted that demeaning or belittling words contribute more to the maladjustment of children than harsh physical punishment.[2] This is consistent with our own counseling experiences involving adults whose greatest pain revolves around early memories of the hurts caused by words from their parents; they carry wounds from "put-downs" for years afterwards.

· · · · · · · · · · · · · · · · · · · · · · · · · · · · · · · · · · · · · · · · · · · · ·

### *Louis Lowdown*

One of my (Karen) sad parenting memories happened when David was in kindergarten. We lived on the 10th floor of an old apartment building with very slow elevators. It was time to take my five-year-old son down to the school bus, but I had not helped David to get ready without rushing. He was struggling to get his shoes on (as five-year-olds do) so I impatiently told him to finish putting on his shoes outside our apartment while we waited for the elevator. Just as David sat down, the doors opened, so we scrambled into the elevator, and I remember feeling embarrassed in front of the other passengers. Why? Because my weird ego was somehow interpreting they were judging my parenting and I was coming up short. (Who cares, right?) Even though David could hear me, I made excuses to the other elevator riders, "I'm so sorry that my son is slow and disobedient. I hope he learns his lesson." By the time we reached the ground floor, I felt like a world-class jerk. Thankfully, the bus wasn't there yet, which gave me time to make amends. I sat with David on the curb, apologized profusely for the belittling words and asked his forgiveness. David was able to go to school happy, if not slightly confused at his mother's strange behavior. If I had not acted immediately, David surely would have gone off to school feeling exasperated. If such interactions had been a "lifestyle" instead of an anomaly, it would have facilitated the development of active lifetraps in him, not to mention that my son would have learned to steer clear of Mom!

· · · · · · · · · · · · · · · · · · · · · · · · · · · · · · · · · · · · · · · · · · · · ·

## Perfectionistic & Conditional

Children will be exasperated by their parents when they feel they can never measure up to a perfectionistic ideal. Parents who cause this kind of frustration usually care very much about how they are perceived by others, how they look in society. They demand perfection and are only satisfied when things go a certain way. These demands put an incredible pressure on the children who become frustrated and sometimes traumatized, and their core emotional needs are not met as a result.

Parents who have such a philosophy about perfection and about looking good care little that their children are feeling sad, disappointed or fearful. *Parents who come across conditional in the love and acceptance of their children are often driven by how they are viewed by others.* Because they view their children as an extension of themselves, when *their children* perform well, they feel that *they* have performed well. They are highly competitive and probably brag about their kids, sometimes bald-facedly. Alternatively, some perfectionistic parents are reserved and withhold encouragement for fear that it will demotivate their children. Conversely, when their children do not "do well", they feel it deeply and take it out on them. These parents are driven by how others perceive their children's "failure", and, when disappointed, it shows up in the way they treat their kids. They withhold affection and love as a result of their disappointment, seen in their body language and their words as well. Life for their children is constantly filled with criticism. Even when they become adults, the parents have the misguided notion they always know what is best, and maintain a sense of superiority.

Celebrative emotions that come with achievements should be welcomed, but those will come few and far between. Or perhaps one child is a super achiever, so the sibling gets compared and criticized for not being as good. The children's preferences, decisions and emotions are not treated as being as important as those of the parents. The parent's shame about a certain achievement not being met is more important than the children's feelings. As a result, the children feel unhealthy guilt and shame; over time, this can cause a lot of anxiety and fear. The following words might be heard during these interactions:

> *Do you have any idea how much we have sacrificed for you?*
> *Stop feeling great when what you did was average. Look at your sister/brother (or cousins or others the children are compared to).*
> *Don't waste time going out with your friends. Get serious with your physics (or tennis or ballet) and be productive.*

## Controlling

Parents who exasperate their children in this way are driven by a variety of factors. Some parents are controlling because of fear their children will make wrong decisions and use bad judgment. This fear drives the parents to micro-manage their children's affairs and as a result, their children feel they have little freedom of choice. They also believe they cannot rely on their own judgment; eventually they will not develop their own sense of direction because their parents are such 'strong' individuals. Other parents' controlling nature stems from the enmeshment lifetrap— they do not permit their children to feel differently from them, and they force their children to be privy to age-inappropriate information, such as their deteriorating marriage, their own loneliness, sometimes even their sexual frustrations. Enmeshed parents instill a strange kind of loyalty in their children. They deprive their children of their own emotions and instead expect them to think about the needs of the enmeshed parent most, if not, all of the time.

These children will not grow up with individuality or a sense of separateness from the parents which creates frustrative experiences growing up, especially in the case of mothers who are enmeshed with her children. They will hear messages such as the following from their enmeshed parent:

*Let me help you choose your after school activities since I know what's best.*
*You're not allowed to have any friends that I don't like.*
*There are no secrets between us, ok? Tell me everything.*
*Let me tell you about how I am feeling about your mother/father.*
*I don't want you to be with your friends. Stay home with me. I need you, stop thinking about yourself.*

Mothers who are enmeshed are usually clueless about how their interactions exasperate their children. They think they are close to their child, but often their child feels exasperated, although the child sometimes gets used to it and becomes dependent on the mother.

## Punitive

Parents who exasperate their children in this way most likely grew up in such an environment themselves. Examples of the punitive exasperation interaction are children being punished for *every little thing* that they do wrong, or for displaying certain emotions, or for infractions that are conventional in nature, as opposed to moral (see Chapter Two); sometimes they are made to feel guilty for past mistakes. Parents who treat their children this way show very little grace. They emphasize "justice" and "truth" rather than mercy, and put their kids "in the dog house" every time they think their child has committed an offence. Words that come out from them may include:

> *You deserve to be punished; I will never trust you again after what you did.*
> *Do you really think one apology is good enough?*
> *I don't spend time with naughty children. Come back when you've learned your lesson.*

## Emotionally Depriving & Inhibiting

Parents who are emotionally inhibited can end up accidentally exasperating their children by depriving them of empathy, comfort and guidance. Parents who fall into this trap often want their children to learn how to behave and be calm. They do not particularly like passionate displays, including crying. Their philosophy is, "Children are to be seen and not heard". They feel uncomfortable with both the high and low emotions—they do not encourage children to laugh out loud, play loud games, or have friends over often, and they certainly are not comfortable talking with their children about heart-felt issues, low times, disappointments, and sadness. Noise is just a nuisance, whether stemming from joy, happiness, pain or hurt. Most parents who exasperate their children in this manner were treated similarly growing up, so this kind of coping mechanism is familiar to them, and as a result, this is what they re-create in their own home. Statements like the following are frequently made to their children:

> *Admit what you did wrong first, otherwise let's not talk about your feelings.*
> *I may not show you a lot of affection, but I do care about you.*
> *If you don't bother with your feelings, then they will not bother you.*
> *I am not emotional like other people. I am a rational, logical person, so let's talk about this logically.*
> *Let's only talk about the positives. I want a positive atmosphere in the home.*

Sometimes parents emotionally deprive their children by being too busy for them. When both parents have demanding jobs, possibly even being very successful at work, there can be a problem with setting aside time for their kids. Children are raised more by their grandparents or by a hired caregiver/day care service. More affluent parents may see going on elaborate holidays as a way of making up for a lack of time spent with the kids but quality does not make up for quantity and the children feel a lack of empathy, nurturing and guidance.

There are other reasons why a parent may emotionally deprive their children. Some adults are incapable of being warm, affectionate, nurturing and showing empathy because of their own upbringing. Some parents go through such difficult times in their marriage that they are consumed with their problems and have little mental and emotional capacity left over to give to their children. Harm is done regardless of the reason, and the children grow up with frustration of not having their core needs met. Another very important aspect of this kind of interaction is when parents do not provide their children with helpful and age-appropriate guidance. This is the opposite of the next type of interaction where parents go to the other extreme.

## Dependent & Selfish

Children whose parents exasperate them in this way may grow up feeling that they are being forced to handle more daily responsibilities than what would normally be expected for a child their age. They may feel like a parent dumps things on them, relies on them for support and understanding, or feels they are strong and should take care of other people. They may feel that one or both parents withdrew from them and left them alone for extended periods, or lied to them, deceived them, or betrayed them. They may feel that a parent used them to satisfy his needs, was moody, unpredictable, undisciplined or an alcoholic possibly even feeling that their parent seemed to get pleasure from hurting people. This kind of exasperation could also occur if one parent died or left the house permanently when the child was young, or if a parent is so structured and rigid that she prefers everything "neat and tidy" to change of any kind. Parents who repeatedly exasperate their children in this way would probably say things such as:

> *Look how smart my six-year-old is—she can iron her own clothes and make breakfast for her little brother and she's only in first grade.*
> *I know you are a child, but you need to support me because you are strong.*
> *I know I did not keep my word but I have a good reason.*
> *I need you to take care of the house and your younger siblings—I have to focus on my career, plus I need a life, too.*

## Overprotective

Parents who are overprotective are excessively worried about their children for the smallest of issues, such as being hurt while playing at the playground, or getting sick when caught in the rain. They convey unrealistic expectations to their children, and at best, react in a way that is very out of proportion to the actual situation, so much so that even onlookers will notice. Children often feel frustrated when regularly exposed to such signals from their parents. They either hang out with their friends much more than they do with their parents, or surrender to their parents' fears and become stay-at-home worry warts. Parents who interact with their children in this way might say:

*I am so mad that your friend didn't choose you to play on his team. Give me his mother's phone number so I can deal with him.*
*I don't want you to play sports because you will hurt yourself.*
*I can't believe they let that boy with a cough stay at day care. Now you are going to get sick. Rest at home tomorrow. Maybe we should find another center.*

## Pessimistic

Children become exasperated when they repeatedly hear the glass is always half empty, not half full. If you were to ask these parents why they were being negative, they would say they do not want their children to be unrealistic about life. These parents probably grew up in negative environments in which they were made to fear making mistakes. Taking risks was not encouraged. So, fuelled with a desire to avoid mistakes and to make sure things do not go wrong, they decide it is easier to not be hopeful at all.

Some remarks from parents who interact with their children in this way might be:

*Don't admire anyone. They will end up disappointing you.*
*I know you are excited about taking up that sport. But it is rough and you will get injured and then your life will collapse.*
*Why are you sad? The world is a horrible place, so get used to it.*

## Overly Permissive

Parents who are overly permissive are not available, or too busy doing their own thing. Sometimes parents feel guilty for not getting involved with their children, so they overreact by not expecting the kids to respect boundaries or learn proper discipline. They are not there to talk about the difficult issues their children are going through. In order to distract their kids from their emotions, they let them watch loads of TV and spoil them with goodies. The parents themselves are uncomfortable getting involved in their children's lives, perhaps for fear of bad news, or perhaps they do not like talking about emotions and so they avoid it by not being available or taking their focus away from their emotions. As a result, children begin to think that it is wrong to talk about their emotions. They also do not take the time to guide them through issues. They allow their children to get away with a lot of mischief before they even say anything. Eventually when children do not feel guided by their parents, this can cause them to feel insecure about the direction they are heading, and they may turn to their peers instead.

> *Sorry, I am too busy. You need to learn to deal with your ups and downs yourself.*
> *You are a grown-up.*
> *I am sorry you feel that way. It is my fault. I am a lousy parent.*
> *Have some ice cream. That is the best way to take your sadness away and make*
> *you feel better.*

Children whose parents are overly permissive feel that their parents are leaving them to figure out how to manage and control their lives. This can easily cause disconnection with their parents and create resentment and frustration, especially when their parents give them advice and finally, on the very rare occasion, decide to talk to them about sensitive issues.

## Why are Lifetraps (Schemas) a Big Deal?

As we mentioned in Chapter One, lifetraps are memories, thoughts, beliefs, and emotions stored in our brain that are triggered when we are presented with familiar situations later on in life. All of us have lifetraps, since none of our "growing up" environments were perfect. The positive experiences help us move forward in life in the face of adversity or challenges. The strongly negative ones affect our self-view and our relationships with people and we get stuck with this over and over again, unable to break completely free and start over. Remember the figure of the woman (see Chapter Two, Figure 2.2) looking into the mirror? It shows a young woman whose views of herself were shaped by the negative messages from her father. She has the lifetrap of defectiveness—she feels there is something wrong with her, that she is not "good enough"; as a result, her self-image is distorted, which is seen in the mirror's reflection.

Our own research, consistent with the findings of others, has found that exasperation (frustrative and traumatic experiences) during childhood is associated with the development of lifetraps.[3] In turn, lifetraps are related to the development of a myriad of personality disorders, psychiatric symptoms, depression, eating disorders, and other dysfunctions. Research has also shown that early negative parenting experiences are related to the development of active schemas or lifetraps (RR4.1).

The fact that lifetraps are associated with early parenting experiences and with many of the disorders and pathologies mentioned above shows that our role as parents is crucial in knowing how to satisfactorily meet the core emotional needs of our children. The stakes are high. Our children's perceived early experiences with us as parents make a huge difference to how they turn out as adults.

SECTION TWO

# THE CORE EMOTIONAL NEED FOR CONNECTION AND ACCEPTANCE

# Chapter Five

# CONNECTION AND ACCEPTANCE

The Core Emotional Need for Connection and Acceptance can be defined as the state children live in when they feel completely attached to their parents in a healthy way, and when they feel like they belong and are accepted and loved unconditionally. Children whose core emotional need for connection and acceptance has been met naturally develop traits and beliefs such as trust, self-acceptance & openness, emotional fulfillment & intimacy, belonging & affinity, emotional spontaneity & expressiveness, and mastery & success.[1] They will *consistently, on an emotional level,* hear and believe the following messages about their parents:

*They are playful with me and spend time with me.*
*They like me, and miss me when I am not around.*
*They care about deep feelings, both mine and theirs.*
*They are proud of me even with my flaws.*
*They talk to me in a respectful way.*
*They believe in me and guide me.*

Denise, 37, grew up in a home where she was made to feel stupid, ugly, fat, and unwanted. Her parents wanted a boy for their first born, and she was reminded of that fact frequently. They also had high hopes for her academically, even though they themselves had only finished elementary school. When she did not "excel" in kindergarten, they called her mean names like "idiot" and "retard" and made it no secret that they wished she had not been born. She was beaten for the slightest offence, and when she was sexually abused by a relative, no one seemed to care. Locked out of the house for minor infractions such as laughing too loudly, she quickly learned to stay in the background. When her brother arrived a few years later, Denise's only value to the family was as a caretaker. In every possible way, her parents did not meet Denise's core emotional need for connection and acceptance, nor any of her other needs, for that matter. This lonely child did poorly in almost every subject, and eventually failed out of high school. As an adult, Denise has been hospitalized for suicidal tendencies, and constantly struggles with relationships, finances, depression, boundaries, and self-esteem issues. It is not hard to surmise that Denise's issues are directly related to her childhood and it is no wonder she continues to have trouble *connecting* with others and *accepting* herself.

Caroline, 32, was never beaten or sexually abused. Her family went on nice holidays. She had lots of friends, attended a posh private school, and excelled in her favorite hobbies. Although her parents both found it hard to express their feelings and had very high standards, they believed in being firm but kind, valued discipline, trying one's best, being humble, and showing respect. Her mother had a flexi-hour job so that she could be at home with the children whenever possible; her father worked long hours as a lawyer. Her older sister was "a handful" and seemed to get the brunt of the discipline, while her younger brother was sickly, so the parents spent most of their time worrying over Caroline's siblings. In this environment, Caroline was overlooked and did not *feel* her parents' love. As a teenager, she yearned to break free and rebel against the disapproving oversight of her fairly strict and emotionally inhibited parents. Although her siblings are doing well in their careers, Caroline never graduated from college, and has many boundary issues. Like Denise, Caroline has been on suicide watch at times, and finds it hard to hold a job or keep a long-term relationship. Many people would look at her parents and family and think she had the ideal home, but her core need for connection and acceptance was not met, and she has trouble feeling *connected* to her family and *accepting* herself or others. What do these two women, from very different families, have in common? Their core emotional need for connection and acceptance was not met by their parents, and now, even though these two women should be able to function as successful adults, their struggle is immense.

Real connection with our children is when the sharing of emotions takes place in both directions; parents to children and children to parents, such that a healthy affectionate bond and an empathic understanding develops between the two sides. The result is children feel their thoughts and ideas, hurts and feelings, and victories and defeats have a place in their parents' hearts and vice versa. Acceptance with our children is when children feel that their parents value them for who they are, with their strengths and weaknesses, flaws and all, and regard them as a blessing in their lives. Authentic connection and unconditional acceptance make home a safe place.

These two constructs go hand in hand. It is impossible to get connected to a child on an emotional level and at the same time not accept them. When a child gets connected, the acceptance usually comes with it; connection and acceptance are interwoven. The reverse is also true; where there is disconnection there is also a sense of rejection. Children will feel discouraged and their behavior will reflect these feelings. When this core emotional need is met well, it lays the foundation for a lifelong enjoyable and fulfilling relationship of genuine love between parent and child.

## Connection is Crucial

Children must feel a deep emotional connection with their parents in order to mature into healthy adults; they must feel accepted by their parents if they are going to develop a healthy sense of self-esteem. In our opinion, most of the harm in today's world is caused by this core emotional need not getting met. Oh, that parents would take heed of the absolute necessity of meeting this core emotional need!

Of all the "four plus one" core emotional needs, connection and acceptance is the need in which emotions play the keenest part. Meeting this core need cannot be done if parents insist on staying in "logical" mode. We repeat, *for parents to connect with their children and help them feel accepted, they must interact with them on an emotional level.* And that does not mean the home needs to be filled with screaming, temper tantrums and crying. It does mean that parents must deal with their own hesitation to have anything to do with emotions, such as anger, fear, sadness, shame, joy, peace, and so forth.

As we think of the importance of emotions in parenting, we should note that our emotions get communicated through many different means, even when we think we are keeping them in check. Experts teach that most communication occurs not only with words but also through non-verbal means such as body language, tone of voice, demeanor and gaze. Albert Mehrabian is the originator of the much quoted "7%-38%-55% rule"; back in the late 1960s, his experiments led to him assert that words account for only 7% of what we ultimately communicate, tone of voice accounts for 38%, and body language accounts for a whopping 55%! His work points to the importance of congruence—that if our words are saying one thing and our tone another, our listeners will believe the tone.[2] So, when we as parents think we are just being "rational", our soulless eyes and flat tone of voice might be telling our children that we do not care about them. When we say the "right" words while our body language repeatedly conveys disdain or disapproval, our children may be experiencing exasperation. Working on eye contact, tone, and body language when speaking with our children is not just a good suggestion, it is crucial if we wish to meet our children's need for connection and acceptance.

When this core emotional need is met, parents and children alike experience satisfying emotions—the "positive vibrations" are almost palpable. You will notice a lighter atmosphere in the home, with parent and child both feeling free to be vulnerable and childlike with each other. This experience is very fulfilling and creates a sense of joy in parenting. When the opposite takes place, both sides feel disconnected and rejected, and parenting feels more like an exhausting chore—three cheers for connection and acceptance!

We notice in the parenting sections of bookshops that most titles tend to be about changing children's behavior. Very few books teach parents how to develop a meaningful and enjoyable connection with their children, yet having such a connection with them is probably the most important need that they have as they grow up.

Some dads think it's a "girl thing"—only daughters benefit from having this core need met. But the core emotional need for connection and acceptance is not unique to a particular gender—research indicates that a father's approval is just as important for the development of healthy self-esteem in boys[3] (RR5.1). Some parents feel connected to their young children but find that they are not as connected to their teens. As our children's level of autonomy increases (see Chapters Nine to Eleven), we should maintain the connection as well as successfully make the transition from leading by authority to leading by relationship/influence.[4] This is where many parents err; they allow the connection level to deteriorate with the increase in autonomy, thinking that this is part and parcel of their child growing up. We need to fight hard to ensure that our children make room for us in their lives. If we are nonchalant about this gradual separation, we will end up forfeiting a valuable on-going connection which teens need as they make the transition from childhood to adulthood. While autonomy (the second core emotional need) is increasing, the connection must be maintained.

In addition, some parents worry that if they have a strong emotional connection with their children, it will *prevent* them from guiding and teaching their children and helping them shoulder responsibilities effectively. This really is not true; in fact, it is just the opposite. Dr. John Gottman has conducted research on marriage and parenting for over a quarter of a century. He has concluded that the more a child is emotionally connected with his parents, the more likely the child is to accept his parent's values.[5] When the level of connection is high, the ability of the parents to influence them is also high—connection isn't just good for the kids, it's good for the parents, too!

When babies are born prematurely and need to live in incubators, hospitals know that they will thrive only if exposed to human touch. We were created to connect with one another, especially with our loved ones—and children need the affection of their parents constantly, not just when they are first born.

One of our favorite studies supporting the need for connection between parents and children is the research done among students who attended Harvard University between the years 1952 and 1954. These students were asked whether their relationships with their mothers and fathers, were close, warm, friendly, or strained and cold. Thirty-five years later when the participants were middle-aged, their medical records were collected. Results showed that 87% of the students who had rated their mothers and fathers low in parental caring had been diagnosed with diseases, such as coronary artery disease, hypertension, duodenal ulcers and alcoholism in midlife, whereas only 25% of them who had rated both their mothers and fathers high in parental caring had diagnosed diseases[6] (RR5.2). While many academically ambitious parents fight tooth and nail to get their kids into Ivy League schools, how many of the put in the same effort to be connected and to show acceptance?

Some parents think that loving their children means that they should provide for their shelter, clothing, food, healthcare and education, and that is it. But what does it take for *our children* to feel connected to us and accepted by us to an adequate degree? Do our children sense that we *like* them? We will only be able to meet this need of connection and acceptance if our children sense that we as parents enjoy being around them *as people*. Many parents are so consumed by their worries that they either do not have room in their hearts to connect with their children or they actually see their children as being in the way of meeting other goals.

## Parenting Pioneers

We would like to end this chapter by sharing the findings of some of the most intuitive family educators over the last 50 years. See if you can spot a pattern, a common thread that runs through their parenting philosophies:

Haim Ginnot was a clinical psychologist and therapist who wrote a best selling book called *Between Parent and Child*. He said that parents should accept the feelings of the children but not necessarily their behavior. He also felt very strongly that parents, and teachers, should connect with and accept their children. He stated:

I am a child psychotherapist. I treat disturbed children. Supposing I see a child in therapy one hour a week for a year. Her symptoms disappear; she feels better about herself, gets along with others, even stops fidgeting in school. What is it that I do that helps? I communicate with her in a unique way. I use every opportunity to enhance her feelings about herself. *If caring communication can drive sick children sane, its principles and practice belong to parents and teachers.* While psychotherapists may be able to cure, only those in daily contact with children can prevent them from needing psychological help.[7]

Rudolf Dreikurs, a student of Alfred Adler, who was trained by Freud, wrote *Children: The Challenge*. Here are two of his well-known principles explaining misbehavior and the importance of non-verbal communication:

A misbehaving child is a discouraged child...In a thousand subtle ways, by tone of voice and by action, we indicate to the child that we consider him inept, unskilled and generally inferior...[8] Parents many times do not know how they go about discouraging their children, starting in very subtle ways, both verbally and with tone and body language.[9]

David Elkind is a professor emeritus at Tufts University, Massachusetts, and wrote several best sellers, including, *The Hurried Child*. Elkind has this to say about how pushing children to learn academically and hurrying them to grow faster than their natural pace puts them in harm's way:

The abuse of hurrying is a contractual violation. Contractual violations are experienced as exploitative and stressful by children because the implicit contracts between parents and children are the fundament of the children's sense of basic trust, a kind of standard against which the children's social interactions are measured. Two different types of contractual violations and exploitations can be identified. One is qualitative and might be called calendar hurrying. It occurs whenever we ask children to understand beyond their limits of understanding, to decide beyond their capacity to make decisions, or to act willfully before they have the will to act. But children can also be hurried quantitatively, and this might be called clock hurrying. We engage in clock hurrying whenever, through our excessive demands over a short period of time, we call upon children to call upon their energy reserves.[10]

This Elkind quote deserves extra attention:

In effect, adolescents pay us back in the teen years for all the sins, real or imagined, that we have committed against them when they were children.[11]

Adele Faber and Elaine Mazlish, disciples of Ginnot, co-authored what is known in some circles as the "parenting bible". They wrote:

If our attitude is not one of compassion, then whatever we say will be experienced by the child as phony or manipulative. It is when our words are infused with real feelings of empathy that they speak directly to the child's heart.[12]

Gottman, who we quoted earlier, believes strongly in helping children deal with their emotions in an empathetic and guiding way (he calls it "emotion coaching"), which in turn contributes to the connection between parent and child. Gottman and his team at the University of Washington conducted in-depth research with 119 families to see how parents and children interact with each other, following children from the age of four until adolescence. His conclusion:

Children whose parents consistently practiced emotion coaching have better physical health and score higher academically than children whose parents don't offer such guidance. These kids get along better with friends, have fewer behavioral problems, and are less prone to acts of violence. Overall children who are emotion coached experience fewer negative feelings and more positive feelings. In short they are healthier emotionally.[13]

Gottman asserts when parents help their children deal with uncomfortable feelings like guilt, regret and sadness, their children feel more supported. He goes on to say:

> If children are emotion coached from a young age, they become well practiced at the art of self-soothing and they can stay calm under stress, which also makes them less likely to misbehave.[14]

Gottman's research demonstrates that the practice of empathy by parents makes children feel supported; they feel like their parents are their allies, and they are much more likely to accept the parents' values.

This is the common thread running through all of the excellent parenting philosophies above—that parents must connect with their children empathically, and not cause exasperation. **This is not just a good idea; it is the foundation of effective and healthy parenting; it is the bedrock of Good Enough Parenting.**

# Chapter Six

## THE DOMAIN OF DISCONNECTION AND REJECTION
·······································································

We mentioned in Chapter One that the 18 lifetraps identified by Dr. Jeffrey Young clustered into four domains—the first of these domains is known as "Disconnection and Rejection". To the extent parents do not meet the core emotional need for connection and acceptance, we believe their children will experience the opposite—*Disconnection and Rejection.* This means that their children will be at risk of developing some or all of the lifetraps in the Domain of Disconnection and Rejection, namely Mistrust, Defectiveness, Emotional Deprivation, Social Isolation, Emotional Inhibition, and Failure. This chapter explains these six lifetraps in detail, and contains an additional segment called "Basic Safety Zone".

### The Lifetrap of Mistrust / Abuse
The first maladaptive schema (lifetrap) in the domain of disconnection and rejection is mistrust / abuse. The core message of the mistrust lifetrap is, *"I cannot expect others to treat me in a fair, considerate or just manner. I should expect to be hurt (emotionally or even physically), lied to, taken advantage of, and manipulated. Others always have their own agenda."*

Children who are abused or who have *witnessed* abuse will almost always develop the lifetrap of mistrust. When their caregivers, especially their parents, are not trustworthy, children receive a very damaging message. When abuse happens, especially repeatedly, children will, out of necessity, stop trusting. They become wary and have a much harder time bonding, making friends, and accepting help. They look for the "agenda" in people and will often read something negative into others' actions and doubt their motives, feeling that others are out to take advantage of them or cause them harm. They are constantly on the alert. They carry the pain and mistrust into their adult relationships and interactions, frequently misconstruing others' words. They have a hard time giving the benefit of the doubt, and easily fall into labeling or judging others.

As crusaders for justice, those with this lifetrap often try to expose others' duplicity, even though there may not be any. They sometimes do not have a good opinion of people who are loving and caring but weak in a "pet" area that they esteem. People with the lifetrap of mistrust see everything in black and white. Rather than understanding people's motives usually lie somewhere in a range, they automatically put people into two categories—those who can be trusted and those who cannot. They give people "tests" (I wonder if she will remember my birthday?) without telling them they are being tested; eventually, everyone fails the tests, proving that they were justified in not trusting.

*Early family environment that might cause this lifetrap to develop:*

- The child was abused verbally, physically and/or sexually, by a parent, a relative, a teacher, a classmate, or any combination of the above. (If the child or adult has never discussed his abuse with his parents or an adult, it will be very painful when he chooses to open up. The listener needs to be patient and understanding, giving him time to talk through it all and not be hurried.)
- The child's siblings fought with him constantly and his parents allowed it and did not protect him.
- There was a lot of tension in the child's home; e.g., he witnessed his father abusing his mother.
- The child grew up in an environment where the abuse was done to others, and he observed the abuse. For example, perhaps a sibling was ill-treated, or the child knew one of his friends was being abused, or he saw peers in school being abused by teachers. (See "Basic Safety Zone" for more info on preventing abuse.)

Figure 6.1: The Lifetrap of Mistrust (Alastair as an adult)

Figure 6.2: A Possible Early Environment Which Would Likely Contribute to the Development of the Mistrust Lifetrap (Alastair as a child) Go to Appendix I

## The Lifetrap of Defectiveness / Shame

The next maladaptive schema (lifetrap) in the domain of disconnection and rejection is defectiveness / shame. The core message of the defectiveness lifetrap is, *"I am not good enough. I am inherently flawed. Anyone who truly knows me could not love me."*

Do you know smart people who do not think they are intelligent, and attractive people who do not think they are nice-looking? People with this lifetrap feel something is wrong with them—that they are strange, short, fat, inept, or just plain lousy. They are over-sensitive to their weaknesses, with an unjustified fear of exposing themselves to others. They do not take compliments well, and believe they do not deserve praise. They get jealous and competitive as well as feel insecure around those they perceive as being better than they are. They make a lot of comparisons, even in common interactions. If the lifetrap is strong, they become consumed with status and position, and they overvalue success, such as academic or athletic achievement. Even though they may be highly successful, they feel deep down that they are not good enough. Because they feel defective, they are rarely satisfied with their present state of affairs. They have not yet learnt to accept themselves, flaws and all, and celebrate their strengths and accomplishments with confidence. If they happen to have the overcompensation coping style, they will be easily offended, and put down the offending person before the other person puts them down. They become more consumed about not being defective than they are about meeting the core needs of their significant others. They push themselves all the time, to the point that their closest relationships get hurt along the way. They also fear that their defectiveness will get exposed and that they will be shamed. This lifetrap is ultimately about shame.

*Early family environment that might cause this lifetrap to develop:*

- The child was compared to others (siblings, relatives, and peers) and felt that her parents were disappointed with her.
- The child was unfairly blamed for wrongs growing up.
- The child was criticized by at least one of her parents for being the "black sheep" of the family, for being useless, slow, dumb, clumsy, ugly, stupid, etc.
- The child's parents constantly talked about their definition of a successful person and how she did not make the cut.
- The child always felt that she did not quite measure up, i.e., not good enough in studies or in sports, or not pretty or talented enough, etc.

Figure 6.3: The Lifetrap of Defectiveness (Sharon as an adult)

Figure 6.4: A Possible Early Environment Which Would Likely Contribute to the Development of the Defectiveness Lifetrap (Sharon as a child) Go to Appendix I

## The Lifetrap of Emotional Deprivation

Another maladaptive schema (lifetrap) in the domain of disconnection and rejection is emotional deprivation. The core message of the maladaptive schema of emotional deprivation lifetrap is, *"I cannot expect others to be supportive of me and care about what I need."* Emotional deprivation is about insufficient empathy, nurturing, and/or not receiving guidance and direction.

Children develop the emotional deprivation lifetrap if they did not feel emotionally close to their parents when they were growing up. This may or may not involve physical separation from their parents, but it definitely involves emotional distance. Some children are left to themselves, and feel empty in their formative years. When children are deprived of love during childhood, they become angry and lonely. As adults, they still have the same feeling that people will never love them enough. They yearn to feel loved but feel that they are neither understood nor loved. Someone with this lifetrap seems to develop a kind of "bottomless pit"—no matter how much love is shown to them, it is never enough to satisfy them. Even in marriage, they frequently feel lonely and feel that no one is there to have care and concern for them. They might not feel a deep friendship with people even though the other parties feel close to them. They combat constant feelings of never having enough love.

*Early family environment that might cause this lifetrap to develop:*
- The child did not have loving and nurturing parents; there were not many kisses, hugs or physical touch. Although the child's parents were physically there, no one was very warm to her, or remembered and celebrated special days, like birthdays.
- The child's parents were emotionally absent and may have had someone else raise her. She seldom went to them for love and affection, and if she tried, it didn't go well.
- The child's mother had a busy schedule (this lifetrap may have more to do with lack of maternal closeness, rather than paternal), and was focused on her own career or social life and did not have time for the child. She may have been ill and not able to meet the child's needs for a legitimate reason.
- Even when the child did talk to the parents, they did not know how to empathize with her. So, the child grew up feeling like her feelings were not important or understood.
- The child was given material things and vacations, perhaps even spoiled, but little interest was expressed in her and what was going on in her life.
- When the child had problems, her parents were not there to listen and advise her.

Figure 6.5: The Lifetrap of Emotional Deprivation (May Lee as an adult)

Figure 6.6: A Possible Early Environment Which Would Likely Contribute to the Development of the Emotional Deprivation Lifetrap (May Lee as a child) *Go to Appendix I*

## The Lifetrap of Social Isolation / Alienation

Social isolation / alienation is the fourth maladaptive schema (lifetrap) in the domain of disconnection and rejection. The core message of the social isolation lifetrap is, *"I am different from other people and do not fit in."* The feelings of isolation and being alone stem from feeling apart from any group or community, and too different to belong.

Children who develop this lifetrap feel different from other people and feel that they do not fit in. They may avoid social gatherings because they do not like to mix with others, and they feel out of place if they do join such a gathering. They may even feel singled out because they *feel* that they are different and not part of the group. What makes them feel different is not necessarily negative—they may be more educated, have more money, or come from a family with fame or power. Ultimately, when they look at those around them, they feel that they are the odd one out. Adults with this lifetrap will focus more on what makes them different and set apart from others than on what they have in common, and consequently end up isolated and lonely. They exaggerate differences between themselves and others rather than focusing on what they have in common with friends, family and others. Although it is related to the lifetrap of defectiveness, it is different from defectiveness, which is related to feeling inferior on the inside; people with the social isolation lifetrap feel out of place because of *external* factors. It is possible to have both.

*Early family environment that might cause this lifetrap to develop:*
- The child felt different from others and felt that he did not fit in.
- The child's friends were of a different race, spoke a different language, or were perceived as being more intelligent than he.
- The child's friends may have been behind him in school or sports or in some talent, which still may have given the child the feeling that he was different from the rest.
- The child felt that his family was strange and different from the rest, and in his heart he felt that something was wrong. This could result from problems in his family, or other factors, such as having more power, fame or fortune.
- The child's parents were divorced, but his friends' parents were not. Or the child's school friends lived in a nice neighborhood, but he did not, or the other way round.
- One of the child's parent's jobs resulted in the family having to move a lot so the child felt different from everyone wherever he went.

Figure 6.7: The Lifetrap of Social Isolation (Chitra as an adult)

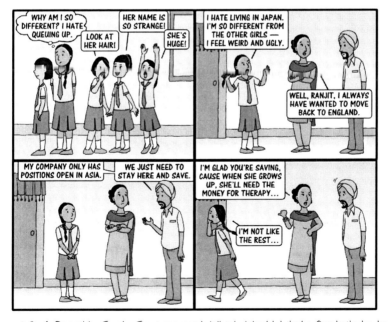

Figure 6.8: A Possible Early Environment Which Would Likely Contribute to the Development of the Social Isolation Lifetrap (Chitra as a child) *Go to Appendix 1*

## The Lifetrap of Emotional Inhibition

Another maladaptive schema (lifetrap) in the domain of Disconnection and Rejection is emotional inhibition. The core message of the emotional inhibition lifetrap is, *"I should not express myself or show my emotions. I should always be in control."*

When children are not allowed to be themselves, are made to feel that their emotions are wrong, and belittled for feeling excited or joyful or angry, they will almost certainly develop the schema of emotional inhibition. These children receive a message that it is safer in their family not to stand out or draw attention to oneself. Some children are even made to tiptoe around the house so as not to offend the highly sensitive parent who does not want to be "disturbed". Adults with this lifetrap are often seen by others as having no emotions. They value being rational as a superior disposition. They do not like anything too loud, too spontaneous, too noisy, or too passionate, though it may not be perceived as such by their spouses or other people. They see such behavior as being ill-mannered, inappropriate, and very much out of place.

In some cases, people from upper middle class backgrounds have been brought up to think this way. In other cases, it may be a cultural issue, associated with ethnicity. Certain societies tend to feel that emotions should be contained, which becomes damaging because in that setting, even intimacy has to be "appropriate". Any emotion or opinion forthcoming is almost viewed as being aggressive. People with this lifetrap struggle to get intimate and are usually unaware of the lack of connection felt by their loved ones. It is difficult for them to share what is heartfelt. What lurks beneath the surface is fear of shame if they were to let out their true feelings or emotions. People with the lifetrap of emotional inhibition are tempted to think that it is weird to laugh loudly, to cry, or express affection because they were looked down upon for being expressive when they were younger. As adults, they have learned to hold things in, rather than seeing emotional expression as being healthy.

*Early family environment that might cause this lifetrap to develop:*

- The child's parents hardly talked when they were at home, even when they were having a meal together.
- The child's parents believed in the old sayings, "Children are to be seen and not heard" and "Big boys don't cry".
- The child was prevented from being a child or expressing emotions. He had to temper his excitement about normal things and control his emotions so as to not bother his father or mother.
- Being loud, excited, and making noise were all viewed as unacceptable behavior.

Figure 6.9: The Lifetrap of Emotional Inhibition (Amir as an adult)

Figure 6.10: A Possible Early Environment Which Would Likely Contribute to the Development of the Emotional Inhibition Lifetrap (Amir as a child) *Go to Appendix 1*

## The Lifetrap of Failure

The sixth and final maladaptive schema (lifetrap) in the domain of disconnection and rejection is failure. The core message of the failure lifetrap is, *"I am fundamentally incompetent and have failed, am failing, and will fail again in the future. I am less talented and successful than other people."* The focus of this lifetrap is on achievement and external status symbols of success, rather than on the internal feeling of shame and inferiority that is present in the case of the defectiveness lifetrap.

Some children have a harder time than others in school, which may make them susceptible to developing this lifetrap. However, other children may actually excel at many things but not in the one area their parents value, or they excel in areas that are not to their parents' liking. When these children become adults, they will always feel down on themselves compared to their peers. Others may tell them that they have done a great job, but they will not believe it. Instead, they always feel like a failure, in relation to their accomplishments, wealth, status, or academic pursuits. Whatever success they have managed to achieve, they will attribute to luck, or they just believe that the people giving them encouragement are mistaken. People with this lifetrap believe they have failed and are destined to fail, and usually do not try very hard to succeed. They make unfair comparisons with others about where they are in life. Some people will not be as successful as others financially, and everyone has limitations in some areas. In fact, it is good for people to be sober about where they are, but people with this lifetrap need to not go to the other extreme. The failure lifetrap is often linked with the defectiveness lifetrap.

*Early family environment that might cause this lifetrap to develop:*
- The child's parents emphasized success in something that was not her strength. For example, they may have focused on the sciences, but she may have been good at the arts.
- When the child did not succeed, her parents were harsh with their criticism and called her a failure.
- The child did not receive much encouragement from her parents about her strengths, and was constantly trying to get their attention.
- The child's parents compared her with her siblings or cousins or she may have heard how much they bragged about them but not about her, so she lost motivation to give her best.
- Friends, teachers or peers looked down on the child due to racism or other reasons, and she may have believed them.

Figure 6.11: The Lifetrap of Failure (Gunther as an adult)

Figure 6.12: A Possible Early Environment Which Would Likely Contribute to the Development of the Failure Lifetrap (Gunther as a child) *Go to Appendix 1*

## Basic Safety Zone

Over the past few pages, we have explained how, if their core emotional need for connection and acceptance is not met, children will be at risk of developing some or all of the lifetraps in the domain of disconnection and rejection. Before we close this chapter, we want to highlight one of the biggest dangers children face today, and one of the biggest contributors to disconnection and rejection: child abuse. Basic safety for this core emotional need revolves around protecting children from abuse for every possible reason, not the least of which is to avoid the development of the mistrust lifetrap. Children need to be protected from all kinds of abuse, be it emotional, verbal, physical, sexual, or the abuse of neglect.

Having counseled hundreds of people who have experienced emotional abuse (discussed throughout these chapters on connection and acceptance) we have found that it is just as harmful if not more so than physical abuse. Having said that, there is absolutely no excuse for physical abuse. It is illegal and in most countries will either land the parent in jail or warrant the child being removed from the home. Neglect is another kind of abuse. In the United States, parents who neglect their children out of ignorance or because of extreme poverty, addiction, criminal activity, or any other reason make up the largest number of abusers, estimated to be as high as 78% of all abuse cases reported.[1] Sexual abuse affects all races, cultures, religions, and socioeconomic groups; it is a scourge of our modern world. For young teen girls, the number one predictor of early sexual intercourse is childhood sexual abuse;[2] and one out of six boys will be sexually abused by their eighteenth birthday.[3] The US based National Center for Victims of Crime website contains shocking statistics as well as helpful advice for assisting a child's healing process.[4] (RR6.1)

It is a given that parents should not abuse their children. Meet the core emotional needs and you will not! In addition, in order to provide basic safety, parents must also do their absolute best to ensure that their kids are not abused by others. This involves getting to know your children's friends, being involved at school, limiting or not allowing unsupervised play, as well as monitoring your children's moods when they play with others and when they come home from school. Specific signs of sexual child abuse can be difficult to identify—e.g. pain while walking or sitting, genital pain, excessive aggression, seductiveness, early sexualization, or a sudden change in mood. Keep in mind that some children resist reporting, as they are afraid of angering the offender, blame themselves for the abuse and/or feel guilty and ashamed. Also, pay attention when someone shows greater than normal interest in your child. You can help by being active in prevention services like public education activities, family support programs, or parent education classes. Don't forget to protect your child from sexual abuse on the Internet. (This will be discussed more in the Basic Safety Zone portion of Chapter Thirteen.)

••••••••••••••••••••••••••••••••••••••••••••••••••••••••••••

### *Louis Lowdown*

We informed our kids early on about "private parts", and how those parts were special, "just for you and one day just for your spouse; that no one outside of Mommy and Daddy was supposed to see or touch them", and how they should tell us if someone else tried to or did anything strange. We didn't want them to be ashamed of sex or of their bodies; at the same time we wanted them to understand the concept of modesty, and we absolutely wanted to empower them with a sense of boundaries and have the ability to say "No". From time to time, we would ask the kids in a very nonchalant way if anyone had tried to touch their private parts, not wanting to alarm them but wanting to provide protection. And we were careful about who spent time with the kids when we were not around. We have heard many stories of children being sexually molested by neighbors, relatives, and kids at school. These stories may have caused us to be a bit hyper-vigilant, but these days, we figure it's better to be safe than sorry.

••••••••••••••••••••••••••••••••••••••••••••••••••••••••••••

# Chapter Seven

# QUALITY TIME TAKES TIME
......................................................................

There are three "must-dos" when it comes to meeting this core emotional need—one is practicing Chapters Three and Four—do not exasperate! Another has to do with processing emotions, which we will deal with in Chapter Eight. This chapter focuses on the all-important "must-do" without which you will never be able to connect: Spend time with your children!

## The Power of One-on-One

As we have helped various parents who are struggling to connect with one or more of their children, the advice they have found the most helpful is to commit to a regular one-on-one time with each child. Most parents do not have a *scheduled* time with each child—their interactions tend to happen on an *ad hoc* basis, i.e., when they go shopping, when they are on a holiday together, when they are driving together after school, and so forth. While these "normal" times have tremendous value in themselves, we believe that most children need more. When parents go the extra mile to set aside one-on-one time for their children, they are sending a loud and clear message, "You are more important to me than anything else right now. You have value because you are worth my time." The busier the parents are, the stronger this message comes across to the children. Children themselves are also busier than they have ever been, considering the pressure to perform academically and athletically, but that is for a later chapter! Suffice it to say, children understand what it means to be busy, and they absolutely know what their parents value and what they make time for. So, when a parent sets aside individual time to spend with each child, it has a great impact.

••••••••••••••••••••••••••••••••••••••••••••••••••••••••••••••

### *Louis Lowdown*

Sonia and I (John) began going on "dates" when she was in kindergarten; I would say, "Hey, Sonia, let's go to McDonalds!" and she'd always say, "Yea!" (In the early years, I wasn't competing with much!). This became our habit; Sonia told me what was happening at school, with friends, and anything else she was felt like talking about. Once I made the "mistake" of asking her what *she* wanted to do for our date that week and she replied, "Draw." "I can't draw!" I exclaimed. Karen smiled maliciously and handed me some colored pencils. "What will we draw?" I asked, and Sonia replied, "Let's sit on the balcony and draw what we see." I was in uncharted waters, but that didn't matter. My daughter thoroughly enjoyed herself, and we felt that much more connected.

I made the mistake of getting too busy with work and neglected our dates just when Sonia entered her preteen years. I tried to "reboot" but Sonia didn't see the need to pick up where we left off. "I want to be close to you", I pleaded. She retorted, "We are already close." Desperate, I bribed her with the chance to order whatever she wanted from her favorite café—that did the trick! We ate cheesecake, I apologized for being too busy, and she chatted about schoolwork. The next week, I brought her to a CD shop where we shared headphones and listened to her favorite music. By the third week, she told me the latest updates on her friends and after a month, our connection was completely repaired.

When Sonia was in high school, the only time she could squeeze me in was early in the morning before school. It wasn't convenient for me, but it was worth it. Sonia and I would talk for maybe forty minutes. Conversations ranged from light-hearted to really opening up about various worries or feelings—especially after a few sips of Starbucks coffee! She left for school feeling happy and secure, and I felt deeply connected to my teenaged daughter.

David and I always referred to our weekly outings as "our time" rather than a "date"—guess it's a guy thing. We did all sorts of fun things in his growing up years. Once he was in high school, we also went for breakfast, but our connection felt the deepest on the courts—from the time he was 14, David and I played racket sports almost every week. Somehow when we were both covered in sweat, after getting out all our aggression, we had the deepest talks! Conflicts got resolved and dreams get divulged—real connection. I wouldn't trade those times for anything!

••••••••••••••••••••••••••••••••••••••••••••••••••••••••••••

Regular one-on-one time has other benefits—as an antidote to sibling rivalry (Junior can't say his brother is your favorite if you make a point to have private time with each child!), to help a child with a more sensitive temperament, or to make up the difference when there is a special needs child in the home. One family we counseled had a child who had been on a strict insulin regime since birth—every two hours the mom had to wake up and check her younger child's readings. Of course the mom was exhausted and barely had time for the older child, who tried her best to gain the mother's favor. After putting this recommendation into practice for just two weeks (and hiring someone to help with housework!), the older child's countenance has changed—the dad says she is like a new kid!

## The Price of Privilege

Research has shown that lack of time spent with our children has a detrimental effect on our children's emotional and intellectual well-being. So isn't it ironic that parents from affluent societies push their children to be accepted into the best schools, fill their children's time up with rigorous competitive sports, extra academic enrichment classes and extracurricular activities such as art, music, dance, debate, and acting, but have no time to build connection? Many of these affluent parents travel for or are consumed by work, and are not available to spend time with the family. Society may consider them successful but they have little or no connection with their children, which begs the question, "Are they *really* successful?"

The unrelenting standards of societies, especially affluent nations, are driving parents to push themselves and their children with a devastating consequence: Poor parent-child connection![1]

In no way are we stating that getting involved in sports or being concerned with academic success is wrong *per se,* but when it is done at the expense of the parent-child connection, it is harmful to the family. There is no substitute for spending undivided time connecting and talking with our kids.

## The Power of Daily Dinners

You've heard it before—one of the most important practices parents can perpetuate is to commit to regular gatherings around the dinner table. Having more meal times together is the single strongest predictor of better achievement scores and fewer behavioral problems such as depression, worry, fear, self-injury and social withdrawal. Parents giving attention to their children, responding to questions from their children, and keeping everyone's behavior at the table well regulated is associated with enriched language development and academic achievement.[2] The Putting Family First community found that from 1981 to 1997, American families had dinner together less often, spent less time talking as a family, took fewer vacations together, and participated together in religious observances less often, and that by the end of the twentieth century, fewer than one third of US families were eating dinner together regularly.[3] (RR7.1)

The researchers also found that watching television during mealtimes is *not* helpful for overall family well-being (but half the families have a TV in their dining area). One reason is that some families turn their television on as a way to avoid further conflict.[4] Another reason is that eating in front of the television is associated with significantly greater caloric intake in children and adults, partly because food ads cue eating behavior.[5] The most obvious reason is that television impairs connection between family members—it's hard to talk when the boob tube (or YouTube for that matter) is on! We strongly recommend that family members be attentive to one another during mealtimes, not be distracted by media of any kind, and spend their time sharing "highs and lows". Make sure to avoid the exasperation interactions—otherwise the process will backfire!

For most families, no other shared activity is done with such regularity as the evening meal. If families spend 20 minutes together during dinnertime, in a given week, that's more than two hours, with no agenda besides fun, (healthy) food, and "fellowship". Such regular connection-building leads to many positive benefits for all family members. Can't do it every night? Shoot for five nights a week. We insist on this whenever we lead marriage and family workshops, without apologies.

• • • • • • • • • • • • • • • • • • • • • • • • • • • • • • • • • • • • • • • • • • •

68 | GOOD **enough** PARENTING

*Louis Lowdown*

We began asking our kids about their "highs" and "lows" after watching the movie *The Story of Us* (1999). Our younger child would almost come out of his seat to share—"I've got five highs! The first high is, I've got more highs than lows. The second high is, I've got no lows." His older sister would be rolling her eyes; undeterred, David would launch into the rest with gusto. If Sonia had a high, it was a real high, and she sometimes shared a low, or sometimes would say, "I don't want to share." (That was a sure sign that we would want to spend an extra long time tucking her into bed that night.) Highs and lows launched all sorts of discussions. Once when I (Karen) was driving David home from first grade, he blurted out, "I've got a low." My instinct was to say, "Wait for dinner so Dad can hear", but I stopped myself and said, "What's that, sweetheart?" "The boy named Jack touched someone's private parts!" Well, let me tell you I was glad I asked! We settled that matter at school the next day. As the kids got older, we shared more and more of our highs and lows, and shared about people we were helping or people who were sick and needed care, etc. Now that John and I are empty nesters, all four of us treasure our rare family dinners so we can share highs and lows together once more.

......................................................

## The Power of Early Attachment

While it may be common sense today for many parents to be close to their infants, this was not always the case even up to half a century ago. After World War II in England, conventional wisdom was that children were attached to their mothers for two reasons: food and "dependency".[6] In other words, the thinking of that day was that if young children were allowed to be too close to their mothers, they would be spoiled and helpless. As a result, it was the norm for mothers to *not* spend time with their infants. I (Karen) remember an article years ago about Princess Diana and how Princes William and Harry were the first men "in line for the throne" who were actually raised up by their own mother. It is hard to believe that this was the mind-set only sixty years ago.

John Bowlby challenged this view. He hypothesized that infants would experience loss and suffering when separated from their primary caregivers, and as a result of his own observations, put forward the theory of the importance of attachment of infants to mothers from birth. Bowlby's findings stressed that children below two and a half years old become secure when they form special attachments to familiar caregivers (RR7.2).[7]

Another researcher found that mothers who are negative and who do not respond to their babies by connecting to them emotionally will end up passing these traits down to their children, even at this age! The infant grows up following suit and becomes depressed as well, with low energy, anger, and irritability. Further, if the mother's depression continues for a year or so, the baby will show lasting delays in growth and development. Our mood and disposition are so important in developing a healthy connection with our infants. Tiffany Field, a leader in touch research, proved that massaging premature babies in incubators greatly improved their health"[8] (RR7.3).

Children learn to relate on an emotional level with others by having a strong attachment. Susan Anderson, a professor of psychology, says when attachment is not satisfactorily achieved, children become concerned about it; but when it is satisfactorily achieved, then the issue of attachment falls to the background.[9] In other words, when children are securely attached, they don't notice that they are attached, and they are free to focus on learning and exploring, eager to explore their new world. Having a healthy connection with the parents, especially the mother at this stage, is crucial. When not securely connected, children become exasperated because their needs are not met. They seek ways to adapt to the mother instead of the other way around. As a result, a false self, as Winnicott calls it, emerges.[10] Later on in life this develops into what we call their "coping style". Secure attachment also brings trust. Elkind says this sense of trust develops when the primary caregivers are consistent and dependable; it gradually instill in children the sense that the world is the same; that it is consistent and dependable and can be trusted. On the other hand, parents who spend time with their children inconsistently, and who are always busy with something else will cause their children to not be trusting of the world, and this will carry into their adult lives.[11]

## The Power of Connect, Work and Play (and Dads Love to Play!)

The way a parent connects with a child varies greatly from stage to stage in the child's development. It is important to take note of the needs of the child at the different stages so we have included these stages here, with an explanation of how to make the connection possible.

## Infancy

Connection begins in infancy; parents should not wait for the child to talk to focus on connection. At around three months old, parents are able to hold their infant's attention. They use a high-pitched voice and talk slowly and repetitively; this type of tone gets a positive response and conveys connection. If the parent is in the right frame of mind, connection takes place throughout the day: during feeding, talking soothingly, cuddling, putting the baby to sleep, singing. Even when parents play with an infant, they are connecting.

We have borrowed from David Elkind, who wrote about the three inborn drives that power human thought and action; we refer throughout this book to the concepts of "Connect, Work and Play".[12] To put things simply, having the right balance of connection, work and play helps us on our journey to be good enough parents as we learn to meet the core emotional need of connection and acceptance without neglecting the other core emotional needs.[13] Like Elkind, we believe that connect, work and play function together, and in the course of time they become increasingly separate. We would like to build on Elkind, and be more specific about the way these three drives evolve with age, as we talk about meeting the core emotional need of connection and acceptance (see Figure 7.1).

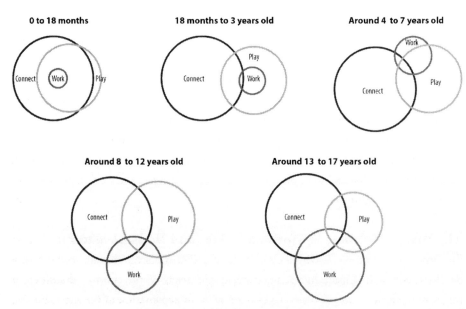

Figure 7.1: Connect, Work and Play

At the infancy stage (see Figure 7.1: 0 to 18 months), connect and play are dominant. Work is done as the child grows, from his five senses, but nothing intentional. Parents should not stress themselves out reading mathematical equations aloud so that their children will be good at the subject when they get older, or playing classical music for them in the womb to make them into geniuses; those theories are probably more urban legend than good science. From what we could gather, listening to classical music may soothe your baby and turn her into a classical fan later in life, but it won't make her smarter. (RR7.4)

When parents are spending time with their infants, they should hold them gently and look at their baby lovingly during feeding time. This can be a special bonding time, since babies are able to respond to facial expressions and even imitate them. How fun when babies smile back—and it's not just gas! Smiles begin at around two months. By the beginning of the second year, sustained joy can be seen in toddlers.

Babies need to feel nurtured and loved. Mothers should encourage them with a gentle and nurturing voice, which sometimes has to be pitched higher than usual (fathers please take note), as babies respond better to such sounds. Of course, this involves lots of affection, such as holding, kissing and cuddling. Infants cry in order to get their needs met. They are not being manipulative at this stage; there is no need for discipline. Their cries are for care, and parents need to respond appropriately. Infants are learning to trust the parents; this comes as parents respond to their baby's cries.

And parents should sing to their babies! By all means, play classical music if you enjoy it! Play fun baby sing-a-long songs as well. Any music that promotes a healthy atmosphere is helpful, whether it's Bach, Beatles, Bluegrass, Bollywood, or Brazilian samba! Did you ever hear the old adage, "You don't sing because you're happy, you're happy because you sing". I (Karen) find that singing calms me down when I am in stressful situations. How nice for children to be surrounded by song.

We have talked a lot about play. Babies love playing and do not need to work! Infants, however, can only handle a certain amount of play, and then they will turn their head away and will not be interested anymore. Do not pursue further, since overstimulation may cause distress.

Parents must provide consistent nurturing and care. We recommend that mothers stay at home with their children until the kids begin to attend school, or at the very least stay home with their infants for a year. In a perfect world, if mothers needed to go back to work, they could get a flexi-hour or part-time job. We applaud progressive countries like Sweden that mandate a three-year maternity leave for mothers and one year for fathers. (Perhaps that's why Stockholm ranks in the top ten most livable cities even though it's dark half the year!) There are many alternatives to the rat race. Perhaps parents can hire temporary help for household chores so that their attention can be devoted to the baby and a part-time job, or a work-at-home, flexi-hour job. Perhaps two couples can live in the same home and share more of the load so that the moms can be full-time with their babies, or they can help look after each other's infants when the other needs to work. This calls for creativity and flexible thinking. We know that this is not necessarily a popular recommendation to make, but for the sake of seeing a generation of children whose need for connection and acceptance was met by their parents, we are willing to stick our necks out and say it.

### *Louis Lowdown*

Having said that, I (Karen) know some mothers who have no choice but to go back to work full time when their babies are small, and they have mixed emotions. This is not meant to make them feel like second-class mothers. I also know some mothers who are so miserable not working that they do not enjoy staying home and then they bring down the atmosphere in the home. The beauty of life today is that we are free to make the best choices we can for our babies and ourselves and we do not have to do what society or anyone else pressures us to do. I benefitted enormously from living in Asia when my children were born. In many developing countries, it is not unusual to be able to hire help at a relatively low cost. Since I was working a flexi-hour job, I spent much of my free time with my babies, but was able to pay someone to do other chores; for that I am eternally grateful. A guilty mother will have a hard time building connection, so whatever decisions you make about your schedule and lifestyle, believe firmly in your decision, don't get "guilted out", and build connection to the best of your ability.

Nigel Barber's research on the windows of opportunity in brain development found that emotional security in future close relationships is determined by a child's first birthday! Parents, this means that you would be giving your child a head start in having good friendships and a great marriage by connecting with them in the first year of their lives! Even more shocking is Barber's finding that intelligence, the kind that is developed while feeling secure, and exploring and bonding with parents (not from rote learning) is determined in the first two years.[14] So rather than spend all that money worrying about how to pay for some supersonic daycare, why not spend two years looking after your baby, giving them meaningful intelligence? You will see the benefits later.

Babies become very attached to their primary caregivers after about six to eight months. (But oddly enough to a parent, a baby will not have figured out that they are a completely separate person until they are around eighteen months old!) If they are crawling, they will enjoy moving away from their parents, empowered by their new skill, but then they will want to come back to as they realize, "I'm too far". When that happens, parents should receive their new explorer with open arms and a big smile, "Where did you go just now?" (Of course mothers are actually watching to make sure the babies are fine; the babies just don't know it!) Parents may become frustrated when their babies are very clingy. Before entering into this stage, babies will usually go to strangers and can be left in the dark without fear, but around eight months or so, they will start showing signs of separation anxiety, such as fear of going to strangers. It is normal. Enjoy this while it lasts—all too soon, babies grow up and the parents are the ones with separation anxiety!

Securely attached babies have mothers who respond quickly to their signals. Since the need for attachment is a natural part of an infant's development, mothers should not get irritated. For example, if a mother needs to leave her infant's room for a moment, she should be enthusiastic upon returning. This will help her baby to learn that the mother is dependable and predictable. If the mother is unreliable, the baby will feel insecure, and this lack of confidence may facilitate the development of lifetraps such as emotional deprivation, mistrust, or abandonment later in life.

Parents should beware of arguing with each other or with their in-laws in front of the baby, thinking the baby is too young to notice. Infancy is the time when pathways of a child's autonomic nervous system are developing (see Chapter One). Gottman says, "Whatever happens to a child emotionally during this first few months may have a significant and lifelong effect on the child's vagal tone; that is the child's ability to regulate the nervous system... which makes a difference in a baby's long term ability to respond to stimuli, to calm herself and recover from stress."[15]

A definite routine for babies is important, especially when it comes to time to sleep. A bedtime ritual is one of the fondest memories for connection that a parent can build with a child. Here are some *recommendations* that parents can adopt in putting their babies to bed (you will probably experiment with many options but these are some that worked for us).

Since we recommend talking to babies almost all the time, parents should begin by telling their baby that it is time to have a bath and go to bed. This gets parents into the habit so that when the child is in the toddler stage, the parents are accustomed to giving them an alert that bedtime is coming. Parents can give the baby a bath, rub their little gums, put on a clean diaper, get them into their pajamas, and sing lullabies during the final feed, all in a comfortably darkened room and relatively quiet environment. (Of course, with tiny babies, they fall asleep frequently for short spurts of time and it is not really your choice when!) Normally, parents will rock and sing to the baby until the baby is asleep, then they will place the baby into a safe crib with walls so that there is no chance of the baby falling, crawling or jumping out in the middle of the night. With newborns, it is not uncommon for parents to put their babies to sleep in a bassinette, or a Moses' basket, that is set up in the parents' bed room, which makes night feeds easier and puts parents at ease.

Once a healthy baby is over three months old, it is our opinion that parents can feel comfortable leaving the room even when the baby is awake. As long as the mother is bonding all day long and responding to the child at other times, the baby will not suffer if left to cry himself to sleep. In our opinion, helping babies learn to fall asleep on their own and stay asleep through the night is crucial for four reasons:

- Without it, the baby may not get enough sleep, and will not thrive
- The mother will not get enough sleep, and will not be able to meet her baby's needs properly during the day
- The parents' Love Connection,[16] especially their physical intimacy, will probably suffer, paving the way for all sorts of other problems.

When babies do sleep on their own and sleep through the night, and when Mommies get enough sleep, then Mommies are happy and excited to see their babies the next morning—they actually miss them rather than be tempted to resent them. In the beginning, most children will cry for a few minutes before they go to sleep. Eventually they will come to accept that the separation will be only temporary and that the parent will be there when they wake up. When the mother sees the baby the next morning, it is important that she greet the child enthusiastically to show that separation is only temporary and that mommy can be counted upon to come back. This repeated pattern is important to the child's sense of security.

By the way, all of this takes connection building with infants takes energy, so we feel compelled to remind parents to *get help when fatigued*. This is very important to prevent depression, neglect, and abuse.

••••••••••••••••••••••••••••••••••••••••••••••••••••••••••••••••

## *Louis Lowdown*

After our oldest turned two months old, she slept for ten hours straight—a miracle—but she was only going to sleep at 3am! I (Karen) was completely wiped out so, after seeking advice from friends who had older children, John and I decided to start adjusting Sonia's sleeping habits from the time she was four or five months old. Our first goal was to stop her from sleeping in the late afternoon which took about a week. The second goal was to make sure she went to bed at 8pm, not 3am. This part was harder but still not that difficult, since she had stopped the late nap. The third stage was the hardest—we had been rocking and singing her to sleep, at night, and we decided it was time for her to be put into the crib to fall asleep on her own. My "mentor" predicted this would take four nights. The first night, we did our bath and lullaby routine, then said, "Ok sweetie, now Mommy is going to go to sleep in her room, and you are going to stay here. I love you, precious." There was a dim night-light, her diaper had just been changed, she was fed and burped, and intellectually I knew she would be fine. However, when I left the room, she started to wail, and I imagined her thoughts à la the movie *Look Who's Talking*, "You guys are leaving me here alone? Mommy, Daddy, how can you be so cruel?" John and I sat in bed and cried, but we knew it was for *her* best, so we let her cry for a whole hour. She fell asleep exhausted…I went in at around 5am when I heard the first little peep from her, and I was so happy that she was so happy. The second night we repeated the routine and the wailing only lasted 40 minutes, the third night it lasted 20, and the fourth night, she smiled at me as I left her in the bed and all was well. The last stage of sleep training was when Sonia was seven months old and was no longer being breastfed; I was hoping to stop waking up to give her milk in the middle of the night. By this time, I was back to work, so I was putting her to sleep around 7pm, then I would work for a few hours. At 11pm I would take off her pajama bottoms, change her diaper, give her a bottle, sing softly, all of this in a fairly dark and quiet room. Sonia mostly slept through the whole thing, and would continue sleeping until 6 or 7am. When she was a bit older, I would leave a bottle of milk (room temperature, so it wouldn't go "off" in her air-conditioned bedroom) in her bed when I was ready to go to sleep. I no longer had to go through the midnight diaper change; she would wake up and drink by herself and then go back to sleep. I know this routine isn't for everyone, and maybe it would not work for all babies, but it worked for both of mine, kept me somewhat sane, and I believe the kids' health prospered because of it.

**The Toddler Years**

During these years, parents have virtually all the say at this stage and can easily be directive all areas like selecting activities, topics of conversations, types of toys, and choices of playgrounds. However, parents need to be directive in such a way that the child can express his feelings and thoughts, not just follow "rigid" instructions of "yes" and "no". Parents should make full use of the opportunity to interact with them at this age.

To quote again from Kagan, who was addressing the danger of very young children being given access to technology too soon:

> There needs to be some preparation, but at the age of two or three, that is too young…A child that age needs to first pick up interaction skills, which can happen only if adults actively engage them in conversation.[17]

Erik Erikson, one of the world's most influential developmental psychologists, says during this period a balance has to be struck between a child's sense of autonomy and his sense of shame and doubt,[18] meaning when children are curious and ask all kinds of questions, parents should respond *cheerfully*, rather than coming across *reproachfully*, else a sense of shame and guilt can result. Kagan says parents should be careful to ask open-ended questions at this stage instead of closed-ended questions that demand only a yes or no answer. Otherwise children can become reluctant to initiate and can become withdrawn and these traits could be carried on into their adult lives.[19]

Of Elkind's three drives, play and connect are still the most dominant (see Figure 7.1: 18 months to 3 years old). Work will start to be introduced, but in small doses, like learning the alphabet or identifying numbers and colors. The work component is therefore a little bigger than the previous stage. As Elkind said, the more their work is in the form of play, the better it will go down with young children. It is not necessary to expand on the work drive too early. Many societies are pushing children to learn at a younger age than in previous generations, even though much research has shown this can do more harm than good. Yet parents out of ignorance and fear are frantic about finding the most effective preschools to prepare their children for the future.

Dr. Sharon Kagan is the co-director for the US-based National Center for Children and families, as well as working in a leadership capacity on children's issues with Columbia and Yale. She had this to say about sending children to school too soon:

> There is simply no evidence to show that preschool would help very young children more than the care of a loving, dedicated parent. When children are young they need intimacy, they need the nurturing of caring adults, they need to be held. Society doesn't necessarily benefit from having children be required to go to an institution when they are very, very young.[20]

So while there may be a rush to get young children educated and exposed to math and in-depth reading, resist going with the flow! Parents should focus on connection, rather than education. And play, not work, is the best way for a parent to connect.

Children enjoy make-believe, and a great way to connect with them is by participating in their fantasy play. Kids enjoy making forts and tree houses, playing dress-up, and pretending to be superheroes on their own, but also have fun when parents join in. (We should note that we are not saying parents have to play for hours on end everyday.)

Mothers should find ways to spend enjoyable time with their toddlers—not just feeding or bathing them, but playing and reading lots of storybooks to them. It is important that they make time for tasks such as putting together simple puzzles with them. Mothers should engage with their children in something that they like. It is tempting for working mothers to use fatigue as an excuse not to play, but if moms only give the leftovers of their energy to their children, then, in the long haul, the children's growth will be affected. We encourage mothers to make sure they are giving the best of their lives to their children and not their bosses. Meeting the core emotional need of connection and acceptance will pay far better dividends than any annual bonus.

Another important aspect of connection with children at this age is related to setting healthy limits. When the core emotional needs are met adequately during the first stage of life, children will be much less likely to act out in aggressive ways towards other children or to get attention from their parents in order to have their needs met.

It is hard for children to develop a proper connection with anyone when they are moaning and whining due to lack of sleep. Sticking to regular bedtimes should be taken seriously. Children need to learn that sleeping times are not negotiable. Young children need to be in bed so they can get to sleep by about 7:00 or 8:00 p.m. They need lots of sleep (See Chapter Seventeen about basic safety and the need for sleep.) Boundaries should be drawn here not just for the good of the children, although that is the main reason, but also so that parents can devote time to each other in continuing to build their marriage, or have friends over, go to the gym, etc. Over and over again in counseling situations, we find that marriages are compromised because young children have not been trained to go to bed at a certain time. This infringes on the time that the parents need for each other, and over time this can damage the parents' marriage. A poor quality marriage will end up hurting the children.

Here are some recommendations for putting toddlers to bed:

Parents should give about fifteen minutes' notice to their children that it is time to begin the bedtime ritual, which would include giving them a bath, brushing teeth, and so forth. At this age, they will still enjoy lullabies, but also bedtime stories. Connection is being built as parents enthusiastically and lovingly read stories with lots of pictures and colors. Toddlers will enjoy books about hugs and kisses and falling to sleep, or even pop-up books, and parents should read in a position that enables lots of cuddling and affection. In addition, at 18 months, children may be able to fill in words as parents read along in a picture book. This kind of repetition is really helpful for their cognitive development. Parents can say "goodnight" with kisses and cuddles.

Some children love to talk just before they go to bed while some do not, depending on their "unique wiring". Parents should not be too busy and get impatient if their child is a talker and needs some time with their parent to get healthy closure for their day. It is not helpful for children's emotional security if a parent sends the message that putting them to bed is a nuisance. They will at this stage be deliberately disobedient and difficult in order to get attention from their parent(s). They would rather face the consequences of being disobedient than not having their core emotional needs met, especially of connection and acceptance. They need lots of cuddling, affection and a feeling that they are special, even if they make mistakes.

....................................................................

*Louis Lowdown*

Speaking of bedtime, from the time they were small, we taught our children to stay in bed and not come out of their rooms after bedtime unless it was really important. This had to be repeated often, and eventually they learned these limits and adhered to them—well, most of the time. This gave us more time for our work, which often included evening appointments. When they were younger, we would put them to bed by 7:00 p.m. By the time they were in primary school, we usually had them to sleep by 8:30 p.m. until third grade; in fourth and fifth grade they were in bed usually by 9:00 or 9:30 p.m. (Bedtimes are a personal preference; see Ch.17 about the need for adequate sleep.) At that age, our reading was quite fun. I (Karen) would read chapters from *The Chronicles of Narnia* or books about heroic characters, and then I would spend time with David for a bit, before going in to talk to Sonia for a while. Even though they are now adults, we still talk about the times that we read the Harry Potter books together!

....................................................................

## The Power of Dads

When it comes to connection and play, fathers should take the initiative. More and more research is showing how crucial fathers are in the lives of children at this age. When it comes to meeting this core emotional need, we must emphasize the relationship between fathers and play specifically. Here are some important findings on the impact that fathers have on their young children:

- One study that began in 1950 showed that children whose fathers were involved in their lives from the age of five grew up to be more empathetic and compassionate adults than those whose fathers were absent. The children also ended up having better social relationships and as a result they tended to have better marriages, better relationships with their own kids and were more likely to engage with others in recreational activities later in life.[21] Wow!
- Another study published in 1986, conducted by Parke and MacDonald, researchers from California State University and University of Illinois respectively, showed that children who had the best relationships with their peers were those whose fathers engaged in high levels of physical play and

who were affirming verbally. Children whose fathers were authoritarian and critical had the worst peer relationships, regardless of amount of physical play.[22] Go dads!

Gottman states, "Many psychologists believe that dad's raucous style of 'horseplay' provides an important avenue for helping children learn about emotions. Imagine a daddy 'scary bear' chasing a delighted toddler across the yard, or lifting and twirling the child over his head for an 'airplane ride'. Such games allow the child to experience the thrill of being just a bit scared, but amused and aroused at the same time…Having roughhoused with dad, the child knows how to read other people's signals when feelings run high. He knows how to generate his own exciting play and react to others in ways that are neither too sedate nor spinning out of control. He knows how to keep his emotions at a level that's optimal for fun-filled play."[23]

Fathers who devote twenty minutes a day during the week and a longer time on the weekends to playing and having fun with their children will reap lifelong benefits from the connection and their kids will reap lifelong benefits in a myriad of areas!

When spending time with your children at this age, try to really enjoy it, and let go of your inhibitions. The house will get messy but that's ok—connection is being built! Avoid prolonged time spent on computers, tablets, etc. In this day and age, many parents buy their kids electronic devices to keep them occupied. Interacting consistently and personally with your children is not something that can be replaced by expensive toys. The most important focus at this stage is learning to interact and socialize. (A wise parent we know said that the best "software" for teaching a child how to read is a parent's lap!)

Playing is a lot more fun if the siblings are close in age; if the age gap is too large, playing may need to be done separately at times. The kind of activities will determine when they should be combined.

As parents, we sometimes get bored with repetition, but children at this age do not get tired of the same old "hide and seek"; they like to hide in the same places! Do not get put off by this—see it as part of the child's development. Learn to enjoy it as much as they do! They will read your face and know if you are as engaged as they are.

Fathers, remember to allow the kids to win some of the time. It's a good idea to win occasionally so you can see their reaction; we believe in helping children to be gracious losers. When siblings are playing, help everyone to win at different times. Even if one may not be the fastest runner, you as a father can work it out to help the weakest child win from time to time. This helps everyone feel confident that playtime is fair.

Mothers need to be supportive about fathers roughhousing with the children. Many mothers caution their husbands about what is or is not safe, which can put an unnecessary damper on the spirit in the home. If the house is too calm, life can become boring, and other needs will not be met. Mothers should not overreact when there are small cuts and grazes. When a child falls, the mother's reaction often has a strong influence on the child's reaction. If the child is crying and the parents are calm, this will help the child take the fall in his or her stride. Do not criticize the child, such as calling on him to be tough. Empathize, but at the same time, do not overreact. Accidents do happen, and in the course of their childhood, hopefully nothing serious will take place.

## Early Childhood

At this age, children generally are still more excited to play with their parents than with their peers; connection and play are still very much a part of the same activity. Work can now be increased, but notice that it sits predominantly within play (see Figure 7.1, 4 to 7 years old). Good enough parents will avoid the panicked mind-set to rush their children and cram information, which does more harm than good. Children need to enjoy their childhood. We need to ensure that our children have time for organized play and free form play; both are important for healthy development. The reason we keep repeating the need for play is that research shows free time, playtime and unstructured outdoor activities have all fallen drastically over the years (RR7.5).

For a quarter of a century, we have lived in Singapore, a tiny country for whom education is practically a religion. The Prime Minister of Singapore recently voiced his concerns about "over-teaching" as he addressed parents who are worried that allowing their children to play will put them behind in school:

Instead of growing up balanced and happy, he grows up narrow and neurotic. No homework is not a bad thing. It's good for young children to play, and to learn through play.[24]

Hot on the heels of the Prime Minister's comments, the Singapore paper, *The Straits Times*, reprinted an article from *The New York Times*, entitled, "Simon Says Don't Use Flashcards". It reported:

Parents who want to stimulate their children's brain development often focus on things like early reading, flashcards and language tapes. But a growing body of research suggests that playing certain kinds of childhood games may be the best way to increase a child's ability to do well in school. Variations on old-fashioned games like "Freeze Tag" and "Simon Says" require relatively high levels of executive function, testing a child's ability to pay attention, remember rules and exhibit self-control—qualities that also predict academic success.[25] (RR7.6)

So parents need to play *with* their children and facilitate their children having time to play, both free play and organized play.

At this age, children need to be exposed to a variety of activities. They are just starting to develop peer relationships, but usually at this stage these relationships are not strong. Gottman says that usually children at this age play best in pairs with another child,[26] but group play on the playground is also very helpful.

Parents should also take advantage of the fact that these are the years when children will not resist being with their parents. In fact they look forward to playing with the parents. These are the years that they think their parents are cool. If parents make sure they are spending lots of time with all the children together and also with them individually, it will serve as a good foundation for the years to follow. Parents finding ways to play and create laughter is absolutely crucial. Habits like spending time individually will be part of their long-term memories, and parents may be able to avoid a stage where their child does not want to speak with them at all. If done in the name of fun, parents, over time, will develop the connection with their children and also lay the foundation for their children to become healthy and capable adults.

Here are more pointers about spending time with children in this age:

- If parents have a certain passion about a sport or hobby, getting children exposed to this will allow them to also be part of their lives. However, this should not be taken to mean that children should just follow and observe the parent. Rather, individual time needs to be taken out to introduce these activities to them. As they get better and better, it may develop into a routine that both the parent and the child enjoys (or not!)

- At this age, they may or may not want to play the same old games over and over; if they like variety, work together to be creative. Some children will enjoy sitting and talking, others will not. In general, play is still the best way to connect. Talk is important, too, but we will cover this in the next chapter.

- Having imaginary friends is not uncommon, especially when children may be going through a transition or feeling upset. Don't worry—Agatha

Christie is one of the top-selling authors of all time. In her autobiography, she recounted that many of her early memories involved imaginary friends, and she continued her conversations with some of them into adulthood—so who knows? You may be nurturing a budding best-seller![27]

·················································································

### *Louis Lowdown*

When our children were two and four years old, we told them we were moving to Australia from Jakarta for work. Around that same time, Sonia started playing with two imaginary (Indonesian) friends who she named Noni and Toto. She would tell me elaborate stories about these two friends. She talked to them and about them in many different ways.. They were around most of the time and I affirmed her little buddies, not wanting to make a big deal out of the phenomenon. Our Australian house had already been chosen by our employers, so the day we moved to Sydney, we were able to go directly from the airport to our new home. Our backyard was filled with trees and birds, something the kids had not seen in Jakarta. Sonia was thrilled, and asked, "Mommy, may I go look around by myself?" She ran excitedly throughout the whole house, up and down the stairs, looked in every room, and came back to where I was standing by the window. With eyes as big as saucers, she happily announced, "Mommy, Noni and Toto are already here and they love this place!" And she never mentioned them again. With the benefit of hindsight, I guess the imaginary friends were her way of coping with the fear and uncertainty of moving to a new country and a new house!

·················································································

Children this age may not want to engage in long talks, but it is still helpful for parents to teach children to identify and be attuned to emotions such as sadness, joy, fear, excitement, disappointment, longing, or anger. This can be achieved by routinely asking about "highs and lows" as previously suggested, and also by using feelings charts, which parents can easily find on the Internet.

Children this age also continue to need lots of affection. Many fathers at this stage withhold from kissing and hugging their children but this is a mistake. Both boys and girls both need this from their fathers.

Children should be encouraged to be involved in cooperative and competitive games, where they can be aware of how other people feel. For example, children can be asked how cheating makes others feel? If someone wins all the time, how would this make others feel? If someone is not cooperative, how would this make others feel? As a parent on the playground with other children, you will be able to observe all of this taking place, and possibly even facilitate some of the games. If so, you can change the games in such a way that different children get to win, not just the fastest or strongest. If you're not facilitating, you can ask questions later to draw out some of the lessons from what you observed. The single best childhood predictor of adult adaptation is *not* school grades, or classroom behavior, but a child's ability to get along with other children.[28] This should be given top priority. Principles such as give and take, trust, sharing, friendliness and selflessness should be taught over and over again so that they will be able to increasingly see things from other's points of view.

It is important for parents to learn to encourage children by being specific about who did what well. For example, parents can be encouraging about who was *cooperative*; who was *honest*; who *played hard*; who *did not give up*; who *was nice to others*; and who *had a good attitude*.

So often encouragement goes to the person who won, or criticism goes to those who made mistakes. If parents make a big deal about winning, then children will follow suit. When winning does not become the parents' focus, then children will be more likely to focus on other people's feelings and not just their own.

Do not choose a game where one child tends to lose continually, assuming the children are close in age, and roughly the same size, etc., else they will eventually not look forward to playing. It may cause them to be envious of siblings who always win. Parents can and should set it up where a different child wins, including the parents, and that the spread is fairly even, or at least not so skewed toward one family member.

## *Louis Lowdown*

During the time our children were in primary and middle school, we had our "family day" on Sunday afternoon from about 3:00 p.m. until bedtime. We swam and played pool games, went for bike rides, and frequented various amusement parks. On rainy days, we played cards and board games. During puberty, Sonia became very distracted and for a few years, playing any sit-down game with her required restraint and patience. I (John) became frustrated and would reprimand her. My wife would politely signal to me to "back off" —that when I acted like this, it defeated the very purpose of playing and having a good time as a family—duh! I was impatient and ruined the atmosphere on more than one occasion. Thankfully, my better half continued to point out the error of my ways, and I was eventually able to prioritize fun and connection over accuracy and efficiency. I am glad to say my children forgave me, and as young adults, Sonia and David have both expressed appreciation to me for choosing to invest my time with them on a regular basis.

. . . . . . . . . . . . . . . . . . . . . . . . . . . . . . . . . . . . . . . . . . . . . . . . . . . . . . . . . . . . .

In terms of the three drives of connect, work and play, work will begin in more earnest at this stage. It is important for parents not to expose children to the pressure of learning at a level more than that for which they are mentally prepared. Connect and play will still be the largest of the three drives.

Elkind frequently speaks up about how parents today are hurrying children to grow up too fast and the harm parents cause by plunging their children into learning that is not age-appropriate. Children who are confronted with demands to do math or to read before they have the requisite mental abilities may experience a series of demoralizing failures and begin to conceive of themselves as worthless.[29] (RR7.7)

Reading loads of books to and with children is a fantastic way to increase connection, teach values, and at the same time, help them academically (in a quiet way!) Bedtime reading with classics by Robert Louis Stevenson, or more modern reads, such as *The Children's Book of Virtues*,[30] or inspirational books with pictures will provide hours of fun, bonding time, and help set the tone for later years. When children are finished reading, and the kids are tucked in bed, this is a good time for parents to ask their children how they felt about the day, or repeat highs and lows. Bear in mind that even though this may have been shared during mealtimes, sometimes there are other lows that they would prefer talking about when alone with a parent, or they simply may have just forgotten to bring it up earlier.

## Middle Childhood

During this age period, the shift among connect, work and play continues. Even though children are approaching adolescence, they still need to play, especially with their father (see Figure 7.1, 8 to 12 years old). At this stage, work will now accelerate a little, especially at school and time for play will decrease correspondingly. Parents should take care that play is not eliminated. Some parents may want their kids to be so well equipped academically that they push them to study hard, even after school hours, with little time to play other than during recess time at school. No matter what, the connection must be maintained, which surely involves play.

Remember, children this age still really want your love and connection, but they may not want others to know it. They may resist open displays of affection and love. Boys especially would rather give high fives than kisses in public, but parents must not stop showing affection in private. Kids this age still love to have bedtime reading along with mom or dad putting them to bed, believe it or not.

This is an age where many issues like winning, losing, looking bad, shame and fear will become real to them. When these emotions are discussed, children should be able to process their feelings and make sense of things without feeling weird. They will still need their parents to help them focus on other people so they understand that life is not just about them, or about them winning. Like we mentioned before, when watching children interact with other kids, or with family members, specific encouragement needs to be given in the same areas.

Also during this stage, play will gravitate more and more toward gender based activities. At the latter part of this stage (ten to twelve years of age), boys would rather play with boys and girls with girls. This would also be a good time for parents to watch team sports in which their children are involved. It is shocking how competitive parents get on the side-lines, more so than their children on the field.

Kids this age will see their strengths and weaknesses more clearly. It is likely that they will talk more. They want and need their parents' constant encouragement and acceptance. If they are taking part in a sport or in a competition, and feel during the course of play that their parent does not value them, or that a parent is spending time with them out of a sense of duty, it will send the opposite message of connection and acceptance. So many times when a child does not win, a parent may say "Great job" or "It's okay, winning is not everything", but the tone of voice, facial expressions, and body language convey that winning actually mattered to him a lot. Most children can sense what their parent is really feeling; this sends a strong signal to the child about what their parent values the most.

In his book *No Contest: The Case Against Competition*, Alfie Kohn talks about the adverse effects of competition that many parents model for and breed in their kids.[31] He posed some of the following questions upon which parents would do well to reflect: Is competition more productive than cooperation? Is competition more enjoyable than cooperation? Does competition build character?

If not being the top or not winning gets in the way of cooperating, enjoying the game and/or building character, then how is competition helpful?

To most parents, getting their children to succeed is about helping them to be more hardworking. However, while this may be the case, parents have no idea about the stronger message that is being sent to their children:

*I am not good enough.*
*I do not fit into my family.*
*I am a failure compared to my siblings and friends.*

This develops the lifetraps of defectiveness, social isolation, and failure. Children who are internalizing these messages may start to feel exasperated and discouraged, and when these feelings are not processed, may become resentful and then perhaps rebel in later years.

## Adolescence

The adolescent period is described as being the years from puberty to adulthood. The American Academy of Pediatrics divides this period into three stages:[32] early adolescence, generally ages twelve and thirteen, middle adolescence, ages fourteen to sixteen, and late adolescence, ages seventeen to twenty-one.

Puberty is defined as the time when biological changes are taking place, and for many it takes place during early and middle adolescence. At this stage, adolescents tend to see things as black and white and are not able to set their sights on long-term goals or the consequences when they do something right or wrong. But by the time they hit late adolescence they are able to think in a far more complex and rational way. Recall the insights of Nucci[33] on the different kinds of morality (see Chapter Two). Some teens will resent parents insisting on adherence to certain rules if they feel that those rules are not truly important. In the interest of connection, parents should not make a big deal out of these things!

Adolescence has been seen as a transition point between childhood and adulthood. They still have their childhood ways, but at the same time, they are also striving to be adults and can react aggressively when parents do not give them the independence they crave. More than any other stage, this is the time when they will start to pull away, and perhaps not want to be as attached to their parents. Even though they inwardly desire to know that they are loved by and close to their parents, teenagers will come across as if the opposite were true. (The Putting

Family First community reports that in a national poll of a representative sample of American teens in the year 2000, 21% rated "not having enough time together with parents" and educational worries, as their top two concerns.[34]) So they will act like they do not need to connect, but parents need to persevere and find a way into their lives. We strongly caution parents to avoid giving up spending time with their teenaged children because of the mistaken thinking that their adolescent children's peer relationships are more important than with their parents. Regular one-on-one time is crucial. It takes hard work and a lot of patience, but the end results are well worth the effort.

Adolescents care a lot more about their peers. Their social circle widens and they want to make their own decisions about who to spend time with and get close to. When they were younger their parents had more influence over these decisions, but at this stage they want to have more say. They are striving to have their own identity as people yet care a lot about what others think of them. There is a tremendous amount of entitlement that creeps in but generally speaking, this type of entitlement is temporary. It eventually disappears as the teens mature, provided parents continue to adequately meet all their core emotional needs.

When children hit this stage, the interplay between connect, play and work will shift fairly dramatically (see Figure 7.1, 13 to 17 years old). They will find new interests and work at school will increase drastically. To parents, it seems like our teens suddenly have little or no time to "play" with their parents, but always manage to find time to play with their friends. Peer relationships are a huge part of an adolescent's life and will continue to be as they progress from being a young adolescent to an older adolescent. However, most teens who spent regular time in the preceding years with their parents and who feel connected and accepted will enjoy spending time with their family. Even then, they may resist. To that we say, persevere, persevere, and persevere!

Spending time with adolescents takes being very purposeful and intentional; it demands that we make our way into their schedule. Some parents have found it helpful to make the most out of the following opportunities:

- When their teens need to be driven somewhere
- When they need help with their school work
- When they need a ride to school—almost all teens would prefer to ride in the car with parents than take the school bus. (Of course, if they have a driver's license, they would prefer to drive!)

So, in the end, the interplay of the three drives of connect, work and play changes as children move from one stage of growth to another. Parents should ensure that they maintain the connection with their children at all stages. Parents who do will never regret it.

We end this chapter on spending time by mentioning the importance of making memories. Our parents had strong convictions about that: John's family has wonderful holiday memories of going to the beach in Malaysia and Karen's family continues to holiday at the Gulf Coast.

No matter what stage of life your children are in, plan holidays with your family. Take pictures. Take the time to file them and create memories. As a family, look at them periodically. Place them in the house where they are accessible, in beautiful frames so that all can be reminded of the precious memories built over the years, adding new ones every so often. Going up and down the stairs of our home, we see photos like these that remind us of many great family times together. A momentary glance sometimes brings out a memory and lifts the atmosphere. As you get older, sweet memories will flood your minds as you reminisce together. Not only will this benefit your family connection directly; this will give your children a blueprint of how they would also want to manage their respective families when they start to have their own in the years to come.

## Chapter Eight

## EMPATHY AND
## VALIDATION OF FEELINGS
·············································

In your journey to be a good enough parent, you've begun to take care not to exasperate your children, and you're spending more regular time with your children. You've gone a long way toward meeting their core emotional need for connection and acceptance. All that's left now is the last "must do"—*validating* their feelings.

### The Benefits of Empathy

Children regularly go through all kinds of emotions. When parents empathize with them and help them understand (process) their feelings, children experience connection and acceptance. Many parents, however, do not attribute much importance to the feelings of their children. Some parents are emotionally inhibited and regard feelings as being unhealthy; others just focus on doing what is right; still others allow their own agenda and worries to take over. In our Good Enough Parenting model, we believe that *not* empathizing with our children's feelings and therefore *not* connecting with them at an emotional level leads to many of the exasperation interactions discussed in Chapters Three and Four.

Empathy is a heart-felt response to another's emotions. We get there by putting ourselves into the other person's shoes, then we respond in a way that conveys understanding accurately and in a caring and respectful manner. Empathy can be compared to watching a movie about another person, immersing ourselves in his issues, and then reflecting back to that person his feelings and thoughts, with a sense of genuineness and care. So how is this related to parenting?

Think about it. Suppose you have a heated argument with your spouse just before leaving the house for work. Flustered, you decide to stop for coffee. What a surprise, while waiting in line, you meet a good friend. You are so happy to have someone to whom you can pour out your feelings, so you just let it all out. How would you feel if, as soon as you finished your story, your friend replied by giving you a lecture about being a better wife or husband? Or maybe started giving you advice? Or told you to stop worrying because you look nicer when you are smiling? Or minimized your feelings, or tried to psychoanalyze you? We bet you would not seek that friend out for a while, at least not when you had a problem! Why? You just wanted someone to listen and show empathy. But what about with our children—what kind of listeners are we? Why do we struggle to show empathy to our children?

One unfortunate consequence of today's lifestyle is that parents have less time to spend with their children than in days past. Moreover when parents reach home after a full day at work and when they should be focusing fully on their role as moms and dads, they often have very little energy left to give to their children. As a result, the quality of relationships between parents and children is on the decline. (That is why we are such big proponents of concepts like downsizing, living on one income, and flexi-time work arrangements for mothers and fathers.)

On top of the economic pressure adults are feeling, children are facing increasing pressure to excel at school, which means more frequent exams and tighter deadlines. Parents and children seem to be rushing from day to day in the pursuit of increasing academic intelligence, at the expense of other important areas of their lives such as emotional intelligence. With less free time, parenting can become very productivity-minded, which leaves less time for play and drawing out feelings. Children with poor emotional intelligence become adults with poor emotional intelligence, unable to bond with the important people in their lives, resulting in shallow relationships and little intimacy. Marriages suffer, since they are less equipped to meet their spouse's needs. It is no surprise that divorce rates are rising sharply across the globe. Unhealthy marriages across the board take their toll on parenting, and dysfunctional behavior is perpetuated through successive generation. Gottman says:

In the last decade or so, science has discovered a tremendous amount about the role emotions play in our lives. Researchers have found that even more than IQ, your emotional awareness and ability to handle feelings will determine your success and happiness in all walks of life, including family relationships.[1]

Gottman proved this by conducting research on families for over a decade. He monitored how parents dealt with their children's emotions, which included the parent's reaction to the children's emotional experiences, such as when their kids were angry, sad and fearful. He also measured the parent's awareness of the role emotions play in their own lives. Gottman's team followed these children from age four to adolescence. Their study found that when parents practiced empathizing with their children and validating their children's feelings, as well as helping their children to be emotionally intelligent, the children fared well in the following areas:

- Emotional well-being – Children with emotional intelligence could regulate their own emotions, which means that they were better at soothing themselves when they got upset. They could also calm themselves down better and faster.
- Physical health – As a result of being able to handle their emotions better, children with emotional intelligence had fewer illnesses.
- Social competence – Children with emotional intelligence could relate to other people better, even in tough situations when they got teased. They also had better friendships with other children.
- Academic performance – Children with emotional intelligence were better at focusing attention and performed better academically.[2]

This research highlights the importance of parents not ignoring their children's feelings, but valuing them by showing empathy and processing their emotions. But validating children's emotions and empathizing with them does not come naturally for many parents. What comes naturally for parents is to respond with a coping style; i.e., to surrender, to avoid, to overcompensate, which inevitably leads to one of the exasperation interactions.

## Zero Degrees of Empathy

Simon Baron-Cohen has been studying empathy for thirty years, and recently published his findings with the eye-catching title, *Zero Degrees of Empathy*.[3] He believes that empathy varies in degrees; it is not an either-you-have-it-or-you-don't quality. In a normal population, people's different levels of inborn empathy will be reflected in a bell-shaped curve. Most people will be in the middle, having some empathy, but a small percentage will be in both extremes; one with a lot of empathy and the other with little empathy, or, worse still, what Cohen refers to as "zero degrees of empathy".

Why do parents need to be concerned about this? Because childhood experiences, including reactions to parenting, affect children's empathy levels. We agree with Cohen's belief that "empathy erosion" results when children's needs are not met over time. Cohen warns, "When empathy is switched off, people operate in the 'I' mode; their primary concern is about themselves," and they treat others as objects.[4] In the case of children whose empathy is being eroded over time, as they get older, they will develop a desire to protect themselves, then a desire for revenge, and later, blind hatred. Scary! Eventually, those with zero degrees of empathy cannot experience remorse or guilt because they do not or cannot understand what the other person is feeling. They lack awareness of how they *come across to others*, how they *interact with others*, and how to *anticipate others' feelings* or reactions. In addition, these individuals "believe 100% in the rightness of their own ideas and beliefs, and judge anyone who does not hold to their beliefs as wrong, or stupid."[5]

If you watch crime shows, you may have heard the terms "borderline personality disorder", "psychopath", or "malignant Narcissist" bandied about—these are the guys who cannot feel for others and only care about themselves. Guess what? They have "zero degrees of empathy". Cohen's research found that a huge percentage of adults with extreme personality disorders like those above have traumatic childhoods or experienced emotional neglect, indifference, deprivation and rejection.[6] Conversely, when children are connected to their parents and confident that their parents will treat their feelings with respect, rather than developing "zero degrees of empathy", their own empathy quotient increases.

## Processing Emotions

Parents' refusal or lack of ability to process their children's feelings is often related to parents' lack of awareness of their own emotions. Children may not always openly show their feelings. Sometimes, they give out only subtle clues, but parents who are trained or intuitive will be able to read between the lines.

Children experience emotions such as anger, happiness, sadness, joy, shame, pride, humiliation, acceptance, guilt, confidence, abandonment, love, embarrassment, excitement, annoyance, and contentment, to name a few, with regularity. The more parents pick up on these feelings and learn how to process them with their child, the better the core emotional need for connection and acceptance will be met. However, parents react differently to the emotions experienced by their child. Many parents do not find talking about feelings or emotions attractive—they prefer to avoid such talk. Some parents get triggered by certain emotions and respond in an unhealthy way, such as by putting the child down, being punitive, pouting, or blaming themselves silently. Parents who are able to gain awareness about how *they* respond to the feelings of their child will be off to a good start in trying to meet their child's core emotional need for connection and acceptance. *Please go to Appendix 2 for an important exercise.*

The three prominent parenting experts who offer the most valuable insights in the area of processing children's feelings are Ginott, Gottman, and the team of Faber and Mazlish.[7] The steps they advocate apply to both older and younger children. In summary these are:

- Be aware that the child is experiencing emotions, and have an initial idea of which emotion(s) he might be feeling. This involves interpreting the verbal expressions, tone, and non-verbal expressions of the child.
- See the child's feelings as an opportunity to connect with him at an emotional level. This will strengthen the bond between the parent and child. Parents should not rush into giving solutions. Both the tone of voice and body language is crucial in communicating this message.
- Draw the child out verbally to be able to express these emotions or feelings, and to label these feelings or emotions correctly. This process will train the child (and in the beginning, the parent) to process his feelings, and thereafter cope in a healthy way.
- Validate the emotion(s), then show empathy and compassion to the child. Again parents should not rush into giving solutions.
- At a suitable time, collaborate with the child and help resolve the issue that triggered the child.

The manner in which the above principles are practiced changes with the age of the children. We echo and support the points below taken from Adele Faber and Elaine Mazlish's bestseller, *How to Talk So Kids Will Listen and How to Listen So Kids Will Talk*. Read the first chapter of their book to get the picture fully.[8]

*Louis Lowdown*

I (John) tended to lose my temper when the kids were disrespectful, which would sometimes happen if they were angry. So when they were young, and said something like, "Janice was mean to me and I felt like punching her in the nose", or "I hate my teacher!" my first reaction was, "You shouldn't be angry", or "Don't be disrespectful!" Instead of empathizing with them first, I would immediately side with the other person. Not surprisingly, that upset them even more. When Sonia was about six years old, a couple with older kids told us that they had regretted telling their daughter, "You're not afraid, you're brave". That statement made me stop and think before dismissing my children's emotions. In the next few years, I read the Faber and Mazlish book, and I saw what I been doing wrong. I made a point to listen to and validate their feelings. Once I learned how to process the kids' emotions, I was able to say things like, "Sounds like you're really angry" and then we could have a conversation from there.

## Accepting Feelings vs. Accepting Behavior

Ginnot and Gottman's writings encourage parents to accept children's feelings, but not necessarily their behavior.[9] For many parents this is confusing. We connect with our kids when we empathize with their ups and downs. However, this does not mean that we will always agree with the behavior that may have accompanied their feelings. A child may feel sad when left out of a game between his siblings, and respond by throwing a temper tantrum. We need to separate the feelings from the behavior. As parents we need to process the feelings of rejection, and empathize with our child, but we also need to voice our disapproval of his *behavior* (not of him or his feelings), and if necessary, apply an appropriate consequence. We need to communicate that there are some behaviors that are acceptable and others that are not. So while we accept their feelings, we absolutely believe there are certain circumstances in which we will not be able to empathize with them. We agree with Gottman that the following are times when it would be inappropriate to validate our children's feelings: when we are triggered either by our children or by other people, when children are with their friends or in public, when the offence is serious, when children are trying to manipulate with their feelings, and when children are not prepared to talk and want some space first.

In conclusion, when you meet the core emotional need for connection and acceptance, and your connection is strong, not only will your children love and respect you, but they will enjoy being *with* you. When the core emotional need for connection and acceptance has been met, children will more naturally imitate their parents' values and this in turn will help them resist being drawn to unhealthy delinquent behaviors, beliefs and ideologies. Spending time with your children, showing them empathy, and validating their feelings are the absolute most important ways to meet this need.

# THE CORE EMOTIONAL NEED FOR HEALTHY AUTONOMY AND PERFORMANCE

# Chapter Nine

## HEALTHY AUTONOMY
## AND PERFORMANCE
·················································

The Core Emotional Need for Healthy Autonomy and Performance can be defined as helping our children develop their own personalities, abilities and self-confidence as they grow into separately functioning healthy adults. When parents meet the core emotional need for healthy autonomy and performance, the child will develop some or all of the following traits and beliefs: confidence about safety & wellness, independence & competence, a sense of self that is differentiated & developed, security & stability, assertiveness & self-expression, and optimism.[1] Children who have had this core emotional need met will *consistently, on an emotional level,* believe the following messages because of the actions and words of (and the atmosphere provided by) their parents:

*I am free to chart my own direction with guidance from trusted advisors.*
*I am allowed to go places on my own as long as I conduct myself responsibly.*
*I think my parents worry about me when I get hurt or sick but not overly so.*
*My parents trust me to make wise choices and the trust grows each year as I prove myself in new situations.*
*Situations in life will turn out for the best, in general.*

If a child really believes those statements, how might that child feel? Confident, encouraged, secure and motivated are just some of the words that come to mind.

Desmond grew up an only child. Both of his parents worked in demanding professional jobs, and his mother was very strict with his schedule. As a child, he was not allowed to play at friends' homes, (might not be a good influence), not permitted to take the school bus (might get bullied), and not taught to ride a bicycle (might be dangerous). He never cleaned his room or made himself a meal, and his mother made sure she had the last word about what subjects he would take and which (hometown) university he would attend.

During college, Desmond was still expected to come home for dinner every night, and his mother became suspicious of any new friends. Surprisingly, he still managed to get married. At first, his new wife thought his dependence on her was cute. "He needs me", she thought. Over the next few years, she realized her husband needed her for everything. Outside of the home this became an issue as well—when they tried to run a business together, he relied on her to do his share of the work. Eventually his wife had enough and gave him a "counseling or else" ultimatum.

Rick grew up in a family of sons with an absent father; his mother lived for her sons. She did everything for them and was involved in every aspect of their lives. Rick was a bit shy, and was sometimes teased for being a "mommy's boy". When Rick became successful and respected in his chosen professions, the mother beamed. But when he married a beautiful and successful young woman, Rick's mother was not ready to relinquish her role. She muscled in on every decision, and criticized Rick's wife constantly. After years of looking like the perfect couple on the outside, the wife had enough and walked out.

What do Desmond and Rick have in common? Their need for healthy autonomy and performance was not adequately met by their parents. One of the goals of parenting is to help our children at different points in their lives make age-appropriate decisions and help them utilize their talents. If we guide and train them, then as adults they will be able to make decisions themselves and achieve a sense of autonomy and competence without having to rely on others in an unhealthy way.

## Autonomy and Self-Esteem

When children are very young, they make very few decisions about what to eat, wear, when to take a bath, and so on. However, as they get older, more and more decisions need to be entrusted to them. Unfortunately, many parents do not understand that helping them to mature is a process: some parents feel the need to control every aspect of their child's life for as long as possible; other parents waive all control as soon as the kid enters secondary school, allowing their child to make many decisions that are not appropriate for their age, which causes just as many problems. If parents are over-involved and too controlling, or under-involved and let go too soon, children do not develop autonomy and competence as they age.

When parents communicate any or all of the messages above, explicitly or implicitly, their children's self-esteem is eroded and they are likely to feel exasperated, insecure and unmotivated. So many parents are not aware of the messages they convey when they are controlling and become over-involved. They think they are being caring and thorough, but their children have a different perception.

## Autonomy and Motivation

What exactly is this sense of autonomy? It is the need to be self-determined and to have a choice in the initiation, maintenance, and regulation of an activity.[2] When older children and adults develop autonomy they believe their behavior is truly chosen by them rather than imposed by some external source.[3] Dr. Edward Deci, a psychology and social sciences professor and expert in the field of human motivation hypothesized that any occurrence which undermines people's feeling of autonomy and leaves them feeling controlled decreases their inner, or *intrinsic,* motivation and is likely to have other negative consequences.[4]

Dr. Mark Lepper and his team at Stanford University studied children whose parents and teachers held them to education strategies such as goals, deadlines, threats, and assessments from the time they woke up till the time they went to bed. It was no surprise that they found this kind of hyper-control having a negative impact on the children's intrinsic motivation and killing the children's sense of autonomy. They also found that some who began as compliant later became defiant.[5] Certainly this does not mean that children should be allowed to do only what they like and that discipline is not appropriate. Limits and expectations are involved in the other core emotional needs, but an overemphasis on discipline, rules and limits proves counterproductive.

When children are maturing in their autonomy and competence, accomplishing tasks that are age-appropriate will be a motivation unto itself. Each victory and new skill adds to their overall self-esteem and their intrinsic motivation. They will eventually believe that they are able to deal with life and the world in which they live. Of course the task cannot be too easy, it must meet what Deci calls the "optimal challenge", which essentially is a meaningful challenge to which one must give one's best.[6]

While we encourage parents to be actively engaged in training their children, sometimes there are simply too many things we have in mind that we want to teach them: table manners, personal hygiene, how to dress appropriately. (We don't want our kids going over to someone's house, leaving things all over the place, and then hearing through the grapevine that people are asking if our kids were raised in a barn!) At the same time, as the kids get older, we have to be able to let go or at least communicate with them in a way that does not show disdain or disapproval when it's not an issue about right and wrong. This will put us well on our way to meeting the core emotional need for autonomy and performance.

# Chapter Ten

# THE DOMAIN OF IMPAIRED AUTONOMY AND PERFORMANCE

·····································································

We mentioned earlier that the 18 lifetraps identified by Dr. Jeffrey Young clustered into four domains; the second of these domains is known as "Impaired Autonomy". To the extent that parents do not meet the core emotional need for healthy autonomy and performance, we believe their children will experience the opposite—*Impaired Autonomy*. This means that their children will be at risk of developing some or all of the lifetraps in the Domain of Impaired Autonomy, namely Vulnerability to Harm or Illness, Dependence, Enmeshment, Abandonment, Subjugation, and Negativity. This chapter explains these six lifetraps in detail, and contains an additional segment called "Basic Safety Zone".

## The Lifetrap of Vulnerability to Harm or Illness

The first maladaptive schema (lifetrap) in the domain of impaired autonomy is vulnerability to harm or illness. The core message of the vulnerability lifetrap is, *"Catastrophe is just around the corner. Something bad is about to happen and I am powerless to do anything about it."*

Children who end up with this lifetrap are made to live in fear that danger is imminent. They are taught to think that it is only a matter of time before they contract a serious illness, lose money, be attacked, have an accident, or have other bad things happen to them. Their fears may become so exaggerated they may manifest in the form of anxiety or panic attacks. They may go for medical check-ups over and over again, since any sign of illness will be interpreted as something serious, like a heart attack. They are often able to function on a day-to-day basis but there is always a sense that danger is very close. Children with this lifetrap tend to be hyper-vigilant and go to great lengths to stop these disasters from taking place. This lifetrap may show up as excessive worry, such as trying to save large sums of money for the future since they believe that they might be left stranded. The worry may in turn induce a stress-related illness, which will then confirm their fears, resulting in more worry. They get stuck in a cycle, and resort to all kinds of medications and special diets in order to be prepared when danger strikes. Children who develop this lifetrap probably observed one or both parents being obsessed about health and safety issues, whose fear of being in danger was probably greatly exaggerated and who talked about tragedies not just as possibilities but as probabilities.

*Early family environment that might cause this lifetrap to develop:*
- The child's parents lived out this lifetrap, talking incessantly about illness, safety, having no money and the tragedies that happened to others.
- The child's parents were excessively in control of his life, forever ensuring he was not in danger.
- The child faced a traumatic event as a child that rendered him fearful of all situations.
- The child had a loved-one who died and he concluded that he should be on guard at all times.
- The child's environment was not a safe place for him, or was unstable and unpredictable.

Figure 10.1: The Lifetrap of Vulnerability to Harm or Illness (Shen as an adult)

Figure 10.2: A Possible Early Environment Which Would Likely Contribute to the Development of the Vulnerability to Harm or Illness Lifetrap (Shen as a child) Go to Appendix 1

## The Lifetrap of Dependence / Incompetence

The next maladaptive schema (lifetrap) in the domain of impaired autonomy is dependence / incompetence. The core message of the dependence lifetrap is, *"I cannot take care of myself. I need to rely on those around me in order to survive. I cannot solve problems or make decisions on my own."*

Children who develop the dependence lifetrap were treated as if they are not able to handle life with all of its responsibilities and tasks. They were not able to develop confidence in their own abilities and they have the need for someone else to be around constantly. Left alone, they feel completely useless, without skills, and unable to make good decisions, hence their dependence on others to do things for them or to help them. They may vacillate and be double-minded about what to do, and worry about whether a previous decision was right. People with this lifetrap may function well in *some* settings, but be very dependent in other settings. Adults with the lifetrap of dependence do not know how frustrated others feel about their unhealthy reliance on them for daily tasks. They think they are expecting normal support from their spouse and friends, and don't realize they are actually dependent on others for almost everything in life.

*Early family environment that might cause this lifetrap to develop:*

- The child's parents were overprotective, and did not allow the child to do things by herself that were age-appropriate. For example, when other children were allowed to travel by themselves, the child was not allowed to do so. When they were allowed to learn tasks, she was not given the opportunity.
- The child's parents valued something (e.g., grades, music or sports), and allowed her to focus only on that. Consequently, the child never learned to do other tasks that her peers learned.
- The child was given unusually strict boundaries. She may not have been allowed to go out of the house, or participate in extracurricular activities, such as sports.
- The child's parents made all decisions about her life, or she was "rescued" by one parent in many situations.
- The child's homework was done, or overly supervised, by one of her parents. When this was repeated many times, the child thought she couldn't do it anyway. She may have also developed a sense of laziness.
- The child was criticized for making bad decisions so she lost her confidence. Her parents gladly stepped in when she hesitated, therefore she never quite developed the confidence to act on her own.

Figure 10.3: The Lifetrap of Dependence (Sierra as an adult)

Figure 10.4: A Possible Early Environment Which Would Likely Contribute to the Development of the Dependence Lifetrap (Sierra as a child) *Go to Appendix 1*

## The Lifetrap of Enmeshment / Undeveloped Self

Another maladaptive schema (lifetrap) in the domain of impaired autonomy is enmeshment / undeveloped self. The core message of the enmeshment lifetrap is, *"I cannot survive on my own without constant contact and closeness with my parent or partner. I need to know what they think in order to be sure of what I think."* This is about an underdeveloped sense of self as a separate person.

Children who develop this lifetrap are intertwined emotionally with one or both parents. For persons with the enmeshment lifetrap, it is hard to tell where one person ends and the other person begins. They are so closely interrelated with the other person that they are unable to tell themselves apart from that person. They feel empty and are often afraid of existing on their own. People can be enmeshed with their parents, their spouse, their children, a sibling, or their best friend. This becomes especially difficult when approaching or entering a marriage. If an adult male is enmeshed with a parent (usually the mother), he will communicate more with that parent than with his wife. His mother will be the first to know about what names he likes for a future child, what kind of house he would like to buy, or which job he will possibly take. Enmeshed individuals feel the need to constantly talk with their parent and tell them everything. There is a sense that the two of them are, in a strange way, one person. People with the enmeshment lifetrap have a hard time making decisions without first considering the opinions of the person with whom they are enmeshed. Enmeshed individuals do not learn healthy boundaries in childhood.

*Early family environment that might cause this lifetrap to develop:*
- There was a very close bond between the child and one of his parents. They were so close they were able to easily read one another's non-verbal communication and know what the other person was thinking. The parent, probably a mother, would also share intimate issues with her child, such as the state of her marriage.
- The child's parents were very controlling and did not allow him to make decisions on his own.
- The child's parents were rigid in their thinking and opinions and did not allow for diversity of opinion.
- The child's parents were over-protective (see "Possible Early Family Environment" under "Dependence Lifetrap").
- The child was taught not to set boundaries with the parents, and if he did, then he would end up with unhealthy guilt.

Figure 10.5: The Lifetrap of Enmeshment (Raj as an adult)

Figure 10.6: A Possible Early Environment Which Would Likely Contribute to the Enmeshment Lifetrap (Raj as a child) *Go to Appendix 1*

## The Lifetrap of Abandonment / Instability

Abandonment / Instability is the fourth maladaptive schema (lifetrap) in the domain of impaired autonomy. The core message of the abandonment lifetrap is, *"I cannot count on anyone for consistent support, caring, and connection. I will be rejected; people I love and need will die; and people I love and need cannot be relied upon to be there when I need them."*

Children who are abandoned will almost certainly develop the abandonment schema. Virtually all children who are adopted will have these feelings, no matter how wonderful their adoptive home is, at least during some point in their lives. The fact is, they *were* abandoned, even if it was no one's fault, for example, in the case of a death. The extent that a new family meets their core emotional needs will go a long way in determining how easy it will be for an adopted child to eventually come to terms with his abandonment, but it may take years. People who have the abandonment lifetrap fear that everyone they love will leave them. They believe that ultimately they will be alone, and that they cannot really count on people to be there for them. They have a constant need to hear that they are loved, and that their close relationships will not leave them. If they are married, and their spouse does not communicate that, they get resentful. Underneath their anger and hurt, they do not feel secure, they honestly believe that they are destined for loneliness. People with the lifetrap of abandonment will have exaggerated feelings of instability in their closest relationships.

*Early family environment that might cause this lifetrap to develop:*

- One of the child's parents left the home, died, or lived separately.
- The child was given up for adoption.
- The child was forced to live with someone other than her parents for a period of time during childhood, perhaps because of difficult circumstances (e.g., divorce, illness, financial problems or war).
- One of the child's parents was too ill to look after her.
- There was intense marital conflict between the child's parents.
- Someone else in the family took the attention away from the child, for example a very ill sibling, perhaps a sibling with special needs, or maybe a sibling who was favored over the child.

Figure 10.7: The Lifetrap of Abandonment (Katya as an adult)

Figure 10.8: A Possible Early Environment Which Would Likely Contribute to the Abandonment Lifetrap (Katya as a child) Go to Appendix 1

## The Lifetrap of Subjugation

Another maladaptive schema (lifetrap) in the domain of impaired autonomy is subjugation. The core message of the subjugation lifetrap is, *"I must submit to the needs and desires of others before my own or I will be rejected by the anger or abandonment of people who are important to me."* The internal slogan is "I'm number two." Subjugation is about *needs*—not showing preferences, desires, decisions and opinions, or *emotions*—not showing feelings, particularly anger.

Children who develop the subjugation lifetrap have been made to feel that their desires, needs and opinions are neither significant nor important. They tend to repress themselves, which leads to passive aggressive thoughts and behavior, withdrawing, and ultimately to intense anger. They believe they *have to always* put others' needs and opinions above their own. They will often neglect themselves and give in to others because they are extremely afraid of conflict, which they fear will lead to some kind of punishment or loss of love and affection. They rarely express their opinions, and even if they do, they will not treat their opinion as being as important as others' opinions because of their fear of conflict or rejection.

One of the dangerous aspects of this schema is, after being subjugated for a while, feelings of anger and resentment start to surface because they have not paid any attention to their own needs, and they haven't asked others to meet their needs. They may feel very little excitement in life, because they have been too busy meeting others' needs. People around them will tell them this is their strength, but it is actually their weakness. People with this lifetrap will not experience the kind of intimacy they want because all of their attention is focused on meeting their partner's needs and wants, with nothing left over for them. They put their needs at the bottom of the priority list for fear of conflict if they do not do what others want of them. When subjugated adults start feeling the need for self-care, they are afraid they will be rejected in anger or abandonment. They have not learned to draw boundaries with unhealthy people. Eventually, people with this lifetrap will hit a wall. They will blow up and become aggressive. If married, this takes their partners by surprise and they think that their subjugated spouse is having a problem, when it is really about them coming out of subjugation, though not in a healthy way. This may lead to the subjugated person overreacting, swinging to the other extreme, becoming defiant to authority, and refusing to follow any form of rules, and may be mistaken for entitlement.

*Early family environment that might cause this lifetrap to develop:*

- The child's parents were abusive and got upset when he did not yield to the wishes of either one or both parents.
- The child's parents were controlling to the point that there was little autonomy on the child's part to make his own decisions.
- The child saw one of his parents give in to the other and learned it was the best way to keep the peace.
- The child was made to feel guilty if his needs were given attention before others.

Figure 10.9: The Lifetrap of Subjugation (Lars as an adult)

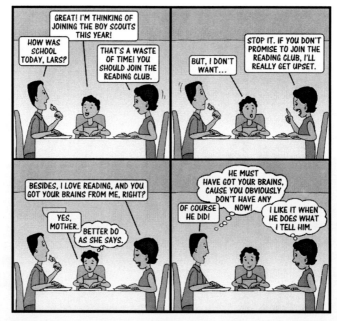

Figure 10.10: A Possible Early Environment Which Would Likely Contribute to the Subjugation Lifetrap (Lars as a child) *Go to Appendix 1*

## The Lifetrap of Negativity / Pessimism

The sixth and final maladaptive schema (lifetrap) in the domain of impaired autonomy is negativity / pessimism. The core message of the negativity lifetrap is, *"I am destined to make a serious mistake that will result in big problems. Things will inevitably go wrong. Bad things will happen to me."* The negative aspects of life are emphasized at the expense of those things which are positive and which will potentially bring joy.

Children who develop this lifetrap are taught it is normal to feel down. Life is seen and experienced with a negative spin on it. The cup is never half-full; it is always half-empty. Those who develop this lifetrap hate making mistakes and fear the supposed consequences that may arise. They worry about the loss and humiliation that may come from taking risks (and experiencing what they see as failure). They would rather be safe than sorry and take the path that would least expose them to such risks. Usually their negativity is not accurate but blown out of proportion. People with the lifetrap of negativity were made to feel ashamed of making mistakes and being wrong when they were growing up. As adults, they still do not realize that making mistakes is part of being human, and that part of learning comes from making mistakes. This often damages relationships; for example, whenever their spouse or friends want to try something new, they may be the "wet blanket".

*Early family environment that might cause this lifetrap to develop:*

- The child's parents talked about things from a negative point of view. Their usual answer would be "no" because they would assume the worst possible outcome.
- The child's parents went through very hard times, and so a strong signal was sent to avoid this fate at all costs, and to avoid making mistakes.
- The child actually experienced many negative events in her childhood, which reinforced what her negative parents told her about the world.
- The child has a more negative temperament, and her parents didn't train her to be more positive.

Figure 10.11: The Lifetrap of Negativity (Nicole as an adult)

Figure 10.12: A Possible Early Environment Which Would Likely Contribute to the Negativity Lifetrap (Nicole as a child) *Go to Appendix*

## Basic Safety Zone

The Basic Safety Zone for this core emotional need is three-fold: the first area of Basic Safety involves protecting children from abandonment, which in practical terms means parents need to protect their marriage. In our experience, the abandonment lifetrap is one of the harder ones to deal with, and we urge all parents to do their utmost to not inflict this on their children (RR10.1).

The second area has to do with making sure children are not neglected; that their basic needs for shelter, food, clothing, and sleep are met. Parents should learn basics of sleep, breastfeeding, nutrition, dealing with illnesses, and so forth.

Lastly, Basic Safety for this core emotional need also means ensuring that safety measures in and outside the home are put in place and that children are not allowed to be too autonomous too soon. Inappropriate (too soon) autonomy can become neglect or can inadvertently promote abuse. Parents should familiarize themselves with childproofing measures so that their homes are safe. For example, poisonous substances should be kept locked away, and babysitter instructions and emergency numbers kept handy. Children need to learn to cook eventually, but they should not be using sharp knives on their own or operating stoves when they are too young. Children should eventually bathe themselves, but infants and toddlers should never be left alone around a pail of water, much less in a bathtub. School age children should be able to walk home from school or take public transport eventually, but not before a certain age. There are all sorts of ways that parents can protect their children under the auspices of meeting the core emotional need for autonomy.

One more thing—while it is perfectly normal to allow an elementary school aged boy to go to the restroom by himself in a public place, the sad fact of today's world is that sexual predators exist and they frequent places where young boys might be unattended. *The Straits Times* has reported several cases of boys under ten being forced to do unspeakable acts in public restrooms, even in a country as safe as Singapore.[1]

. . . . . . . . . . . . . . . . . . . . . . . . . . . . . . . . . . . . . . . . . . . . . . . . . .

### *Louis Lowdown*

When our son was young and felt the call of nature while out in public, my husband would accompany David. If David and I (Karen) were out on our own, I brought him to the ladies' room. Not surprisingly, once he hit about seven years old, he was no longer open to that arrangement, and I didn't blame him. However, I told him that the only way I would allow him to enter the men's room by himself is if he would keep a semi-running conversation with me while he was inside. I would walk up to the door of the men's room in such a way that I could not see in, but as David walked in, I would shout, "David, I'm standing right by the door, ok?" He would answer, and I would ask another question about every fifteen seconds. I absolutely would have charged in if he hadn't answered me—luckily that never happened. Incidentally, when recounting this to my son as I was writing this book, he told me he had no memory of me standing guard anywhere, and congratulated me on keeping him safe while at the same time not making him paranoid.

• • • • • • • • • • • • • • • • • • • • • • • • • • • • • • • • • • • • • • • • • • • • • • • • • • • • • • • • • •

# Chapter Eleven

# AGE-APPROPRIATE EMPOWERMENT

·····································································

Adequately meeting the core emotional need for autonomy and performance means balancing between providing the right amount of protection with increasing freedom and empowerment. There are five "must-dos" when it comes to meeting this core emotional need—the first two are simple—watch out for the exasperation interactions and don't neglect the first core need while working on the second, since they are all intertwined. Here are three more steps that will help parents steer clear of the Domain of Impaired Autonomy.

## Provide Age-Appropriate Choices

As part of Deci's research on motivation (which we mentioned in Chapter Nine), he found that people who are given more choices regarding tasks showed more enthusiasm and spent more time doing tasks than those not given a choice at all.[1] They tested this by giving two groups a puzzle-solving experiment. One group was given a choice as to which puzzles they would work on and how long they would spend completing them. The other group was not given a choice but had the same amount of time at their disposal. As suspected, the group that was given a choice spent more time on the puzzles and reported enjoying the task more than the other group. There is something about having our say in a task that will get us to be more fully involved, and then greater intrinsic motivation will develop from within us.

Providing choices is a very important part in developing our children's autonomy. It draws them into the task and helps them take responsibility for it. But more than anything, it shows our level of respect for them. Even adults are much more motivated when they are given the choice to own a task rather than having the task forced upon them; rigidity and inflexibility with children may prevent the core emotional need for autonomy from being met.

Part of children becoming autonomous in a healthy way is knowing where their rights end and others' rights begin.[2] If children are old enough, parents can explain why it would be inappropriate for them to engage in certain tasks. This will help them to accept limits without feeling inadequate. The following examples are not absolutes, as some children mature quicker than others, but should be useful as general guidelines.

### Infancy

While it is helpful for babies to learn to be at ease around others, most parents are wise to not expose their newborns to too many people for the sake of protecting them from germs. Once babies hit the stage where they are a bit clingy to Mommy (see Chapter Seven) parents can encourage their babies to not be fearful around others by holding their children securely in their arms while introducing them to other people. Parents should speak with a gentle and encouraging tone of voice, and never have an angry and disappointed tone if their babies are not yet ready to go to others.

From about three months onwards, babies can learn by being around other babies. Especially after babies can sit up, there can be interaction between them and their parents. Babies should also learn to play alone and keep themselves occupied. Many parents never allow their children out of sight at all. A child lying down can play with a mobile above the bed. A child who can sit up can play with safe and appropriate crib or play pen toys. Otherwise, these children will not be able to be by themselves at all when separated for only a few minutes. Parents should be able to leave their child for a few seconds at a time with toys, always ensuring the baby is safe in the room. Parents can leave the door open and supervise without their children actually seeing them.[3] This in no way implies that parents are to ever leave a baby for more than a few seconds, and always within view, and not at all if they can crawl.

## The Toddler Years

One thing to keep in mind at this age is that children's brains develop faster in the first three years than at any other time—how exciting! Of course everyone has heard of the well-known stage at this time that is specifically related to autonomy—"The Terrible Twos". Toddlers want so desperately to do things themselves but they do not want to separate from their parents, so they are frustrated. They also do not know how to do many things and will have to learn and make mistakes, and this also frustrates them.

They should be allowed to explore their room, toys, and other safe objects, and learn to interact with their surroundings. Remember that parents are to provide "age-appropriate" autonomy, which means reasonable limits on one side and basic safety on the other.

Play is their primary work, up to five to six hours per day. They want to run, climb, and jump. Notwithstanding toddlers love of repetition, when fathers are spending time at the playground with their children, they should ensure that their kids try a variety of physical movements.

• • • • • • • • • • • • • • • • • • • • • • • • • • • • • • • • • • • • • • • • • • • • • • • • • • • •

### *Louis Lowdown*

When Sonia was about a year old, I read a baby book that said when babies are able to sit up in a high chair comfortably that they should be able to start feeding themselves, and to not worry about the mess—put newspaper down under the high chair, and give them a bath afterwards, the book said. What the book did not say was to use common sense—that was probably implied! One day a friend came into town and we went to a restaurant for lunch—after fifteen minutes, the older and more experienced parent begged me to stop the madness. I proceeded to help Sonia finish her lunch, helped the waitress clean up the disaster area, and waited another year or so before trying that again in public.

• • • • • • • • • • • • • • • • • • • • • • • • • • • • • • • • • • • • • • • • • • • • • • • • • • • •

To encourage healthy autonomy, parents can provide choices, such as what type of toys to play with, which books to read and which playgrounds to visit. Sometimes children this age will be overwhelmed by choices, so a parent may want to offer just two choices, e.g., "Darling, would you like to do some painting or read a book?" "Which DVD would you like to watch—*Busytown* or *Sing Along Songs*?" Different children will have different preferences. Our son couldn't care less what he wore at this age whereas our daughter practically came out of the womb with an opinion about which hairclip she would use, and which dress she would wear. Our son was more concerned with which toy he would carry around with him for the whole day.

Again, we have to stress that these decisions need to be age-appropriate. Parents will still need to make important decisions, and take charge in many areas, such as when to go to sleep, take a bath, eat, watch TV or be on a computer. Also, children should not get the impression that it is their right to choose everything; more on that in the next section.

## Early Childhood

By four to seven years of age, children are able to do many more things on their own. Some examples of tasks that children this age can do on their own, or with just a little help, are getting dressed, tying their own shoelaces, helping to set the table before dinner, picking up their toys, packing their own bag (6-7 years of age), taking care of a pet and feeding it (6-7 years), and doing their own homework (7 years).

Parents will still need to take charge of, or at least monitor, things like going to bed on time, waking up on time, doing homework (ensure that homework is done by the child, not the parents!), taking a bath (boys especially needs reminders at this age), spending time with parents, and facilitating other interests or activities.

In everyday situations, problems that they encounter should be brought out in the open for some discussion. At this age, parents need to be more directive, but whenever possible, they would do well to provide opportunities for their children to express their opinion, rather than always telling them what to do. Remember that play is still more important than work (e.g., if they are taking piano lessons, and you want them to practice a bit everyday, you may want to sit with them and make it into a fun activity or else it may become a battle which would be counterproductive).

## Middle Childhood

Children who are at the pre-teen stage may develop strong tastes about their clothes or hairstyles. Allow them freedom in this area with a bit of guidance (but parents should follow their own conscience—they do not have to let their daughter wear a micro-miniskirt just because the neighbor's kids are wearing them). Parents should continue to encourage autonomy, allowing their children to do their own tasks without interfering, which will be a temptation for many parents. Some kids will continue to enjoy using their imagination and playing games in a pretend world, and parents should not embarrass them when they want to talk about such things.[4]

*Choices that can be provided:*

- Choice of extracurricular activities
- Choice of clothing (especially around twelve years old)
- Choice of music (parents should monitor lyrics to see what they are promoting)
- Kind of birthday party they get to have (if they are having a nice party that year)
- What they would like to do during "dates" with each parent
- Whether or not to have sleepovers—parents should ensure basic safety is implemented.

## Adolescence

As the child grows older and her need for autonomy increases, the need for parents to be directive decreases. When children encounter difficulties, parents should talk about the problem and ask them what choices they have about how to overcome them. Parents should draw out their children's opinions, not just lecture them and tell them what to do. After drawing them out, parent and child can discuss things together. For navigating autonomy in the pre-teen and adolescent years, we strongly recommend reading the book *Teen-Proofing* for help with autonomy and limits. The author (John Rosemond) hits the nail on the head when it comes to figuring out the right balance.[5] On this topic, Rosemond echoes Dr. Michael Popkin, founder of Active Parenting, who says, "Make the problem their problem."[6] And who could forget the quote from Spiderman's Uncle Ben, "With great power comes great responsibility."[7]

## Communicate Respect

So let's assume that we are trying to give our children choices. Even then, the style of communication could send the wrong message. Parents can give their children a choice but may communicate it in a way that makes the child feel "put down", as opposed to letting the child feel "we are on the same team". Especially when dealing with young children, the gentleness of a parent's tone and the words a parent uses are crucial.

For example, a parent may say in an authoritarian tone, "Today we are going to the park; decide quickly which toy you want to play with." This is giving the child a choice, but how was it said? The harsh tone communicates that the child is secondary to the parent's agenda. As mentioned in Chapter Four, words only account for a small part of what we communicate to others; tone of voice and body language/facial features are much more important. A better way to talk to the child would be, "Hi sweetie, we are going to have fun today. Which toy would you like to bring to the park?" This conveys a vastly different message to the child. Or imagine a mom speaking with her very young child about having lunch. Instead of impatiently barking, "I want you to eat now. I will only let you go to the park if you finish eating," wouldn't it be better if the mom kindly but assertively beamed, "We will eat lunch first, and when we are finished, we can go to the park."

There is a world of difference between the two. Both are spelling out a task but one is done in a way that shows parent and child are allies, not "I am up here" and "You are down there." (There are obviously times when a parent may have to raise his or her voice, such as when a child is in danger or about to hurt herself or another child. When we raise our voice only in *rare* circumstances, the child will know that something serious is being conveyed.) Of course, these instances are not a big deal if they occur as one-off interactions, but repeat them day after day as part of your lifestyle and you will end up with exasperation. The temperament of the child will determine how long that will take, and in what way it will surface.

## Keep Agenda in Check

Sometimes we have underlying motives, not always obvious to us, that are pushing us to accomplish things through our kids. This motivation is so strong and forceful that it is done at the expense of our children's need for healthy autonomy and performance. In order to meet this core emotional need, parents need to honestly ask themselves, "What is my agenda?" Here are some questions for further self-examination:

> *Do I live through my children? Am I trying to meet an underlying need in myself?*
> *Do I feel the need to be ultra close to my children because of the poor quality of my marriage?*
> *Do I feel the need to protect my children because in my heart I believe the world is a dangerous place?*
> *Am I negative about them making their own decisions because a pessimistic parent raised me?*

If you answered "Yes" to any of the above, go through the questionnaires in Chapter Three of our marriage book, *I Choose Us*,[8] so you can identify the lifetraps you have, and how they specifically relate to meeting your children's core emotional need for healthy autonomy and performance. If you have any of the lifetraps from this domain to a strong degree, then there is reason to believe your drive to be over-involved with your children is a result of your own upbringing and some unmet need. Parents who are able to gain awareness in these areas will be able to identify their underlying unhealthy drive and motivation. Being aware is a huge first step.

We frequently say, "Dysfunction is the gift that keeps on giving." Here are two real-life examples of parents whose own lifetraps caused them to pass down similar lifetraps to their children.

*A mother enmeshed with her twins*: Gayle had twin daughters. She doted on them and gave them every advantage she could, monetarily and in education. Gayle was also over-involved and controlling. She did not allow her daughters to do what normal teens do on their own and protected them from taking risks of any kind. In a city where all kids either rode the school bus or took the subway, Gayle forbade her kids to do either. When it came time for the teens to go to university, they decided to live in different cities from their mother and each other. One of the girls was able to cope because of her temperament, but the other girl was not. Filled with fear, she had to drop out of school, move home, and was not able to go out alone. Now over 30 years old, she is still dependent on others, is enmeshed with her mother, and frozen in fear—truly trapped by vulnerability to harm and illness.

*A father passing down negativity*: Ben's son, Zack, was all excited about entering an art competition. Although Zack was good at drawing, Ben was not happy when he found out about it and completely berated and humiliated his son. Ben barred Zack from entering any such competitions because he thought they were a complete waste of time. Ben was so deeply filled with negativity that he could not imagine how anything good would come from such an attempt. This left a painful scar on Zack emotionally, which he brought into his adult life when he became a father. Now Zack finds it very difficult to try anything new, and constantly hears a voice, "It's no use, why bother, what's the point?"

When it comes to letting our children grow up, it is so tempting to hold on tightly, or even to give up in despair. At the end of the day, we reason with them and plead our case, all the while showing them that we love them and trust them. When we let our children make choices and give them age-appropriate freedom, we are meeting their core emotional need for healthy autonomy and performance, and we are also maintaining our connection.

SECTION FOUR

# THE CORE EMOTIONAL NEED
# FOR REASONABLE LIMITS

# Chapter Twelve

# REASONABLE LIMITS
..................................................

The Core Emotional Need for Reasonable Limits can be defined as giving our children a sense of right and wrong, a sense of boundaries, and the tools they need to get along in the world and work well with others. Children whose core emotional need for reasonable limits has been met naturally develop traits and beliefs such as reciprocity, fairness & equality, self-control & self-discipline, and a sense of mutuality.[1] In addition, they will *consistently* and *on an emotional level* believe the following messages about their parents:

> *They challenge me in a respectful way when my behavior and words are out of line.*
> *They encourage me to persevere with tasks that I find frustrating.*
> *They guide me to consider multiple factors in order to avoid rash decisions.*
> *They don't always let me have my own way; they say "No" when it's best for me.*
> *They expect me to be responsible and contribute to the well-being of our home, such as by doing chores.*
> *They expect me to be wise when choosing my closest friends, and to be able to say "No" to some of my friends when the need arises.*

Carly's parents were not financially well off but they worked hard and looked forward to the birth of their first child. When baby Carly was born, her parents talked of nothing else. Other siblings followed, but to her parents, she was always special—the smartest, prettiest, the most talented. As all the children got older, the parents' favoritism became more blatant—when the other children got a toy, Carly got two; if her siblings got a single scoop ice cream cone, Carly got a double. The other children had set bedtimes with no television on school nights, Carly was allowed to stay up to watch TV as late as she wanted. Naturally gifted, she didn't have to work hard to stand out in class, and she was easily accepted into several universities. However, out on her own, success did not come so easily—after being dumped by her boyfriend, she could not get out of bed to take some important exams. Carly managed to get hired after graduation, but quit due to boredom, and drifted from job to job, falling for "get rich quick" schemes along the way. She cheated on her husband who then left her, and was fired from her last job. Carly declared bankruptcy and now lives alone, bitter about how life has been unfair to her.

Peter was born into a wealthy family, surrounded by hired help. He had a nanny, a chauffeur, a cook, and a nurse to make sure he always had everything he wanted. The moment he cried, someone was there to offer him a cookie. The second he fell down, someone was there to coddle him. If he did not like his kindergarten, he was moved immediately. If he wanted the latest toy or a new pair of shoes like the ones he saw on television, he got them. Peter never heard the word "no" and never experienced frustration. He became an insufferable bully on the playground, a shallow friend to the other kids at school, and an obnoxious older brother. The rest of the world wouldn't put up with his nonsense, and eventually, when faced with some challenges at his first place of employment, he attempted suicide. After a stint in a psychiatric ward, he was able to get another good job, but so far he has never had the discipline or follow-through to have another serious relationship or move up the corporate ladder.

Carly and Peter may have been from different socioeconomic backgrounds and raised in different countries, but they had the same kind of parenting—their need for reasonable limits was not met when they were growing up.

## Everyone Needs Boundaries

Limits and boundaries provide markers and guides so that children know what is acceptable and what is not. In a very real way, both children and adults need boundaries to live in a world with others. Of course, every family is different—some parents are comfortable with loud voices, messiness and spontaneity, others will more naturally opt for "inside voices", keeping the house tidy, having a strict schedule, etc. The important thing is that parents should have conviction about their personal values, and their boundaries and limits should reflect their beliefs consistently.

There is no one in the world who likes to be around smart-alecky, whining, ungrateful children. Dr. Phil, an American TV talk-show host and self-help guru, says that kids without limits become entitled. Instead of feeling guilty for giving children boundaries, Dr. Phil says, "If you want to feel guilty, feel guilty for not teaching them to understand how the world works, that everyone goes on green and stops on red."[2] Psychoanalyst Dr. Ruth Sharon co-authored the book *I Refuse To Raise A Brat*. She says when it comes to helping people have breakthroughs in therapy, the most difficult clients are *not* those who have been disadvantaged and abused; rather those who as children were pampered, over-indulged, and spoiled.[3] Every day on the news we witness the fallout from the rise in entitlement—not mentioning any names, but more than a few famous athletes, entertainers and politicians could have done with some reasonable limits when they were growing up!

*Meeting this core emotional need by teaching our children limits and expecting them to live within these limits is a very loving thing to do as a parent.* Children are not born programmed to learn to follow rules and to respect limits. In fact it is the other way round—they are born without any knowledge of limits and rules. Children come into the world thinking that they are the centers of the universe. They love to explore, investigate and test the world, which seems colorful, fun and inviting. However, at what point is it fine (or even safe) for them to "explore" without consequences? When is it not wise to do so? Modern culture is confused on this point—society mocks limits and sees restricting children as old fashioned and cruel; those with more common sense do want to set boundaries but seem at a loss as to how to do so. Children are certainly not going to learn reasonable and healthy limits on their own; the only way parents can make sure they learn is by meeting this core emotional need.

Just as important as ensuring that they convey limits is *how* they convey them. On the one hand, parents must take care to meet this need in a respectful and healthy way, lest they end up causing frustration and exasperation. (When parents correct their children with harsh and disrespectful words, it leads to exasperation. This complicates the process of learning and awareness because the exasperation is separate and apart from the original act of misbehavior and lead to resentment and rebellion in the adolescent years.) On the other hand, *not* conveying reasonable limits with appropriate seriousness brings problems of its own. Whatever happens, our children need limits if they are to become healthy adults—children who are not able to follow simple rules, be it in the classroom, in public, or at home, will face huge problems in life. They will cause burdens for others as well as bring heartache to the people who love them the most.

## The Benefits of Self-Control

Ancient wisdom literature contains many references about discipline and self-control, and modern research concurs that we are better off when we practice curbing our appetites. A study out of Stanford University in 1972 found that "...young children who were able to resist grabbing a fluffy marshmallow placed in front of them for 15 long minutes in order to get two of them later scored an average of 210 points higher on the SAT [an entrance exam for American universities which the kids took 12 years later] than kids who could not wait. About one third of the four to six year-olds studied were able to withstand the sweet temptation. Follow-up was done 18 years later, and the kids with more self-control in the marshmallow trial had better life outcomes across the board."[4] A more recent study reveals that self-discipline has a bigger effect on academic performance than intellectual talent, and contributes more than "IQ" to positive report-card grades, standardized achievement-test scores, and school attendance[5] (RR12.1).

Parents often vacillate from one extreme to another. Some are very strict and rigid, while others are permissive. Many also have a mixture of both styles. As a result, mixed signals are sent and both parents and children enter into a "Vortex of Conflict Escalation" where they trigger and re-trigger one another (see Chapter Fourteen). When this gets repeated multiple times, many parents end up losing their patience and resorting to exasperation interactions, throwing their arms up and giving up altogether, or tightening the screws and mandating strict obedience regardless of the state of their relationship, only to see animosity and a loss of connection down the road.

Our children were both fairly strong-willed and opinionated, so it is no surprise that we had to start saying "No" early on in their lives. We doubted ourselves as young parents do, wondering if we were being too strict at times. But we noticed a difference whenever we got soft and backed down from boundaries—chaos reigned, and the kids did not seem any happier for it! Limits and boundaries give children security and comfort because they know what to expect. They may try to fight them; they may even temporarily "hate their parents", but they are secretly grateful. (And when they get older, they will tell you so!) Dr. Gary Solomon calls it "CPR": parents who are *consistent, predictable* and *reliable* are more likely to produce children with good mental health.[6]

Limits help kids to see that, contrary to every fiber of their young beings, the world does not revolve around them and they must respect others if they want respect. Limits are a way of teaching children how to live out "The Golden Rule"—to treat others as they would like to be treated. Unfortunately this does not fit the direction the world is moving. The enlightening book, *Why Is It Always About You? The Seven Deadly Sins of Narcissism* reports that entitlement is widespread and that an ever-increasing percentage of Americans are narcissistic![7]

One caveat—when parents are helping children follow limits, they must ensure their children are not just obeying out of "approval seeking" but that their children genuinely understand the limits and why they are important. This will help them understand "why", which enables them to eventually adopt the parents' values as they grow, and to fully benefit from having this core emotional need met.

# Chapter Thirteen

# THE DOMAIN OF IMPAIRED LIMITS

The third domain of schema clusters is known as "Impaired Limits". To the extent that parents do not meet the core emotional need for reasonable limits, we believe their children will experience the opposite—*Impaired Limits*. This means that their children will be at risk of developing some or all of the lifetraps in the Domain of Impaired Limits, namely, Entitlement, Insufficient Self-Control, and Approval-Seeking. This chapter explains these three lifetraps in detail, and contains an additional segment called "Basic Safety Zone".

## The Lifetrap of Entitlement / Grandiosity

The first maladaptive schema (lifetrap) in the domain of impaired limits is entitlement / grandiosity. The core message of the entitlement lifetrap is, *"I am special and better than other people. Rules should not apply to me. I should always come first."* This lifetrap is rooted in a desire for power and control.

Children with the entitlement lifetrap will grow up to believe that what they want or need should always be a priority. It is okay for them to cheat on tests or at sports, and they minimize it. They do not need to fasten the seat belt when the plane is taking off, they can drive while under the influence, and they generally get angry when they do not get what they want. Entitled individuals do not care if getting their way disadvantages others; they don't think twice about changing the rules when playing a game. As long as they win, that is what matters, and they do not have any awareness of the pain others feel. They have a warped sense of fairness, and may accuse others of being selfish instead. They rarely, if ever, put themselves in other people's shoes. They are usually not in tune with others' feelings, but are totally in tune with their own. When challenged about their behavior, they often think that people should accept them the way they are.

Children develop the entitlement lifetrap in two ways. Being told that they are more special than other kids, having no limits, and never being made to take responsibility for their actions, words or moods, produces "pure entitlement." In her revealing book, *Disarming the Narcissist*, Wendy Behary says these children grow up into "purely spoiled narcissists," unable to be thoughtful of others.[1] It is this kind of entitlement we are trying to prevent when we talk about meeting the core emotional need for reasonable limits. The second way that entitlement is produced is a bit more complicated. This is called "fragile entitlement". This form of the lifetrap comes not from being spoiled, but is a *reaction* to unmet core emotional needs for connection and acceptance or realistic expectations, and is rooted in either the defectiveness lifetrap or the emotional deprivation lifetrap. When needs for caring and recognition are not met, a response of "I have to take care for myself" and "No one else is looking out for me" develops. The lifestyle and behavior look the same as "pure entitlement", but it is important to understand that the behavior of these narcissists is covering up a lot of pain from unmet needs.

Entitled children will often become leaders (at school, in sports, or in gangs) who boast about not taking "No" for an answer. Highly entitled individuals do not like to hear the word "No". They may even receive compliments for their natural leadership qualities and for being so determined in life. They do not like to work under others, since they do not like rules, but they do not mind enforcing rules with others. Adults with the entitlement lifetrap generally hate being vulnerable and sharing about their weaknesses, but they love to boast about their strengths. Because of their bullying, they have power, and they achieve results by infringing on other people's rights. Very few people with this lifetrap volunteer to seek help or see their need to change. Why? Life is good, since they get their way most of the time. Without intervention, entitled children who grow up to be entitled adults rarely get to the point where they can see that relationships are a two-way street, and that by becoming open and vulnerable, rather than being demanding, self-serving, or bullying, they are more likely to get what they *really need*—a satisfying and caring relationship. We believe that adults with narcissistic and entitled behavior can change, but it makes much more sense to nip it in the bud when we see it in our children than trying to change them when they are older.

*Early family environment that might cause this lifetrap to develop:*

- There were no proper boundaries in the child's life early on; he set his own limits. Even if there were limits, they were few, and revolved around him achieving excellence in one or more areas.
- The child was shamed a lot growing up, and to avoid feeling shame, he overcompensated and shamed others.
- The child was allowed to throw tantrums and often got his way because of his strong will. His anger was a manipulative tool to get what he wanted.
- The child was not taught to care about others.
- Insufficient attention was given to recognizing the child's accomplishments and he was unduly criticized. His response was to become excessively demanding.

Figure 13.1: The Lifetrap of Entitlement (Javier as an adult)

Figure 13.2: A Possible Early Environment Which Would Likely Contribute to the Entitlement Lifetrap (Javier as a child) *Go to Appendix I*

## The Lifetrap of Insufficient Self-Control / Self-Discipline

The next maladaptive schema (lifetrap) in the domain of impaired limits is insufficient self-control / self-discipline. The core message of the insufficient self-control lifetrap is, *"I should not be uncomfortable."* This lifetrap leads people to express their emotion negatively, avoid difficult tasks, and give in to temptation. It interferes with healthy adult behavior like relationship reciprocity, and setting and achieving goals.

Children who are not given limits, are neglected or not given disciplined role models, will usually develop this lifetrap. Almost all children struggle with self-control growing up, which is normal. However, if they develop this lifetrap, they may, as adults, have difficulty controlling their impulses. Their fits of rage or sexual promiscuity or over-eating or whatever may evolve into an addiction. They also may have trouble working at a task for what others would consider a reasonable length of time because they feel bored. People with this lifetrap may set out to do a task, but they easily get distracted. If a task seems too difficult, they will give up.

People with the lifetrap of insufficient self-control have a hard time making themselves uncomfortable, or delaying gratification. As children, they did not learn the value of persevering to accomplish tasks, or the principle of not giving into short-term pleasure. If they are in a position of authority, they will delegate more than they should. Discipline is a challenge for them. Much of what they do is based on their desires, and they can be rash in their decision-making. Only when this lifetrap brings them to a low point in life will they start to realize that have to deal with this problem. It is worth noting that people with this lifetrap are sometimes quite likeable because their spontaneous side is very attractive. This charm may carry them far, in spite of a lack of discipline.

*Early family environment that might cause this lifetrap to develop:*

- The child's parents were not very involved with her while she was growing up. Her parents left her to set her own limits at too young of an age, such as when to sleep, how long to play, what to eat, how much TV to watch. Early on, she was allowed to act on her desires.
- No consequences were set when the child got out of line. Because the child's parents were not involved, they did not know what she was up to. They were too busy with their own work and schedules.
- Since the child's parents were too busy, she was brought up by grandparents or by nannies, who spoiled her and gave her whatever she wanted.
- The child was naturally talented. She did not have to try that hard to succeed early on in life, and her parents did not sense the need to teach her

perseverance. As life became more challenging, the child avoided pursuits that would require much perseverance.

Figure 13.3: The Lifetrap of Insufficient Self-Control (Young Jin as an adult)

Figure 13.4: A Possible Early Environment Which Would Likely Contribute to the Insufficient Self-Control Lifetrap (Young Jin as a child) *Go to Appendix 1*

## The Lifetrap of Approval-Seeking / Recognition-Seeking

The third and final maladaptive schema (lifetrap) in the domain of impaired limits is approval-seeking / recognition-seeking. The core message of the approval-seeking lifetrap is, *"I must seek the approval of others above all else. If other people do not approve of me, something is very wrong."* This pattern of thinking is about defining who we are through the eyes of others rather than paying attention to our own needs and desires.

Children who develop this lifetrap will struggle to form an opinion about themselves outside of what others think and feel about them. They are not secure enough to trust their own instincts. This lifetrap is not about achieving a self-imposed high standard, or about feeling superior, but about craving other people's approval.

People with this lifetrap feel that their world collapses when they sense that others do not think highly of them; when the opposite is true, they feel elevated and happy about themselves. They put a lot of energy into drawing attention to their good deeds. Given how much they are controlled by what others think, they do not really develop an authentic sense of self with their own values and preferences. As a result, they cannot truly be fulfilled. At work, people with this lifetrap are consumed with what their colleagues and especially their boss think of them. Even if they are doing a great job, it is the approval of others that will decide how they feel about themselves. They lack their own convictions and suppress their preferences at the expense of being liked by others.

*Early family environment that might cause this lifetrap to develop:*
- The child's parents emphasized the need for status, looking good, or recognition in such a way that it was part of their normal family conversation.
- The child's parents boasted about themselves. If and when they were praised by others (e.g., appearing in the papers or on TV), they made it into a big deal.
- The child's parents bragged about their achievements and who they knew.
- The child's parents focused more on how things looked at home, rather than what was inside the hearts and minds of their children.
- Self-esteem had nothing to do with the child liking himself, and everything to do with others approving of him.

Figure 13.5: The Lifetrap of Approval-Seeking (Jono as an adult)

Figure 13.6: A Possible Early Environment Which Would Likely Contribute to the Approval-Seeking Lifetrap (Jono as a child) *Go to Appendix 1*

## Basic Safety Zone

An extremely important component for this core emotional need involves protecting children from the dangers of early/inappropriate exposure to sex and violence. In particular, this is related to dangers on the Internet (porn, revealing personal information on social networking sites, lurking pedophiles, scams, inappropriate YouTube videos, and the like), listening to inappropriate song lyrics, as well as inappropriate and sexually explicit books, movies, and TV shows.

Parents need to understand how using the Internet without limits can have dire consequences, affecting their children for life. In an age where two-year-olds surf the Internet on their dad's tablets, parents must be urgent about setting healthy limits for their children. Given the fallout, this is not something that should be taken lightly.

## The Influence of Media

Contrary to the opinion of those who argue that watching TV and playing violent computer games have little negative effect on children, there is overwhelming support that the opposite is true.[2] We strongly believe that parents need to exercise control regarding what they allow their children to watch on TV and online, how often they are allowed to access social media, and what kind of video games they are allowed to play.

Studies show that kids who play inappropriate video games and watch inappropriate TV programs, YouTube videos and movies are exposed to thousands (maybe tens of thousands) of murders, along with hundreds of hours of vulgar language and unhealthy relationships.[3] Even if children are not influenced to act out what they are watching, they risk strengthening the vulnerability lifetrap (see Chapter Ten), convinced that the world is a mean and a dangerous place; this would inhibit autonomy and interfere with forming healthy adult relationships.

Parents who doubt whether they should limit their children's "screen time" have to ask themselves if they are happy with their kids being raised by "the other parent". *The Other Parent* is the title of a book authored by James Steyer and Chelsea Clinton; it is also the nickname Steyer and Clinton have given to the media. This "other parent" directly and indirectly teaches our children material things buy happiness; looks are more important than character; women are objects to be used and thrown away; drunkenness, drugs and the like are part of growing up; aggressive and violent behavior is no big deal; killing people is part and parcel of everyday life; sex outside of marriage is fine, even without commitment; flirting is no big deal, even if you are married; children always need more freedom; and strict parents are old-fashioned.[4]

Most experts advise parents not to allow children to have a TV or computer in their bedroom, as it is difficult to monitor and promotes isolation. They also advise parents not to turn the TV on during meal times and when the family is talking. Media experts also agree that parents should establish guidelines about how much TV should be viewed during school days, and talk about limits for holiday times as well.

We would add that parents should discuss what movies the children should watch, what to avoid and why. Parents would do well to make use of websites like www.kids-in-mind.com. (Kids-in-Mind rates each movie according to the amount and intensity of sex, violence, drugs, and vulgarities.)[5] Parents and children should have frequent discussions regarding gaming, TV and Internet content, song lyrics, and social media, and content of texts/chats. It should be a given that all computer, tablets and cell phones have filters to avoid access to pornographic websites.

Parents must impress upon children how what they watch and hear will have a big impact on their future choices. Parents should not underestimate the powerful influence of TV, computer games and the Internet. In the end, parents who take this kind of basic safety seriously and introduce healthy limits (and help their children to agree eventually with these limits) will increase their chances of protecting their children from many harmful outcomes.

*We have included a long "Research Revealed" portion to correspond to this Basic Safety Zone. Here are a few tidbits—please read the rest when you have time.* (RR13.1)

- Heavy online users are more likely to get into trouble, and are often sad, unhappy or bored.[6]
- Young people are spending about 54 hours per week consuming media which is more than some adults spend at work.[7]
- The strongest factor associated with early teenage sexual intercourse for male adolescents was viewing pornography between 14 and 19 years of age.[8]
- Researchers studied a remote village in British Columbia before and after television was introduced; they found that two years after TV arrived, violent incidents had increased by 160%.[9]
- Among children ages 8-14, incidences of psychological trauma (including anxiety, depression and post-traumatic stress) increased in proportion to the number of hours of television watched each day.[10]

••••••••••••••••••••••••••••••••••••••••••••••••••••••••••

## *Louis Lowdown*

When Sonia and David were in the same kindergarten, I (Karen) organized a play-date with a mom from the school. It was our first and last one. (I should have known better; my kids had told me the boys were bullies! Still, the mother was so nice; I had thought, "How bad can they be?") During our time in their home, my kids ran to me in the kitchen for protection several times. The misguided mother would shake her head helplessly as her children disobeyed her every word and ran riot throughout the house. I'll never forget how dumbfounded I was when the mother uttered, "I always thought that if I gave my children everything they wanted and didn't say 'No' to them, they would be so happy they would obey me out of gratitude." Summoning all of my self-control, I politely said, "Wow, that's an interesting parenting philosophy. My philosophy is a bit different." At that moment, I truly thought the mother would say, "Oh please, tell me your philosophy; what do you do?" However, she just stared at me blankly, then smiled and said, "Oh well, I guess that everybody has their own way." I almost fainted. A few minutes later my kids gave me a look that said, "Mum, we gotta' get out of here!" Boy did we have lots to talk about on the way home!

••••••••••••••••••••••••••••••••••••••••••••••••••••••••••

# Chapter Fourteen

## WHAT INHIBITS LIMITS?

·······························································

Despite understanding rationally that their children need consistent boundaries, parents' good intentions sometimes get "bottlenecked;" sometimes there is confusion about "wants" and "privileges"; and sometimes parents get caught in "The Vortex of Conflict Escalation" before they know what hit them. This chapter explores various scenarios that work against parents, preventing them from meeting the core emotional need for reasonable limits.

### Frequently Seen Bottlenecks

**Parents feel guilty** – guilty they are not perfect, guilty they cannot buy everything for their family that they deserve, guilty they are not doing what their neighbors are doing with their kids, guilty they are not spending enough time with their kids. Whatever the reason, guilty parents often give in to their children's complaints and excuses. They neither follow through with previous agreements nor enforce family rules.

**Parents overreact to their own childhood** – parents who grew up in a strict environment often hear a voice in their heads reminding them how painful it was to live under rigid and strict rules. This is also true when a parent was subjected to a harsh schoolteacher, leader or boss. In a noble effort to never emulate such treatment, parents go too far to the other extreme.

**Parents don't understand "grace and truth"** – too much focus on grace alone and not on obedience, truth and character. A friend asked us why sometimes the brattiest children have the sweetest and kindest parents? How can that be? Because the parents love their kids so much that they cannot bear to say "No" to them! They are good and kind individuals who serve their children unceasingly, and wonder why the kids turn out entitled. They are sure that patient smiles alone are all they need to guide their children. These parents usually have compliant temperaments, are easy to get along with, and would never hurt a fly, so they do not see that their "differently-tempered" children occasionally need correction.

**Parents think their kids will develop limits by themselves** – but few will. Parents sometimes believe children will eventually grow up and learn when they are more mature. We have not found this to be the case. Children without limits become adults without limits. When they are not trained at a young age, it becomes harder and harder as they grow older. Adults with healthy limits were trained to respect and obey healthy boundaries as they were growing up.

**Parents want to avoid conflict** – they are not ready to go "toe to toe" with their child. In an effort to make the home atmosphere more pleasant, some parents avoid setting rules and talking about healthy limits. These parents usually make excuses to other parents, "well, kids will be kids", Such short-term peace often comes with a huge price later on when the children have to face the consequences of their actions.

**Parents want to be liked by their children** – similar to the above but with an element of "need". Most of us "hate being hated"; some parents absolutely cannot bear the thought. Emotionally deprived parents are vulnerable to making choices to help their children *like* rather than *respect* them. They do not wish their children to harbor *any* ill feelings towards them. Some parents, intentionally or not, use their children to meet their own emotional needs. In their desire to be friends, they compromise and do not train their children to honor healthy and reasonable limits.

**Parents are just too busy** – this is probably the saddest one, but all too common these days. The amount of time many parents set aside today to spend time talking with their children is shockingly low. Schedules become too busy and family time is not prioritized. These parents often wake up to a nightmare, surprised when they find out their own children don't want to speak to them, or what their children have been doing behind closed doors. The irony is family crises take up far more time than simply nurturing good relationships and enforcing limits along the way.

## Needs vs. Wants; Rights vs. Privileges

Something can be said to be **"a need"**, as defined by Merriam-Webster, if it is "a physiological or psychological requirement for the well-being of an organism";[1] in other words, without it, a person's well-being will suffer. **"A want"** is something that is desired, which a person may get if circumstances go their way i.e., a person works hard and pays for it or receives it from another; alternatively, the "want" may remain elusive. Merriam-Webster defines **"a right"** as "something that a person is or should be morally or legally allowed to have, get, or do."[2] With "rights", adults don't need permission, and in some cases, kids don't either, i.e., children have the right to education and to grow up in a safe home; however, the exercising of a right cannot deprive the equal rights of others. **"A privilege"** is a benefit given to some but not to all; it is something a person cannot do unless the person is given permission.

Parents do their children a disservice when they don't help them to understand these differences, when they get confused and give their children "wants" but communicate they are giving "needs"; ditto for "rights" vs. "privileges". This in turn confuses the kids, who begin to expect things as their "right", or as "needs", instead of understanding they are "privileges" and "wants". Many a destructive conflict has arisen over a child thinking he needs a particular toy, a pre-teen thinking a cell phone is her right, or a teen not realizing that getting the car is a privilege. (We were amused by how many children we know said confidently that having access to Wi-Fi was a "need" and a "right"!) Go to www.gep.sg for an exercise that will help families get rid of confusion, as well as encourage teens to *be responsible* with all four categories.

## Parents' Expectations

Just as we admit that as parents none of us is perfect, we also acknowledge that our children do not always live up to our expectations—whether or not our expectations are healthy will be left for the chapter on Realistic Expectations. The fact remains that all humans who are connected with each other have certain expectation. Just as children have core emotional needs, parents have normal, healthy expectations. In saying this, we emphasize that this is not about the emotional needs of the parents, but about healthy expectations in a family. *(Parents should have their own needs met in their marriage, and in their community, or with peer groups. It is not the children's place to meet the emotional needs of the parents. Just as children can become exasperated when their core emotional needs are not met, parents will not be fulfilled or at peace when their core healthy expectations are not met.)*

So, what reasonable and healthy expectations can and should parents have of their children? Here are some expectations that we think are normal, reasonable, and healthy. These sit well with our experiences, and are parallel with the core emotional needs of children:

- **Connection:** This involves children responding to the parents, in an age-appropriate manner, as the parents do their best to meet the core emotional need for connection and acceptance. Parents want an on-going, life-long connection with their children.
- **Growth and Performance:** This involves children learning and growing in age-appropriate ways (emotionally, physically, mentally and spiritually). Parents want to see their children living up to their potential and utilizing their strengths and abilities as they respond to the parent meeting the core emotional needs for healthy autonomy and realistic expectations.
- **Responsibility and Respect:** This involves children adhering to rules and taking care of themselves in an age-appropriate manner, as parents do their best to meet their children's core emotional need for Reasonable Limits. Most parents want to see their children develop character and be respectful; this is linked with children understanding that they need to be responsible when it comes to *needs, wants, rights, and privileges.*

These three areas define the core expectations of parenting; when children make progress in them, parents feel that their kids are maturing properly and that their parenting amounts to something worthwhile.

Bear in mind even if a child is not able to make much progress, it is still the responsibility of the parents to accept and love children unconditionally. Unconditional love is critical to parenting. Many parents get disappointed when expectations and limits are not to a certain mark. Parents need to take stock of each child's potential and inclinations, and be grateful for the individuality and gifts of each child. (More on this in the section on Realistic Expectations.)

## The Vortex

When parents (rightly or wrongly) feel that children are not meeting their expectations, or when children (rightly or wrongly) feel that parents are not meeting their core emotional needs, there will be conflict. If parents are able to practice the principles of Good Enough Parenting, hopefully the conflicts will be sorted out constructively.

However, since the emotional part of our brains seems to work quicker than the rational part, this does not always happen! When conflict escalates, parent and child enter into what we call "The Vortex of Conflict Escalation" (see Figure 14.1). This vortex may involve the exchange of harsh words, throwing of tantrums, or stonewalls of silence and sulking, but either way, it will harm the connection, mar the feeling of acceptance, and damage the relationship. Let us consider how the vortex might occur when dealing with reasonable limits.

# Vortex of Conflict Escalation

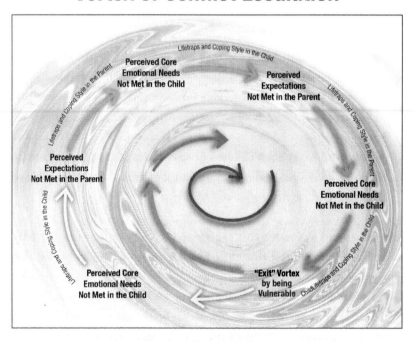

Figure 14.1: The Vortex of Conflict Escalation

Picture a case in which a 14-year-old boy is defiant about obeying rules. He tests his parents' limits to see how far he can go. What may escape unnoticed is the role parents play in teaching limits. Let us suppose that in this case, when the father tries to teach his son reasonable limits by giving instructions, the boy refuses to cooperate, and the father becomes stern. The child debates with the father. The parent becomes frustrated and raises his voice. The teen also raises *his* voice and walks out. The parent keeps going, following his son out of the room, perhaps issuing threats. The boy retorts with an insult, then both get tired and retreat to their own corners. In the meantime, other family members may witness this scene. Typically, the other parent joins the fray, either against the child or against her spouse. Finally, someone gives in… But is the fault always with the child?

Typically in a situation like this, people will leave thinking the child has to learn a thing or two about limits. While this may be the case, it is also true that the parents may have been more focused on their own triggers in the vortex of conflict than on the needs of their child. It could be that one or more exasperation interactions were hindering the child from learning about limits. These further exacerbate the formation of a vortex between the child and the parent. It then escalates, causing emotional pain and damage. Unnecessary words are used. Verbal or physical abuse can take place. Some parents give up and then the child "wins". Sometimes the parent "wins" and the child develops resentment. In both cases, the parent-child connection is damaged.

••••••••••••••••••••••••••••••••••••••••••••••••••••••••••••••••

### *Louis Lowdown*

When our children were younger, we had rules for TV and computer usage (what, when and how long). We facilitated outdoor play, sports, and music; add in homework and friends, there wasn't much time left for "screen time". However, when David started high school, we found that he would try to sneak in extra computer games. While his grades were not plummeting, we were worried more about the deceit and addiction factor, and noticed that it was starting to have a negative effect. I (John) talked with him and made a written agreement about his limits. He agreed and for the first few days, it went well. Then one day I caught him red handed—he tried hard to exit the video game, but it was too late. I lost my patience, shouted at him and went off angrily to my office. David was hurt at my outburst. Later, after my wife's intervention, we talked and I apologized. David also apologized for his lack of seriousness in sticking to the agreed limits, and for being secretive. Looking back, even though he blatantly disregarded a rule we had agreed on earlier, I should not have blown up. I allowed myself to walk straight into a vortex of conflict escalation, which potentially hurt our connection and was counterproductive. Most of the time, I managed to *not* cause exasperation; I expressed my disappointment in a firm voice and let him reflect, making time to talk later, showing acceptance to him but not accepting his behavior. Staying out of the vortex helps our kids to learn from their mistakes.

••••••••••••••••••••••••••••••••••••••••••••••••••••••••••••••••••••

In addition to blocking our children's core emotional needs, the exasperation interactions are major contributors to the development of the vortex. Subtly and unintentionally, a parent exasperates the child, which does not help the child to listen and obey. At the same time, if the child is defiant, his nature either diminishes the firmness of the parents in staying committed to their expectations, or causes them to blow up further. The interplay between meeting the core emotional needs of children and the expectations of parents has to be harmonized and balanced, failing which, parent and child will trigger each other, and the vortex of conflict escalation will emerge, leading to more exasperation. Please review Chapters Three and Four, and then read the two vignettes below, after which you can go to our website www.gep.sg for more vignettes and an exercise that will help parents become experts in navigating the vortex.

Alice (12) comes home from school frustrated—she has extra homework and several projects due soon. She goes to her room. Her brother, Sam (10), comes into her room without knocking. She yells, "Get out of my room!" He says "sorry" in a sarcastic tone. She shouts, "You're insincere and have no boundaries!" He then brings out examples of how she is mean to him. Their parents hear the exchange and the father tells Alice to settle down, which is his normal response whenever the kids have a fight. Alice responds angrily, accusing her dad of taking Sam's side. The two children continue to call each other names. The father goes into the room, raises his voice and says, "Why can't you both just get along for once?! Even animals behave better than you both! Your arguments are so stupid. The house was a lot more peaceful before you two showed up!" As he blows up, they become quiet. The father then commands them both to apologize. They do so, but silently still resent each other and their dad. The dad then calls them names and issues threats as he storms out of the room. At dinner, they do not speak to each other and the atmosphere is uncomfortably quiet and unpleasant. Later in the evening the father blurts out the good news that he got an email from his boss to say he got a promotion at work. Sam congratulates him, but Alice does not say anything and walks up to her room. The father is disappointed but does not say anything back to her, leaving the issue unresolved.

Ben comes home from school and plays computer games, as he always does. His mother reminds him about his promise to be reliable at his new part-time job and to go to work on time, but he ignores her. She pleads with him and he agrees to go to work, but procrastinates and leaves the house late, as usual. Later that week, Ben gets fired. His mother works up the courage to ask, "Honey, would you like to talk about your resolutions?" Ben gets angry and says, "Why don't you just give me a break? I'm old enough to choose what I like and if I don't like something, why should I do it?" When Ben's mother serves dinner, he hardly eats, preferring to eat the junk food he purchased when out with his friends. He plays computer games until the wee hours of the morning; he frequently does not get enough sleep and falls sick. His parents know what is going on, but are afraid to say anything. Ben's mother, in particular, blames herself and becomes depressed.

In these examples (and the ones in our website), the interactions quickly escalated into the vortex. The children fell short of their parents' expectations in some way, and their parents' response was more about how the situation triggered them than about addressing the situation from the point of view of a parent mindful of meeting a child's core needs. It does not matter which one came first, the child not cooperating or the parent exasperating the child. Either way, parents owe it to their children to learn to stay out of the vortex of conflict escalation. The next chapter contains Ten Tips on staying out of the Vortex all together!

# Chapter Fifteen

# STAYING OUT OF THE VORTEX

································································

A big part of avoiding "The Vortex" is related to laying a good foundation; therefore, the first seven of these ten steps are about what parents can do to set things up well. Once the foundation is in place, parents will usually find that conflict escalates much less often.

## 1. Give Clear Instructions (with Strategies in Place)

It is imperative that clear instructions are given to children as to what the limits are. Infants can understand the word "No"; toddlers can learn to pick up their toys. As children get older, it may be helpful to have regular family meetings to discuss household chores, limits, discipline, and responsibilities.

Having strategies in place during known and predictable times of stress can be very helpful in avoiding the vortex of conflict escalation. Roughly 150 families in California allowed researchers to place audio recording devices in their house for a sixteen-month period in hopes of discovering the most frequent times for conflict. No surprises on their findings—most arguments took place during the rush to get out of the house for school/work, right before bed, and at the end of the month when finances were getting tight![1] Therefore, it makes sense to think about clear instructions and strategies to prevent meltdowns before they happen.

We can surmise that the "hot spots" picked up by that study are the times when the pressure of parents' expectations and children's core needs are most likely to be in conflict. For example, the parent expects the child to be mindful of the need for everyone to get out of the house quickly in the morning, but the child may need time to get ready quietly and methodically, or to feel connected before beginning the day. The parents' rushing triggers the child's anxieties and prevents emotional needs from being met.

Different children have different issues and needs—not all children need limits for all things, only those that pertain to them personally. For example, the subject of how much time to spend playing computer games did not come up in conversations with our daughter, and budget concerns seldom came up with our son. Other issues are age-sensitive. Here are some issues you may want to discuss with your children, depending on your values and their ages (feel free to add your own!):

| Issues | Expectations |
| --- | --- |
| Tidying toys away | How tidy? |
| Having friends over | How often and expected behavior? |
| TV on school nights | Allowed? How much? Which shows? |
| Bedtime | During weekdays vs. weekends? |
| Pocket money | Allowance? |
| Phone bills/Texts/Chats | Limits? |
| Morning | Waking up, leaving house on time? |
| Computer games | Which and how often? |
| Chores | Which and how often? |
| Family dinners | Regularity? (We recommend five times a week) |
| Curfews | Weeknights vs. weekends? |
| Movies/TV/Online content | Age-appropriate? |
| Music lyrics | Acceptable? |
| Internet access | What kind and how much? |
| Teenagers rooms | How tidy? |

| Moodiness and temper tantrums | Tolerance level? (Feelings are acceptable but not necessarily behavior—see Chapter Seven, section on accepting behavior vs. accepting feelings) |
|---|---|
| The big NOs | Decide what they will be for your family. |

When children disobey because parents were not clear about limits, frustration sets in, and the vortex might be right around the corner. With some children, it may help for both parties to write out an agreement and keep a copy each, as a point of reference. (This is not meant to be legally binding!) When something is written down, it is amazing how it shuts down potential ambiguities. With the proliferation of smartphones, tablets and other gadgets, there is no reason why agreements about instructions and limits cannot be easily recorded.

## 2. Be United

When trying to prevent a vortex, it is important to make sure that mom and dad are on the same page. Since most of us seem to marry our opposite, this will take planning ahead and lots of discussion. At times, getting united on training and disciplining our children will feel a strategic battle discussion. Do not be discouraged. Persevere—it is worth it. Children are very smart; they know which parent is weak in a particular area and some kids will milk that weakness for all it's worth, so be united!

## 3. Be Optimistic and Encouraging

Be optimistic *when setting limits* and encouraging *when limits are followed*. It is important to convey confidence in your child's ability to follow limits and to recognize success at every opportunity. Sincere praise is more reinforcing than criticism. Shinichi Suzuki, founder of the world-famous music school, said, "Notice everything, focus on a few, mention one."[2]

Here are some examples of the way we can encourage our children as they show signs of improvement in accepting limits:

*You're doing such a great job with your household chores—it really shows how much you care about our home.*

*The way you handled that conflict was brilliant—you showed empathy and humility but you also spoke the truth.*

*Your Mom and I noticed how much effort you have been putting in to get up on time when your alarm goes off and we are so proud of you.*

The focus is not on the actual achievement, but on the effort and what it shows about their character and level of responsibility.

## 4. Role Play during Family Time

Another idea for pre-empting mistakes and teaching limits in a pro-active way is to role-play during family time or game nights. We particularly recommend this for children between ages two and ten.

Experts have proven that role-play helps children explore imagination, think in the abstract, acquire language skills, build social skills, problem solve, understand someone else's perspective, learn essential life skills from adults, discover leadership skills, safely explore the world beyond, and acquire confidence and a sense of self.[3]

Children love to role-play mommy, daddy, teacher, fire fighters, and so forth. When role-play is based on principles such as honesty and obedience, the role-play becomes "the spoon full of sugar that helps the medicine go down". If your children are below ten, do not let the opportunity slip away—using a myriad of different scenarios, you can role-play topics such as obedience, learning to say "no" properly, being polite, being respectful, not hitting but requesting politely, ignoring troublemakers instead of fighting, working together to get chores done, being hospitable with guests, and a host of other topics for your family.

In role-play you can demonstrate what to do and not to do. Sometimes you can have your children act out both parts; kids especially love to give feedback when mom and dad play the "bad-guy" roles! You will have lots of fun and the kids will get the picture about limits.

## 5. Engage Cooperation

This is another helpful tip from Adele Faber and Elaine Mazlish's book, *How To Talk So Your Kids Will Listen and Listen So They Will Talk*.[4] As long as parents are already consistently practicing our first four steps mentioned above, they will find that "engaging cooperation" helps parents to avoid exasperation interactions and stay out of the vortex. Read the second chapter of their book to get the picture fully.

## 6. Maintain an Excellent Connection

We return to the first core emotional need again. When the connection is high, children want to please their parents, because, in the words of Elkind, the parents have fulfilled their part of a "loyal-commitment contract" and the children want to reciprocate.[6]When parents expect children to comply with limits but do little to enhance their emotional connection, they are inadvertently saying that this contract applies to the children, but not to them. In essence, the parents do not need to follow the rules, but the children must. This becomes a problem for two reasons, the first: when children feel the "contract" is broken, they will feel exasperated and this may result in rebellion and retaliation. This often shows up in their refusal to accept limits they are given, especially later on in their adolescent years, which inevitably leads to the vortex. When a father, for example, hardly spends time with his children, yet stays on top of them about their schoolwork, their computer usage or their bed times, the children will rebel (either inwardly or outwardly). Often when asked, they will not even know where their rebellion comes from. Maintaining a deep connection will inhibit this kind of rebellion from taking root in their hearts. As long as we are meeting the core emotional need for connection and acceptance, then mild disapproval and mild anger will already be a form of discipline because they care about their relationship with their parents.[5]

Secondly, this kind of role modeling will become a breeding ground for the development of the entitlement lifetrap, in which mutual reciprocity is not respected. This lack of reciprocity may come out in their relationship with their teachers and even with peers. Be in touch with their highs and lows, have dinners regularly, play with them and spend time with them, including regular one-on-one times with each child. Passing down limits is so much easier when the connection is healthy. (Remember, this is about "good enough" parenting, and mistakes of the past can usually be healed by careful attention to the need for connection and acceptance as children develop.)

## 7. Revise the Rules Periodically

While children must learn to abide by rules and limits, parents need to be aware that some rules will need to be amended as time goes by as children grow older and demonstrate good behavior. Children need to know that they are able to earn their parents' trust and that with greater trust they will enjoy greater privileges and more freedom. This is also related to meeting the core emotional need for healthy autonomy and performance. Examples may include extending curfews, bedtimes, and giving more pocket money, to name a few.

Sometimes rules need to be revisited because parents may have been too rigid with both limits and consequences. Other times, this may not be the case— the child may simply be chafing against the consequences of reasonable expectations and limits, which is all part of the learning experience.

## 8. Give Options and a Second Chance

When children misbehave, it is sometimes helpful for parents to give them awareness by alerting them to the undesirable act and saying, "Would you like to try that again?" This gives children a chance to pause and take stock of what they have done, and make a decision to correct themselves. It is like Round Two of engaging cooperation. If the children still choose not to, consequences should come into play. However, before they even get there, give them a chance. (Exceptions would be if they were caught stealing, lying, or doing something in your "Absolute No" list—or doing something dangerous). See vignette below:

*Eight-year-old Sheila comes through the door and drops her bag on the living room floor. Daydreaming about trying out her new colored pencil set, she hurriedly heads for the stairs.*

Mother (*smiling*): Hello, sweetheart, how was your day?

Sheila (*quickly*): Not now, Mom, I'm in a hurry.

Mother (*politely*): Rushing for the bathroom?

Sheila (*impatiently*): I wanna try out my new pencils!

Mother (*kindly*): Did you forget something, dear?

Sheila looks confused. The mother stares directly at the bag, and then smiles back at her daughter.

Sheila (*rolling her eyes just a bit*): Mom, I'll get it later.

Mother (*still kind and smiling*): Would you like to try that again?

Sheila (*surrenders*): Yes, Mommy…

Sheila got the point, picked up her bag and took it to her room—she actually knew she wasn't supposed to leave her things lying around in the common areas of the house. Two minutes later she was in her room, at her desk, doodling away, and humming a song. If she does it again soon, her mom could mete out consequences or it could be the subject of a role-play during a family meeting.

Constant repetition of this simple, yet powerful principle makes a big difference. Children forget all the time. If consequences are imposed immediately, it causes tension in the house and strains the relationship between parent and child. Parents who tend to exasperate their children—especially by belittling, being punitive, being perfectionistic, or being controlling—should take note. Give them at least one other chance. Learn to be patient. Do not resort to consequences straight away, unless they are older and the misbehavior is something very serious.

## 9. Allow Consequences to Take Effect

In the context of teaching children discipline, consequences should be related to undesirable behavior or attitudes that can either cause harm to the children or to others. Learning from natural consequences helps children be responsible. Rudolf Dreikurs highlights both natural and logical consequences in his groundbreaking book entitled, *Children: The Challenge.*[6]

When parents do not allow their children to reap what they sow, either by jumping in to protect their children from consequences or by failing to provide consequences, they are doing untold harm to their children's character. We believe, if used properly, consequences are an effective way of halting undesirable behavior, preventing a vortex of conflict escalation, improving children's overall behavior, helping children take their parent's words and instructions seriously, and helping children realize how serious their misbehavior is to themselves and others.

Consequences work with adults, too. Have you ever received a speeding ticket? How did that affect your driving thereafter? Have you ever paid a credit card bill late only to have a hefty penalty imposed? Have you ever been conned by a "get rich quick" scheme? Consequences work for people of all ages. We prefer that children learn the lessons when they are young, before the consequences become more serious.

### Natural Consequences vs. Logical Consequences

Natural consequences are about children reaping what they have sown as a direct result of their behavior, not as a result of a penalty or consequence imposed by a parent later. Here are some scenarios to illustrate natural consequences:

- If children lose their mobile phones, they will not have one until *they* buy a new one.
- If children do not study for their exams, they will get poor grades.
- If children do not get up on time in the morning, they will be late to school.
- If children are mean to their friends, people will not enjoy playing with them.

- If children spend all their pocket money, they will have no money to spend until they receive their next allowance.

One caveat—do not use natural consequences when the outcome of an undesired behavior will harm the child, e.g., crossing the street without holding the parent's hand or touching an electrical socket.

Logical consequences result in children having to face the music when they break a rule, in ways previously established by the parents and children, perhaps in a family meeting. Such consequences should be talked about and decided collectively with the children. This way, parents cannot be accused of being unfair later. With logical consequences, they do not follow automatically, but come when parents intervene and offer discipline, as seen in these real life examples.

Jim was an easy-going kid who had not gotten in much trouble over the years. However, around the age of 14, he became extremely fond of online games, at the expense of doing homework. Eventually, his teachers commented on his underachieving performance. His parents established rules for playing: only after his schoolwork was satisfactorily done and only for a limited time, failing which, his laptop would be taken away for two weeks. Jim's parents caught him breaking the rules and followed through with the promised consequences. While it came as a shock to Jim that his parents meant what they said, subsequently his behavior greatly improved.

While Karla (10) was swimming with a group of friends, a girl from another group made catty remarks to Karla about how her bathing suit made her look fat. Karla felt humiliated, ashamed, and angry. She pulled the rude girl's hair, got out of the pool, and threw the girl's handbag into the water. The friend's parents quickly intervened, and told Karla's parents about it when they arrived. After hearing both sides of the story and empathizing with her humiliation, Karla's parents told her they would decide on the consequences after thinking about it, but she would certainly pay to replace the handbag and the contents of the bag with her allowance, which would probably take four months. Later they barred her from parties and sleepovers for the next two months. This was a wake up call for Karla, who found it hard to control her temper; her self-control greatly improved after that time. (Effort was also made to help the girls reconcile but the other party wasn't interested. Karla had to learn that even though the other girl "started it", it did not give her the right to behave the way she did.)

When administering consequences:

- Watch your tone - A proper tone is not just a good idea—it is crucial in communication. It is okay to show disappointment when misbehavior is demonstrated, but the tone should not move from indignation to rage and contempt. Otherwise, the child will face the added components of shame and humiliation plus resentment and bitterness. Parents need to be mindful of the exasperation interactions they tend toward, such as Belittling, Punitiveness, or Pessimistic.

- Exercise the consequence immediately - This is especially important for younger children. If there was negative behavior, the agreed-upon consequences should be put into effect immediately—quickly and calmly.

- Persevere if change does not happen - Often parents give up when change does not happen, in which case they need to revise the consequences and perhaps even intensify them. Eventually, if administered correctly, consequences will have an effect.

- Ensure consequences fit the misbehavior – This is an important principle parents need to understand when deciding on possible consequences. If the level of seriousness is small, then the consequence should also be small. Parents who tend toward Punitive, Controlling or Belittling interactions often come up with consequences that are out of proportion to the level of misbehavior. Those who tend to exasperate by being Overly Permissive will have the opposite problem.

## 10. Reconcile with Meaning Attribution and Closure

After consequences have been administered, parent and child should take time to sit down and evaluate the entire scenario. Repair must be done satisfactorily—leading to forgiveness and reconciliation. Without proper closure emotionally, resentment and bitterness will set in and cause disconnection between the parent and child (see Chapter Twenty). As mentioned before, if repair is done well, conflicts between parent and child will have a benign effect on the mental and emotional health of children and parents.

............................................................

SECTION FIVE

# THE CORE EMOTIONAL
# NEED FOR REALISTIC
# EXPECTATIONS

............................................................

# Chapter Sixteen

# REALISTIC EXPECTATIONS

·······························································

The Core Emotional Need for Realistic Expectations can be defined as helping your children understand what is expected of them, while giving them the freedom to be themselves; it involves fine tuning expectations so that they inspire and motivate your child. When parents meet the core emotional need for realistic expectations, their children will develop some or all of the following traits/ beliefs: realistic standards, graciousness, and self-sacrifice with boundaries,[1] and they will *consistently* and *on an emotional level* believe the following messages from and about their parents:

*They know my strengths and weaknesses.*
*They encourage me to do my best, while letting go of perfectionistic expectations.*
*They help me to achieve balance between work and play.*
*Their love for me is not based on the outcome of my achievements.*
*They value my strengths and aspirations even though they may be different from*
    *theirs and not as valued by society.*
*They give me the benefit of the doubt when something goes wrong.*
*They guide me in taking care of myself and endeavor to ensure that I enjoy life.*
*They truly forgive me when I mess up.*

Charlene and Rebecca's father is a highly successful individual who hails from an established family in the USA—their grandparents have a second mansion exclusively for holidays and are well connected politically and socially—status and achievement are highly valued in their extended family. As much as the girls' parents have tried to infuse healthy values in their parenting, they have not been able to protect their daughters from the on-going scrutiny of their father's relatives, who constantly compare them with their cousins: "Freddie got a 2300 on his SATs, but I heard that Charlene only got a 2100!" "And Rebecca didn't get accepted into riding camp this summer either!" Although Charlene and Rebecca are doing well academically and are attending Ivy League universities, they are struggling in several areas of emotional intelligence. Harboring anger issues, they lack empathy and do not relate to others well. They view themselves as superior and do not want to have much to do with those who do not meet their expectations. All in all, they are not pleasant people to be around. One of the girls has struggled with suicidal thoughts and has recently begun to go to counseling, as have the parents who want help with "repair and reconnection" and with guiding their daughters emotionally and socially.

## Exaggerated Expectations Are Not the Cure

All of us have expectations. We *expect* the sun to come up tomorrow. We *expect* our friends to return our calls. We *expect* our spouses to be faithful. We *expect* our children to grow, to, make friends, explore hobbies, and learn to take care of themselves. When we explored reasonable limits in the previous section, we discussed the healthy and normal expectations parents have for their children. However, in some families there are few, if any, expectations; this can leave children adrift and uninspired, and convey a lack of appreciation for and belief in their strengths and capacities. Conversely, in other families, there are too many expectations, spoken or unspoken; exaggerated expectations can cause undue pressure and anxiety. Hence, the name of this core emotional need is *realistic* expectations. (The bulk of this section addresses tempering expectations; however from time to time we will speak to those who "under-expect".)

We live in a world where both adults and children are experiencing increasing stress. Demands and expectations at work and school are pushing people to the limit. Although we are surrounded by timesaving devices, we do not seem to have more time. Children have not escaped the fallout—some are buried under piles of homework, some are involved in endless afterschool activities, and some practice sports for hours a day, not for enjoyment but to help them get a college scholarship, leading to even more pressure.

Children at increasingly younger ages are expected to do more and learn more difficult concepts, beyond what is age-appropriate. Moreover, competitiveness in schools discourages students from helping one another and produces an "every-man-for-himself" mind-set. Parents are pressuring children to get into the best schools and universities, causing households to be rife with tension. Children cringe when parents make comparisons ("Your cousin went to Harvard"), deliver lectures ("When I was your age, I understood the value of hard work…"), and nag them about being number one in class or in a sport.

Parents striving to bring out the best in their children are not helped by parenting philosophies such as those espoused in the "Tiger Mother" article published by the Wall Street Journal on January 8, 2011, in which a Chinese-American Yale Law Professor boasted about her own parenting. One of her more outrageous paragraphs reads as follows:

A lot of people wonder how Chinese parents raise such stereotypically successful kids. They wonder what these parents do to produce so many math whizzes and music prodigies, what it's like inside the family, and whether they could do it, too. Well, I can tell them, because I've done it. Here are some things my daughters, Sophia and Louisa, were never allowed to do: attend a sleepover, have a play date, be in a school play, complain about not being in a school play, watch TV or play computer games, choose their own extracurricular activities, get any grade less than an A, not be the No. 1 student in every subject except gym and drama, play any instrument other than the piano or violin, and not play the piano or violin. [2]

We think it is unfortunate that these principles have received so much publicity; not only do we find them unhelpful, we find them harmful—they go against the findings of good research about how to connect with our children and raise them to become healthy adults emotionally, spiritually and psychologically.

## The Barrenness of A Busy Life

Many parents these days, even without reading such extremist urgings, overreact out of fear and worry, and force their children to attend extra classes during the weekends, or to sign up for multiple sports activities. Even holidays are filled with make-up classes and camps, fewer periods where families can relax and connect[3] (RR16.1). Where does this lead? To the hospital—some doctors estimate that 75% of all medical conditions begin with stress; to the mental hospital—it is well-known that stress causes anxiety and depression; and to the divorce court—many divorces are caused by neglect due to lack of work-life balance, arguments about the lack of it, or lack of unity regarding expectations for the children.

It is time to wake up! This reminds us of a quote attributed to William Sloane Coffin, chaplain of an Ivy League school in the 1950s, "Even if you win the rat race, you're still a rat."[4] More than two thousand years earlier, the Greek philosopher Socrates said, "Beware the barrenness of a busy life."[5]

Since there is interplay between the core emotional needs, we remind readers that parents cannot meet the need for realistic expectations without ensuring that the core emotional need for connection and acceptance is also adequately met.

••••••••••••••••••••••••••••••••••••••••••••••••••••••••••••••

## *Louis Lowdown*

Our children began learning tennis when they were very young, while we were living in Australia. (We knew we would eventually move back to Asia so we figured that we should make the most of living in such a sporty nation!) When our oldest turned eight, she insisted on entering tournaments. We are not sure if she was born with a perfectionistic temperament and naturally competitive nature, or if I (John) passed it to her, but my wife and I decided to intervene early on. We sought advice from fellow tennis parents who taught their children that winning isn't determined by the score—in their family, a match would be considered a "win" if the player gave his best effort, had a good time, and was a good sport/gracious winner or loser. Conversely, when the child had won *solely* in terms of the score, the parents would consider the match to be a loss. By helping Sonia to have healthy expectations, she not only enjoyed her matches, she also grew in her character.

••••••••••••••••••••••••••••••••••••••••••••••••••••••••••••••

# Chapter Seventeen

# THE DOMAIN OF
# EXAGGERATED EXPECTATIONS

························································

The fourth domain of schema clusters is known as "Exaggerated Expectations". To the extent that parents do not meet the core emotional need for realistic expectations, we believe their children will experience the opposite— *Exaggerated Expectations.* This means that their children will be at risk of developing some or all of the lifetraps in the Domain of Exaggerated Expectations, namely, Unrelenting Standards, Punitiveness, and Self-Sacrifice. This chapter explains these three lifetraps in detail, and contains the "Basic Safety Zone".

## The Lifetrap of Unrelenting Standards / Hypercriticalness

The first maladaptive schema (lifetrap) in the domain of exaggerated expectations is unrelenting standards / hypercriticalness. The core message of the unrelenting standards lifetrap is: *"I must work very, very hard to meet very high standards, or I will be criticized. I do not have time to relax, or have fun. I must always be efficient."* The driving words for this lifetrap are *"I should ... "*

Children who develop this lifetrap are propelled by their incessant need to push themselves. They are constantly striving to work harder in order to get to a better place because their present position is never good enough. In fact, this lifetrap is related to the lifetrap of defectiveness—for contentment is always going to be one position away, within sight, but unreachable. As they grow older, they develop standards that must be in place, thus making them critical of people who fail to meet these standards. These self-made rules accompany them everywhere they go as they impose them on everyone. They frequently look down on others who do not live up to their exceedingly high expectations and pick on small issues that no one else would have noticed. Moreover, they show a lack of grace towards others' mistakes.

People with the lifetrap of unrelenting standards actually think the standards they impose are normal and that others are stupid, shoddy, careless, lazy, unkempt, inept, or slow. They are completely unaware of the fact that their reactions to situations, along with their opinions and condemnation of others, are usually out of proportion with the reality of the situation. They are usually hard on themselves as well as others; taking time off makes them feel guilty. They find it difficult to relax, and all of these factors combine to take a toll on their health. While they may achieve success in life, it usually occurs at the expense of relationships. Because they constantly expect others to comply with their rules, they are difficult companions. (Those with the unrelenting standards lifetrap do not notice that they only have these standards in certain areas but that in other areas, they fall short as well; for example, the no-nonsense academic whose desk is a mess, or the doctor who works tirelessly but has no time for his children).

*Early family environment that might cause this lifetrap to develop:*

- One or both parents had very high standards in areas such as cleanliness, academic achievement, and good manners. Even though the parent might not have directly imposed these standards on the child, the parent still might have modeled the trait.
- The love of one, or both, of the child's parents was performance-based; thus the child did not experience unconditional love from either, or both, of them.
- The parents' conversation was frequently about what the child should achieve, what others were achieving, or how the child should measure up. Character was defined more in terms of achievement than inner qualities.
- The parents were hypercritical about others in their conversations and did not encourage the child.
- When the child did not achieve, she was criticized and shamed; nothing was ever good enough for her parents (or a teacher or a coach).
- The child developed these standards to soothe the inner pain in her life possibly from an inability to forge deep relationships with others—in order to feel good.

Figure 17.1: The Lifetrap of Unrelenting Standards (Francois as an adult)

Figure 17.2: A Possible Early Environment Which Would Likely Contribute to the Unrelenting Standards Lifetrap (Francois as a child) *Go to Appendix 1*

## The Lifetrap of Punitiveness

The second maladaptive schema (lifetrap) in the domain of exaggerated expectations is punitiveness. The core message of the punitiveness lifetrap is: *"Mistakes have consequences. I should be punished for making mistakes and so should everyone else. It is not okay to make mistakes. We should constantly strive for and demand perfection."*

Children who develop this lifetrap have usually been brought up by parents who do not show grace or mercy either to themselves or to others for mistakes. The parents have a "justice at all costs" mentality and inculcate the same mindset in their children. As with their parents, these children grow up to become adults who do not forgive easily; they view all mistakes as crimes that should be punished. With a rigid sense of justice, they see things in black and white. Mistakes are mistakes, whether committed unintentionally or deliberately; they are quick to assign blame when something goes wrong. They often view people who show mercy as weak.

*Early family environment that might cause this lifetrap to develop:*

- The child's parents frequently blamed and berated him and his siblings when things went wrong. Consequences were usually disproportionate to the mistakes made, and even in adulthood, his parent's voice is still in his head.
- The child attended a school where others were punished frequently for their mistakes and little grace was shown.
- The child's parents did not talk much about forgiveness. They had a negative view of people who held such a perspective.
- The child's parents were "always right", blamed others and held grudges.
- The child's parents were hurt growing up and ruminated on memories of this hurt.

Figure 17.3: The Lifetrap of Punitiveness (Kong as an adult)

Figure 17.4: A Possible Early Environment Which Would Likely Contribute to the Punitiveness Lifetrap (Kong as a child) *Go to Appendix I*

## The Lifetrap of Self-Sacrifice

The third and final maladaptive schema (lifetrap) in the domain of exaggerated expectations is self-sacrifice. The core message of the self-sacrifice lifetrap is: *"I must meet the needs of others before my own. I do not want to feel selfish, or cause any pain to others."* While this pattern of thinking and behaving seems altruistic, it can create problems in the long run, as it results in imbalanced relationships, and problems with unmet needs.

Typically, children who develop this lifetrap are endearing. They empathize and genuinely care for others, and take on responsibilities in order to relieve others of discomfort. In fact, they would prefer to suffer, rather than allow others to be inconvenienced. Ultimately, they strive to make other people feel better. Their decision to help others does not come from a desire to please, or to avoid conflict or a threat; these children are so in tune with others' pain and feelings, and genuinely empathize with others so much that they actually feel that it is their responsibility to provide relief for others. When they do not sacrifice for others, they feel guilty. One might wonder, why is this a lifetrap? Because such a selfless mind-set becomes a danger when these self-sacrificing people give and give without getting their own needs met; eventually, they experience burnout, as well as physical and mental health problems.

*Special Note to parents who are in caring occupations:* If you are a healthcare provider, a counselor/therapist, a minister, or any helping professional, you probably already struggle with balancing your work and family life, and no doubt are aware that you need to develop a routine of "self-care". Should you choose to go the extra mile for others, as many noble individuals do, make sure that you do not demand the same of your children: it may not be what they want to do—maybe they will be happier and more productive working in another line of work.

*Early family environment that might cause this lifetrap to develop:*
- The child's parents were unable, for whatever reason, to take care of her and/or her younger siblings. So she stepped in and assumed this responsibility, going beyond what should have been expected of a young person.
- The child's parents role-modeled self-sacrifice for her. Perhaps, they were working in one of the helping professions, or highly involved with volunteer work.
- The child had to work, or help out, in her parents' business early on in life because of her parents' financial problems, or poor health.
- The child assumed the role of the parent (parenting their parent) at too early an age, instead of the other way round. For example, one of the child's parents might have been an alcoholic, had a chronic illness, or was being abused by the other parent, or other relatives.

Figure 17.5: The Lifetrap of Self-Sacrifice (Daniella as an adult)

Figure 17.6: A Possible Early Environment Which Would Likely Contribute to the Self-Sacrifice Lifetrap (Daniella as a child) *Go to Appendix 1*

## Basic Safety Zone

Parents are responsible for protecting their children's welfare. By meeting the core emotional need for realistic expectations, parents are protecting their children against a myriad of problems brought on by today's stressful lifestyle.

## Sleep Deprivation

One of the world's leading medical journals, *The Lancet*, revealed that among developed countries, Singapore has the lowest mortality rate for young males—this is something to celebrate![1] (The US has the highest.) On the down side, the increased education-related expectations placed upon Singapore boys and girls by parents and teachers means they are experiencing sleep deprivation, which results not just in crankier children, or shorter tempers, but also in serious mental health issues.[2]

Forgive us for including more stats, but they speak volumes!

- Children with trouble sleeping at 12-14 years old were more than twice as likely to have suicidal thoughts at ages 15-17 as those who didn't have sleep problems at a younger age.
- Studies show a 50% increase in children having anxiety disorders in their twenties when they had persistent sleep difficulty at age nine.
- Singaporean children get an average of two hours less sleep than their peers in Switzerland. One professor said, "My personal experience is that many children and teenagers (in Singapore) are quite sleep-deprived..." and when they get more sleep, they show "markedly improved academic ability."[3]
- Most parents are unaware of the long-term effects of sleep deprivation, in combination with other stressors, on the mental well-being of their children.
- Singapore leads the world in mental illnesses among youths.
- Staying awake for 24 hours in a row is on par with legal intoxication with alcohol (in driving) in impairing performance. Sleeping six hours per night for two weeks causes a similar level of impairment as staying awake for 24 hours.[4] (RR17.1)

## Heavy Backpacks

Research has revealed the dangerous effects of excessive expectations of educational institutions on the physical well-being of young children. Specifically, students in different parts of the world are carrying backpacks that exceed the recommended weight of 15% of their body weight. Carrying these heavy backpacks has an adverse impact on their bodies by undermining their lung volume and causing chronic back pain[5] (RR17.1).

## Myopia

How does eyesight fit into this discussion? Myopia has emerged as a major health issue in parts of Asia, affecting most children. The causal factors include the over-emphasis on education and inadequate time spent outdoors; the latest research links lack of exposure to sunlight with myopia. Parents need to ensure that their children spend two or three hours a day in the sunlight. In Asia this is affecting 80–90% of graduating school children compared to 10–20% in other parts of the world.[6] No wonder our family doctor, Dr. Malcolm Lim, told us his biggest gripe with Singapore parents is not protecting their kids' eyesight! (RR17.1)

So please take this issue seriously: we owe it to our children and the future of our societies not to let our exaggerated expectations inflict physical and mental harm on the next generation!

••••••••••••••••••••••••••••••••••••••••••••••••••••••••••••

### *Louis Lowdown*

This is not about our family but it is based on something I (Karen) saw in the leading Singapore newspaper called *The Straits Times*, and I wanted to show that all is not gloom and doom—One Singaporean mother, a Madam Poh, responded to the articles on sleep deprivation by sharing her family's schedule, which we consider to be a recipe for healthy parenting, albeit difficult to follow in today's climate. Nevertheless, we have included it as a good example for which to strive. In short, Madam Poh wrote that she and her husband, who both work full-time, have three girls aged five, seven, and ten. They have breakfast with their daughters, put them on the school bus, and then head straight to work; thus, they are able to start work by 7:30am at the latest. Their daughters come home by school bus and do their homework before their parents get home, supervised by a caregiver. On a typical day, Madam Poh and her husband leave work by 5pm to have dinner with their girls by 6pm and address any homework questions after dinner. They play together or watch a bit of television. By 7:30pm, they are reading a storybook with their girls and lights are off by 8pm. The older two wake up at 5:50am after ten hours of sleep. The five-year-old wakes up at 6:30am and takes a one-hour nap in the afternoon. Thus, all the Poh children meet the requirements stated in the National Sleep Foundation's suggested sleep guide. Well done, Poh family!!

••••••••••••••••••••••••••••••••••••••••••••••••••••••••••••••

# Chapter Eighteen

# PARENTAL INVOLVEMENT—
# ASSET OR LIABILITY?

································································

When looking at outcomes in the areas of academic achievement, sports achievement, and all-round success, parental involvement can be either a liability or an asset[1]—it all depends on *how* parents go about meeting the core emotional need for realistic expectations (RR18.1). Based on the huge amount of expenses, worry, and anxiety that accompany parents' expectations in the area of their children's academic performance, we will speak mostly about academic expectations; however, this discussion can be applied to other types of expectations.

**What Causes Parents to Be A Liability?**
Parental involvement must take into account the parent's dynamics with the child. For example, when some parents hear about the positive outcomes of parental involvement, they decide to monitor their children several times a day, and push their children to achieve at exceptional levels, while being critical of their children's mistakes. These parents, in the name of love, are unaware of the harm they are inflicting on their children!

How parents convey their expectations, the quality of their relationship with their children, whether their children still feel accepted after making mistakes, and the level of criticism from parents all make a huge difference in the outcome of children's academic performances. We are not advocating low expectations—it is all about what kind of expectations and how they are communicated, i.e., that's why it is called the core need for *realistic* expectations.

### What Helps Parents To Be An Asset?

When parents are meeting the first three core emotional needs, especially when connection is strong, parental involvement will be an asset. At the risk of sounding repetitive, we will remind parents yet again how important it is for them to take care to meet the first core need for connection and acceptance. The Heritage Foundation in 2008 revealed that a sensitive, warm, and responsive style of parenting and engaging in play activities with young children bolsters not just their social and emotional development, but also their communication skills and ability to focus, both crucial for achievement.[2] And teens whose parents are more involved and who feel they receive more support from their parents are more likely to participate in structured after-school activities that, in turn, are positively correlated with achievement and social competence.[3]

••••••••••••••••••••••••••••••••••••••••••••••••••••••••••

### *Louis Lowdown*

Parents of sixth graders in Singapore wait in agony every November— that's when the grades for the national standardized Primary School Leaving Exam (PSLE) come out. In my work as a family educator, I (John) always remind anxious parents not to get too worried. (No mean feat, since this particular exam determines which "high school" their children will attend; the students are ranked according to their score and only those with the highest scores are eligible for the more sought-after schools.) One year, I asked a group of mothers whose children had tested well above the national average how they "felt" about their children's scores. Their answers were telling—most of them were disappointed; from their perspective, their children should have done even better. I also spoke privately with their children. Even though their scores would get them into good schools, they were disappointed by their results and felt that they had let their parents down. For some, their parents hadn't said anything negative, but their mom's facial expression or their dad's body language had revealed it all. I felt compelled to let the mothers know their exaggerated expectations were endangering their children's mental health, not to mention ruining any connection they might have. I told them that their children would put two and two together: if they only got praised when they did *exceedingly* well, they would conclude that their parents only accepted them when they "performed"; they would feel exasperated; and their need for connection and acceptance would not be met. Eventually, these moms understood how they were hurting their children and began working on repairing and reconnecting.

........................................................................

Parents who have a good connection with their children and desire healthy involvement should monitor children's activities outside the home and school; set rules; engage in conversations about and help with school work and school-related issues; establish educational expectations; discuss and plan for future; help them with important decisions; participate in school-related activities such as meeting with teachers and volunteering in the classroom; read together, and do other enrichment and leisure activities together.

The rest of this chapter contains strategies about how parental involvement can be an asset, rather than a liability.

## Parents Must Prioritize Their Marriage

Before we discuss the dynamics between parent and child, we have to again remind parents that the quality of their marriage has a direct correlation to the quality of their parenting. Please re-read the portion of Chapter Two devoted to making sure parents understand how crucial this point is!

We add this specific bit of research here since it is directly related to expectations about school achievement: the overwhelming research indicates that divorce has a significantly negative effect on children's academic performance. In fact, children whose fathers have *died* do better in school than children whose parents are divorced.[4] It is speculated that children are able to attribute a more positive meaning from a death, however painful, than when their parents go through a divorce. In the case of divorce, children have been known to blame themselves, which usually does not happen in the event of a parent's death. In fact, children from divorced families are statistically less likely to graduate from higher education and more likely to have difficulties obtaining employment.[5]

*Please note: we are making a big deal out of all of these marriage statistics not to shame single parents—in fact, we salute you for your hard work and perseverance. To you we say, beat the odds! These are statistics, not an absolute indicator of your future. What we mean to do is to impress upon readers who are married the importance of prioritizing their marriage.* (RR18.2)

## Set Learning-Oriented Goals, Not Performance-Oriented Goals

The combination of the two different studies below shows how setting learning-oriented goals helps parents to be an asset rather than a liability.

Stanford psychologist Dr. Carol Dweck has received worldwide recognition for her decades-long study of motivation. Her work on academic expectations distinguishes between two kinds of orientations: parents who encourage their children to focus on learning for learning's sake, and parents who push their children to attain high grades.[6] Dweck and her colleagues called the former "learning-oriented", and found that learning-oriented parents tend to (a) emphasize the need to enjoy learning, (b) encourage progress towards their child's potential, (c) inspire their child to seek out challenges, and (d) reward effort over results. The parents who were more concerned with high grades and outcomes they called, "performance-oriented". These parents tend to (a) believe that success in performance signifies competence and a high degree of intelligence, (b) feel that having a highly intelligent child brings personal recognition, (c) have a desire for that kind of recognition, and (d) expect their child to secure a prestigious job and earn a high salary.[7]

Sixth-grade students (12-year-olds) at the Johns Hopkins University's Center for Talented Youth were measured for perfectionistic tendencies and then divided into two groups—healthy perfectionists and dysfunctional perfectionists.[8] "Healthy perfectionists" were defined as children who had high scores on being unusually organized and driven, but had relatively low scores in areas related to fear of making mistakes, concern about parents' criticism and self-doubt after taking action. Conversely, the "dysfunctional perfectionists" had high scores in all the aforementioned areas, and were more likely to describe themselves as defensive, anxious, moody, and socially detached—characteristics that hinder academic achievement and lead to social and emotional problems.[9]

The Johns Hopkins' researchers used Dweck's categories and discovered that *children of "performance-oriented" parents were significantly more likely to fall into the "dysfunctional perfectionism"* group than children of parents with learning-oriented goals, leaving them vulnerable to social and emotional problems,[10] such as depression, anorexia nervosa, bulimia, obsessive compulsive disorder, migraine, procrastination and suicidal tendencies. Another bit of research on motivation found that children who feel loved conditionally based on academic achievement were more likely to develop the schemas of defectiveness, failure, social isolation (see Chapter Five), entitlement (see Chapter Twelve), and unrelenting standards (see Chapter Sixteen). (RR18.3)

Special note from John: Those of us from Asian backgrounds need to listen up—The Johns Hopkins' researchers also noted that 69% of Asian parents had performance-oriented goals, while only 25% of Caucasian parents had them.[11] (This is such a common state of mind in Singaporeans that there is actually a local slang word for it: "kan cheong".) Whether it's over grades, sports, music and other hobbies—the performance-oriented disposition almost always brings disastrous results. How many children have we seen who struggle with the maladies listed above, or at the very least with migraines and digestive system malfunctions, all because of parent-generated anxiety? Remember the Basic Safety Zone—we should not let our unrealistic expectations put our children in harm's way. This is not Good Enough Parenting.

∙∙∙∙∙∙∙∙∙∙∙∙∙∙∙∙∙∙∙∙∙∙∙∙∙∙∙∙∙∙∙∙∙∙∙∙∙∙∙∙∙∙∙∙∙∙∙∙∙∙∙∙∙∙∙

### *Louis Lowdown*

During our daughter's first two years of elementary school, I (John) was a performance-oriented/*kan cheong* parent: when Sonia didn't perform up to "my standard" in math, I assumed that she was not trying hard. It did not occur to me that her strengths might lie in other areas, or that she might need some extra work or have a different learning style than I have. My wife challenged me about the way I was speaking with my daughter and showed me the folly of my ways. As I grappled with this knowledge, I saw my daughter really, really trying, and it moved me. In fact, one day she told me that she felt "stupid". My heart went out to her and I realized I had contributed to her feelings. From then on, I focused on her effort. We even celebrated when she got a 'C'. It was an occasion that I truly enjoyed. I changed, and I was happy that I had changed. Even better, Sonia was encouraged and became more joyful, and didn't run so far away when it was time to do math with Dad!

∙∙∙∙∙∙∙∙∙∙∙∙∙∙∙∙∙∙∙∙∙∙∙∙∙∙∙∙∙∙∙∙∙∙∙∙∙∙∙∙∙∙∙∙∙∙∙∙∙∙∙∙∙∙∙

## Do Not Control with Punishment, Praise or Reward

A child's level of curiosity will drive him or her to investigate, ask questions, and make numerous attempts at one task. They are enthusiastically driven to explore and grow; like sponges, they absorb everything around them. They rarely distinguish between work and play because they are having so much fun doing both at the same time.

Edward Deci, the motivation expert we mentioned in Chapters Nine & Eleven, has spent years studying children of all ages. Deci noticed that most of the learning done by preschool children is done not because it is instrumental for achieving something else, but because the children are curious: they want to know. Deci would say children are intrinsically-motivated,[12] but that made him wonder, given their natural propensity for learning, what causes children's attitudes to change as they grow older? Deci performed many experiments to evaluate the effect of rewards and punishments on motivation. What he found was that motivation through rewards over time actually did not promote an excited state of learning, but a sad state of apathy.[13]

When he used money as a reward, Deci observed that once the participants started getting paid, they lost interest in the activity and did not do as well. Rewards, he concluded, turned the act of playing into something controlled from the outside. When this happened, play became work and the player, a pawn. Deci deduced that rewards eventually have a negative effect on people's intrinsic motivation.

Not surprisingly, Deci obtained even worse results when he used punishment as a motivator. Deadlines, goals, and tight surveillance are frequently-used methods that are supposed to help people to get results. Deci strongly believes that both materialistic rewards and threats of punishment ultimately destroy children's (and adults') enthusiasm and interest.

Unfortunately, many parents rely on short-term strategies, but progress made based on threats and even rewards rarely lasts. Deci and his colleague, Richard Ryan, argue that rewards given with a controlling style have a negative effect on intrinsic motivation and leave people feeling more pressured and less interested. On the other hand, when rewards are extended in a non-controlling way as an acknowledgment of good work, they will not produce detrimental effects. Their perspective seems to suggest that it is the controlling intent of rewards that sabotages one's attempts to motivate others, by destroying the very motivation that they had been intended to promote.[14]

We have to be very careful about *how* we administer rewards: It is a real test of parents' motives to offer rewards to their children in a non-controlling way! The next time you consider saying, "If you get all As, I will give you….", or even the alternative "If you don't make an A, you'll be grounded...", change your mind, reject these so-called "motivational techniques" and decide to be an asset, instead of a liability.

When parents praise their children in front of visitors, from time to time, it sends a positive message. Even if children are pretending that they are not listening, parents should do it anyway. I, John, remember a time when my dad encouraged me in front of my siblings for having a tidy desk. I was doing terribly at school, and two of my brothers were A students, but my dad noticed my desk. That did a lot to cement the connection with my dad, and eventually my grades turned around anyway. Now, it is important to note that we are not talking about boorish parents who boast about their children's achievements non stop; rather, we are highlighting a way of encouraging tentative children and letting them know that they are believed in.

Another fun yet indirect way that parents can encourage their children in front of others is to try "Resource Gossip"—a tool devised by Mark McKergow, a Solution-Focused consultant based in the UK. He recommends "gossiping" positively about a person in front of them with colleagues, or in the case of a child, with the family.[15] You speak as though the child were not there, and say, for example, in the case of an eight-year-old girl, "Honey (wife to husband), do you know what I heard about Janie? She is kind to the girls at school, even though that sometimes upsets the popular girls." "Really? Wow, I bet she is proud of herself for having her own convictions." "I bet she is, too." or "Freddie, what did you notice about your little sister recently?" "Well, I'm happy that she doesn't come into my room and take my stuff so often." "Hmmm... looks like she is growing up to be a considerate and caring young lady." Just watch little Janie beam and blush as she hears sincere comments from her favorite people!

However, there are some parents and teachers who resort to aggravating children with pessimism, an approach that they call "Negative Psychology". Essentially, they use negative threats in order to induce fear, and employ put-downs by telling the children that they are not good enough, in an endeavor to motivate the latter to do better. These adults genuinely believe negative messages and fear will offer greater motivation than positive messages!

Now, when parents and teachers alike are so stingy with encouragement, such that a kid has to distinguish himself on a supersonic level just to get any encouragement, what kind of message is the child receiving? How often in life does that kind of achievement happen? Once a year? Once a decade? Surely this would lead to some kind of exasperation.

## Focus on Who Your Children Are, Not What They Do; On the Inside, Not the Outside

Do you truly appreciate effort, instead of grades? One mother we know who has a son with learning difficulties threw her child a party after he received his PSLE / end of elementary school grades, not because they were "high" compared to the other kids, but because she appreciated the work and effort he had put into his studies. She wanted him to know that she was very proud of him. We hold her up as a mom who understands how to be an asset in her child's academic life, not a liability.

When we praise our children for doing something well because of the effort they put in, we should do so without making any comparison with others. Thus, we should *avoid making statements* such as:

*You made us proud by becoming first in the class.*
*You made us happy by doing what you should, like we expected.*
*You made us look good because you scored straight A's.*
*You were the best actor/actress in the entire play.*

If your encouragement is based on what they actually achieve, what happens when they do not achieve the same results the next time round? Then no matter what you say, it will have little effect on them.

Rather, you should direct praise at their effort, and not in a comparative way:

*You worked so hard for your exam…*
*You gave it your best and I am proud of you.*
*I really admire the heart and spirit you put into playing basketball.*
*Wow, you were amazing in the musical! You are really good at acting.*

Look out for other qualities that you may not have noticed or thought were important. This list will get you started:

- helpfulness—helping siblings, classmates
- empathy—putting self in another's shoes
- cooperativeness—cooperating with others in the house
- effort—making the effort to do well in their studies, not just getting good grades
- tidiness—in own room or in whole house

- joyfulness—showing joy and being fun
- forgiveness and compassion—with family members or others
- sense of humor—making others laugh but not at anyone's expense
- patience—waiting without grumbling
- politeness—takes patience
- caring—having a heart for others.

When you witness these qualities, take your child aside and tell them how much you appreciate them. This is much more effective than just praising the outcome of an exam or a competition. Encourage them. Our children do a lot of good things, but we do not always notice; we should not miss the opportunity to acknowledge the good in our children.

Furthermore, when you encourage your children, be specific. General and ambiguous praise can have a negative effect on children because they may think their parents are insincere. Just saying, "Great job", or "You are awesome", without referencing any specific actions, will not lift their spirits.

One of the children we have known since he was born developed anxiety and stress issues. His mother has hounded her son year in and year out to the point that we were worried for him. He had even talked about suicide. I (John) had a counseling session with the boy who told me that his number one source of stress was the fact that he stopped getting first place in his class (just that year). He cried and said, "I do not have any other talents and by not getting first, I feel useless."

Deci and his colleagues found that university students who said they had complied with their parents' conditional love/controlling approval when they were younger ended up resenting and disliking their parents! Yikes! They also found that moms who had felt this way to their parents more often than not turned around and did it to their own children[16]—truly dysfunction is the gift that keeps on giving! So while children may perform for a time when their parents have exaggerated expectations for them, they also suffer from pressure and unhappiness trying to live up to the expectations. Moreover, the adverse effects of conditional parenting apply not only to high school and college students, but also to adult children [17] (RR18.4)

When parents focus on what their children do instead of who they are, their children will very likely conclude that they are not accepted and loved by their parents unconditionally. Their negative thinking will slowly erode their emotional security towards their parents and undermine their self-esteem. This is why we have heard so many adolescents say:

*I don't care about my exams, why should I?*
*I am just working to get my parents off my back.*
*I need to do well so that I can get a job that pays me a lot one day.*

These children have very little natural drive. They lack spark and joy, and project a flat demeanor. They are sometimes knows as underachievers—a subject we will now discuss in greater detail.

## Learn to Motivate "Underachievers"

Underachievement relates to the discrepancy between the child's ability and his or her actual achievement.[18] These students tend to be disorganized, lose assignments, misplace books, daydream, and forget to do their homework. They spend most of their energy and time on television, computer games, and phones. Underachievers often blame their teachers or school for their poor grades, and prioritize sports or computers or music or social life (anything!) over academics. However, beneath the carefree facade:

- Underachievers don't believe they can reach their goals, even if they were to work hard. The defectiveness and failure lifetraps are triggered at the thought of trying harder. If they have a surrendered coping style, they "fulfill the prophecy" of their inner voice that says that they can't reach healthy goals.

- If underachievers do not think that they can win, they will not bother trying. Essentially, they would rather not try than to try and be disappointed out of fear their flaws will be exposed. Instead, they opt to brag about the low grade they managed to achieve without studying.

- While this attitude helps them feel better about themselves temporarily, there is a constant inner voice that tells them to counterattack their sense of defectiveness and failure. As this voice grows stronger, they will become even more afraid of losing. What underachievers should realize is that, even when they lose, they can still learn valuable lessons that will enable them to triumph at other times.

- Some underachievers are driven by the dependence lifetrap. They do not feel confident about performing their own tasks and believe they always need someone beside them to guide them and to succeed. They have low self-esteem about their ability to perform tasks by themselves.

- Some underachievers have magical thinking, associated with the entitlement lifetrap. They believe that things will suddenly change for the better later in life and they will become extremely well off. Indulging in magical thinking helps them alleviate their sense of defectiveness by reassuring themselves that everything will turn out alright even when they make no effort.
- Many struggle with the lifetrap of insufficient self-control—they have not learned how to persevere through a task. They do not know what it means to really make an effort; thus, the have an unrealistic view of what it takes to perform a task well.

In the case of underachievers, giving them realistic expectations will increase their confidence. As they learn to complete tasks and even excel, their motivation will increase. Parents—if your child is in this category, do not insist they jump through the same hoops as their peers—take your expectation down a few notches and work up to things gradually. Otherwise you risk your child feeling that their failure is a confirmation of the little voice that tells them there is no point trying.

Our advice is that if children are not motivated, parents should allow the natural consequence of school to take effect. Research has confirmed that children are more likely to apply themselves with determination when they receive less pressure and criticism from parents (RR18.5); they will understand where they had gone wrong when the feedback comes from another source like their teachers.

## Learn about Multiple Intelligences and Identify Your Children's Gifts

We do not have the space here to do this subject justice, but we implore you, if you are struggling with having realistic expectations for your children, to read up on the theory of "Multiple Intelligences". Howard Gardner, from Harvard University, is the pioneer on the subject. For several decades, he and his team of researchers and scientists have validated his theory of the existence of different intelligences in the brain. Gardner advocates exposing children to different experiences, media, and learning styles so that all children have the possibility to be their best.

When we teach this part of our workshop, we describe the eight intelligences that Gardner has proven to date: logical/mathematical, verbal/linguistic, musical, spatial, environmental, kinesthetic, interpersonal, and intrapersonal.[19] Based on this theory, we try to help parents see that statistically, it is not possible for children to be gifted in all subject areas, nor is it probable for all children to be gifted in math! We beg them to not be disappointed if their children do not excel in mathematics and science—there are other paths to success and happiness! Then we explain how to nurture all eight intelligences to see which ones their children seem to naturally gravitate toward.

••••••••••••••••••••••••••••••••••••••••••••••••••••••••••••

### *Louis Lowdown*

My mom taught me to read when I (Karen) was four and I devoured everything in my small town school's library by the time I finished elementary school. Reading came easily to me so I'd always assumed that my daughter would be a voracious reader as well. We read to her since she was born, and her room was filled with books. However, when Sonia still didn't get into reading by the time she was in the fourth grade, I felt like the world's worst mother. I had followed all the tips, but still, she just wasn't like me, and my narcissistic parent self couldn't help but feel disappointed! Thankfully, my wonderful husband, who had recently stopped being a freak-out math dad a year earlier, opened my eyes by pointing out that Sonia had won a national tennis tournament when she was just nine years old—how many trophies had I won at nine? Or ever? "Let Sonia be Sonia and she will develop her own strengths, and don't be so egotistical that you think she has to be just like you!" (He probably was a bit nicer than that, but I remember it that way!) That was very sound advice; I stopped worrying about Sonia's reading. The irony of it all—in university she ended up majoring in English Literature!

••••••••••••••••••••••••••••••••••••••••••••••••••••••••••••

## Don't Let Yourself Jump to the Worst Case Scenario

Such a mind-set can make meeting your children's core emotional needs difficult, because it is hard to have realistic expectations when you are always in a worst-case scenario mode. Below are two stories of people we have counseled, still traumatized by the memories of their parents' overreaction to relatively small issues.

Because her mother expected everything to be perfect, Sterling was petrified of doing anything wrong. One evening, as the family was getting ready to go out for dinner, Sterling's mother yelled at her for taking too long to put on her shoes. In a panic, Sterling put her shoes on the wrong feet. In the car, the yelling continued because her mother then berated her for not just being slow, but also being so stupid as to confuse her left with her right feet. Sterling was so upset and traumatized by the event that even at 40 years old she can still remember how she felt when her mother completely overreacted to her "mistake".

Each day, after coming home from work, Zach's father would watch his son do his homework. After Zach completed it, his dad would test him to see if he knew the material. On several occasions, when Zach did not quite grasp the material, his father would be physically abusive to him. Zach ended up hating school, studying only to please his father and escape punishment. Due to burnout, Zach eventually dropped out of school, traumatized by his father's overreacting.

These parents were overreacting as if their entire world were coming to an end. A good question to ask would be, "What could the worst possible outcome of this mistake be?" Really, what concerns are worth worrying about? Is the child's well-being or health in jeopardy, for example? Is he sick? Does he have to be admitted to a hospital? Does the child have to be taken to the police? Has the child committed grievous hurt against another? Most of the time, 90% of our worries and concerns do not even come true. Even if they do, what is the worst thing that can happen?

Let's look back at our examples: What would be the worst-case scenario of a child taking a bit more time to get dressed? You might be a bit late for dinner! And if you have to catch a flight, one of the parents could help dress the child on the way. Is that such a bad thing? The parent could use the car ride to have a great time singing as a family, or if the appointment were not so urgent, the parent could have allowed time for the child to get dressed herself and then praised her for doing a great job. A wonderful experience is lost because the parent's reaction is disproportionate to the mistake made.

What is the worst-case scenario if a child cannot remember all the material he has studied? Not to worry—he just needs to keep working and eventually he will get there. And should he fail a test, he will learn how to do better next time. Is this situation worth imprinting a negative emotional scar on your child?

Mistakes can be a good opportunity for teaching, bonding, and connecting. Mistakes, when not viewed negatively by parents, can lead both sides to engage in meaningful conversation, with everyone reflecting together. Both parent and child can turn the entire situation into laughter; a potentially heavy moment is instead transformed into a light moment. Sadly, parents often turn small mistakes into lifelong scars.

Let us seek to transform day-to-day mistakes into discussions in which the child learns; at times, the very nature of these discussions may even lead to laughter and light moments. Through mistakes, taking calculated risks here and there, trial and error, our children will learn to spread their wings. They will be boys and girls, and eventually adults, who are neither compliant nor defiant; they will acknowledge their strengths and limitations, embracing life, and us, with zest and enthusiasm.

· · · · · · · · · · · · · · · · · · · · · · · · · · · · · · · · · · · · · · · · · · · · · · · · · · · · · ·

### *Louis Lowdown*

I (Karen) attended a small West Texas farming community high school with a graduating class of 40 kids. In my sophomore year, I took Chemistry and had absolutely no interest in the subject whatsoever. When the end-of-quarter exam came, the teacher gave all the top students an exemption; so only a few other non-science types and I took the test. I scored 57/100 (the passing grade was 60) and worried about how I would tell my dad. (Though my parents were not overbearing in the least, it was a given in our home that one should strive to live up to his or her potential. Plus, I had never flunked an exam before, so I was a bit nervous.) The ensuing conversation went like this:

Karen (with a big smile): *Dad, we got our exam grades back this week. I've got some good news and some bad news.*
Dad: *Tell me the good news.*
Karen: *The good news is that I scored the highest grade in the class on my Chemistry final.*
Dad (with a surprised look): *Well, that is good news. And what's the bad news?*
Karen (looking a bit sheepish): *It was a 57.*
Dad (silence): *...Well, I've only got one thing to say.*
Karen (with trepidation): *What's that?*
Dad (with a cheeky smile): *When you go to college one day, you'd better major in business so you don't have to take any science classes!*
Karen (relieved): *Thanks, Dad!*

The sequel to this story is: 30 years later I attended a workshop called "Helping Children Deal With Stress". The Australian lecturer asked for a volunteer from the audience to share a personal story of how they dealt with failure. I shared this story and when I got to the punch line about not taking science in university, the crowd of over 100 people burst into spontaneous applause!

What a wonderful story of a father with realistic expectations (in this case, extremely realistic!) and a daughter who benefited from having her core emotional needs met. (I've wondered my whole life, why I got such nice parents!)

••••••••••••••••••••••••••••••••••••••••••••••••••••••••••••••

······································

SECTION SIX

# MOVING TOWARDS A HEALTHIER OUTCOME

······································

# Chapter Nineteen

# SPIRITUAL VALUES AND COMMUNITY

······································································

The Plus One Core Emotional Need for Spiritual Values and Community can be defined as parents impressing a "worldview in line with their own positive values" on their children, and connecting children with something bigger than themselves, perhaps (but not limited to) their faith and traditions. It is also about parents helping children experience "kin-ship" with like-minded people who will treasure the same values and beliefs, and be there for one another.

Throughout this book we have referred to our research that resulted in the identification of the four core emotional needs and the nine exasperation interactions. So where does the "plus one core emotional need of spiritual values & community" come in? We did not have time to conduct a separate study on spiritual values & community, so we don't have *empirical evidence,* but we have read related research—plus we know it from our experience! We believe that to the extent parents do not meet the need for the plus one core emotional need for spiritual values and community, their children may experience the opposite, meaning they may *lack values, lack a moral compass* and be at risk for *loneliness & isolation.*

In our experience, children who have had this need met will *consistently* and *at an emotional level* hear and believe the following messages from and/or about their parents:

> *They base their lives on certain principles and hold to them even when things get difficult, and they expect me (and my siblings, if applicable) to do the same.*
> *They want me to hold to their values because they love me and want the best for me, but they hope that I will do so with my own personal convictions.*
> *They love being a part of their community.*
> *They make sure that I get to spend lots of time with friends who hold similar values.*
> *They encourage me to help the less fortunate, read inspirational literature, and be active in a community.*

Even though we have said it repeatedly, we will once again remind readers that none of the core emotional needs "lives in a vacuum"—parents will find meeting the plus one core need almost impossible if they have not met the other needs as well, particularly the core emotional need for connection and acceptance. Parents who communicate unconditional acceptance, who create connection, who believe in their children without frightening them off with exaggerated expectations, and who have been consistently firm but not rigid with limits are admired by their children; these kids will want to imitate their parents' values.

## Spiritual Values

"What Do Parents Want?"—Therapist and best-selling author, Peter Levine, researched the topic for ten years and found that the top three qualities American parents hope for in their children are honesty, having good sense and good judgment, and being obedient at home (being studious got a mere 3%).[1] In the deep recesses of their hearts, parents value values! On the other side of the globe, Singapore residents were asked to rate a variety of qualities, in order of importance to them personally; honesty, kindness, gratitude, fairness, and forgiveness came out tops.[2] In a nation that prides itself on excellence in education, we were encouraged to see the highest rankings given to values accompanying good character.

For many parents, teaching their children values, and the limits that come with having values—even getting children to obey simple rules at home and at school—has been made confusing by modern culture, and has brought its own set of heartaches, stress and frustrations. Parenting experts Dr. Diana Baumrind and Dr. Michael Popkin feel strongly about the "whys" behind passing down values: Baumrind, best known for coining the terms "authoritarian, permissive and authoritative parenting styles", believes practically the whole point of parenting is to develop character and a sense of competence.[3] Popkin, known for his "Active Parenting" series, advises parents to hold out obedience to a set of values as something that benefits the child, not the parents, that the parents' concern for the children developing principles is not to satisfy the parents' agenda but totally for the child's own good ("It's *your* life…you're the one who's going to live with the decisions you make now…").[4]

Meeting this core need is really about parents shaping their children's belief systems, their values, in essence, their hearts. It is not about a one-time talk or even a once a week talk; it takes parents sharing the "whys" behind what they think, say and do, attributing meaning to everyday conversations and occurrences. There are many values (gratitude, service, integrity, empathy, respect, loyalty, forgiveness, kindness, and embracing diversity are but a few); different families may have differing opinions on which are the most important. Rather than tell parents *which* values they should be passing down, we put forward five "views" that we feel parents should impress on their children in order to meet the plus one core need: the way they view themselves, the way they view others, the way they view right and wrong, the way they view taking correction, and the way they view conflict in relationships, forgiveness & reconciliation.

**Shaping Our Children's View of Themselves**

By striving to meet the four core emotional needs and avoiding the exasperation interactions we have identified in this book, parents will automatically be helping their children to have a healthy view of themselves. Kids will unconsciously play reassuring messages from their parents over in their heads, which will over time reinforce positive messages and a healthy self-image. Parents who give their children space but are also committed to spending time with them and listening to them are the ones who will be invited into the private thoughts of their children. If parents are (appropriately) open and vulnerable about their own feelings with their children from a young age, their children will be more likely to follow. When this becomes a two-way relationship, parents will know exactly how the children feel about themselves and have a window into their children's hearts which provides opportunities to shape their thinking about themselves.

· · · · · · · · · · · · · · · · · · · · · · · · · · · · · · · · · · · · · · · · · · · · · · · · · · · · ·

## *Louis Lowdown*

When our children were three and five years old, I (Karen) began talking to them about the need to be open and share their thoughts and feelings regularly. This was partly so that they wouldn't get in the habit of hiding things from us that may have happened during the day, such as when they were at kindergarten. But with Sonia, I had a second motive. I worked with her on having positive thoughts about herself and the way she viewed herself in relation to the world around her, because from a very early age, she would sometimes tell herself negative messages. She would actually say them aloud, but under her breath; I could hear a kind of mumbling coming out of her. I would ask her what she was saying; at first she wouldn't tell me. Eventually it would come out, "I'm saying I am stupid" or something to that effect. I seem to remember these conversations happening when I was driving her home from school, so I would park the car, turn around, look her in the eye, and tell her positive messages to counter the negative ones she was telling herself. (Knowing what I know now, I am not sure what was happening in our home that caused her to have "defective" thoughts, which come from the domain of disconnection and rejection. We must have been exasperating her in some way—possibly the Perfectionistic & Conditional Exasperation Interaction. At this stage in life she hasn't been able to come up with anything but I bet if/when she has children one day, some of the memories will come flooding back.)

· · · · · · · · · · · · · · · · · · · · · · · · · · · · · · · · · · · · · · · · · · · · · · · · · · · · ·

Tapping into the power of community, which we will cover later in this chapter, can also help your child's view of himself. When your adolescent child has other adult friends whom they like and respect, they will also be willing to share with them about their inner thoughts and issues. It's amazing how much of a difference this makes in helping a child view himself in a healthy way, and in being tied into the community. There may not be a better gift parents can give their children than helping them have a healthy view of themselves.

## Shaping Our Children's View of Others

If our children do not feel for and show compassion and empathy for people, they will feel that having concern for others is a task or duty, and their relationships will not be long lasting or fulfilling. Lecturing them about the need to care for people is ineffective; we need to help them feel it from the inside and it starts with the way they *view* others.

### a. Create a Home Environment That Fosters Empathy

We have spoken about helping our kids empathize by getting them involved in volunteer work and through other means. However, caring about others does not just come from visiting the needy and those who have less than we do. Parents need to help their children take others' feelings into account as they go about their day-to-day lives. Parents should explain things *as they are happening* so that they are able to attribute positive meaning to situations, not just be a good example for the sake of it.

We talked about the need for parents to show empathy to their children, and to not dismiss them or put them down. We mentioned that by listening to their children's hurts and showing empathy, parents are modeling what they want their children to do as well, and exhibited a wide array of good that comes when parents show empathy to their children (see Chapter Eight). Sadly, there are some parents who show little empathy with other members in their home, and then expect their children to become people who care. When parents do not model empathy, it is doubtful that it will be deeply embedded in the hearts of their children.

### b. Focus on Cause and Effect

Marilyn Watson popularized the idea of talking to children about cause and effect. We have to stress the need to keep talking about the manner in which our children's actions affect other people's feelings. If we just point out our children's mistakes and wrong doings and tell them how much they are messing up, they may eventually get fed up. Many parents exhibit this kind of zeal in their parenting, but do not take the time to explain and process the effect of the misbehavior. Such opportunities should not be missed. They can be turned into valuable life lessons instead of times when we as parents are trying to "teach them a lesson" by harshly correcting them.[5]

On the flip side, when they do positive things, focus on how it helped other people feel. This will teach them that part of loving people is taking into consideration their feelings. Incidentally, it also helps them with the previous "view" of right and wrong, because children learn best about right and wrong when they see how their right and wrong actions affect other people. This is the heart of 'The Golden Rule": *Do to others as you would have them do to you.*

More from Nucci, our moral development expert (remember his different domains of morality in Chapter Three?): Nucci's research found that children feel helped when parents correct them with statements about their actions (rather than exasperation interactions) such as, "That really hurt Mike," "How would you feel if someone had called you a name like that?" "Do you think it is fair for you to get two toys when everyone else gets one?" He wrote, "a child's moral development is affected by experiences (including conversations) having to do with feelings and thoughts about the ways actions affect people."[6] Focusing at the feelings level is crucial here, as opposed to using one of the exasperation interactions, or even just labeling an act is wrong. Imagine a home atmosphere where negatively labeling actions dominate the way parents teach their children. What would that atmosphere be like from the children's perspective?

### c. Parents as Role Models

One of the most important "others" in the lives of parents are their very own children. As parents we have many opportunities to teach our children this principle, situations when they do well by taking into account other people and those when they do not. This would include speaking to our children in the way that we wish people would speak to us, correcting our children in the way we wish others would correct us, giving our children the benefit of the doubt in the way that we wish others would give us the benefit of the doubt, and encouraging our children in the way that we wish others would encourage us.

Children are very smart; not much gets by them. When they see their parents having a good marriage (not perfect but always working things out and loving each other), and feel that they are treated with love, respect, kindness, and firmness and given appropriate freedom as well as limits, they will put two and two together and admire parents' values. Before we pass virtues on, we need to live them out ourselves first. An example is extremely powerful, and can become a legacy that we will leave behind for our children.

Our children will see us through the good times and the bad, through our highs and lows, and when we go through our "normal" days. All these put together give our children numerous opportunities to see what we really are on the inside, what values we really hold dear. It goes without saying that they will carry these memories with them till they themselves become adults. It is amazing what they pick up from our behavior on a daily basis. For example, they will see the way that we do the following:

- Work (our work ethic)
- View money, wealth and status
- Share with others (generous or stingy)
- Handle conflict, anger, and forgiveness
- Apologize and display humility (or not)
- Talk about others
- Treat our spouse
- Treat waiters, cashiers, and the "ordinary" people the same as the rich and powerful
- Treat and talk about our own parents, or their grandparents, and our siblings.

The list goes on and on. If there is duplicity between what we teach and what we practice, it will have an impact on them. No doubt, we have weaknesses, but there is a difference between parents who are imperfect and admittedly "works in progress" versus parents whose lives are riddled with hypocrisy and duplicity. Being good examples is crucial; but we also need to verbalize and teach them what we believe.

In their book *The Altruistic Personality*, Samuel and Pearl Oliner tell how they interviewed 406 persons who rescued Jews from the Nazi Holocaust and 126 people who lived in the same parts of Nazi-occupied Europe but did not get involved in helping the Jews. The rescuers were much more likely than non-rescuers to say:

- Their parents modeled caring values. In contrast, parents of non-rescuers were more likely to have emphasized economic values, such as getting a good job. (This should make us really consider what kind of conversation we have around the dinner table!)
- Non-rescuers also said that their parents were more likely to use harsh punishments. Rescuers instead cited that their parents would occasionally punish them but more often they would teach and explain things.
- Rescuers' parents also were much more likely to explicitly teach a positive attitude and tolerance towards people of different culture and religion.[7] (RR19.1)

The bottom line is parents who show compassion are more likely to have children who are empathic and show compassion to others themselves, and who are more likely to know the difference between right and wrong. Wow! Which leads into our next topic…

### Shaping Our Children's View of Right and Wrong

Similarly, we must help our kids learn how to make wise choices and to see that there are consequences for choosing unwisely.

Nucci observed that disputes over issues in the conventional, prudential and personal domains comprised virtually all of adolescent-parent disputes.[8] Disciplining and training children about issues within the Moral Domain, which are truly about right and wrong, is always correct. Protecting their safety with boundaries within the Prudential Domain is also a must for parents. However, when parents argue with and discipline their children for "offenses" within the conventional and personal domains, they are on slippery ground. As parents fight with their children about the arbitrary and personal choice issues that are not truly a matter of right and wrong, their children will become exasperated and will experience frustration of their core emotional needs.

There are many issues that tend to get parents frustrated, for example, poor table manners, vulgar language, dishonesty about grades, unusual hairstyle and hair color, to name a few. Think about the types of disputes that you frequently have with your children. Are they about making you look good? Are they about conventional issues? Or are they about helping your children develop morally? Studies have also shown that children who are given control over the personal domain are much more willing to share their personal information with their parents, even when it concerns involvement in sexual behavior. Controlling parents have less chance of knowing their children intimately, especially those at an adolescent stage. Parents can expect a rude awakening about the secret behavior of their children when they sabotage their children with exasperating behavior such as belittling, being punitive, perfectionistic, or controlling. Trying to control the behavior and appearance of children will only lead to these children keeping parents in the dark about their personal struggles and challenges.

Go to our website, www.gep.sg for an exercise in categorizing issues into domains (Nucci's domains mentioned in Chapter Three) in order to gain insight about guiding your children's view of right and wrong.

························································

## *Louis Lowdown*

When I (John) was 15 years old, my parents sent me from Malaysia to England to attend boarding school. As you can imagine, the boys there misbehaved and got into all sorts of trouble, including all sorts of bad language, lying, stealing, you name it. However, rather than address hidden issues that could scar boys for life, the school usually focused on the conventional domain. For example, when we spoke to our teachers, we were not allowed to place our hands in our pockets, even in the dead of winter, because it was construed as disrespectful. If we forgot, we would be punished by getting up 45 minutes earlier the next morning and reporting to a prefect. Here were some of the other rules to which we were required to adhere:

Cheering on the rugby field while facing the winds from the Atlantic Ocean with a very high wind chill factor (and no hands in pockets!)

Going for walks in the open farm fields at set times (Sunday afternoons).

Holding our knives and forks the proper (British) way; we were told off if we did it in the American style.

While I am not against conventional rules, it strikes me as very skewed that we had the same severe punishment meted out by kids practically our age (prefects) just for "improperly" holding a fork as we had for being disrespectful to our teachers. We were punished for the dumbest things. These rules were totally arbitrary. Needless to say, I developed a lot of bad attitudes towards the prefects' authority while schooling there.

························································

When parents focus too much on conventional and personal issues in teenagers and reprimand them for not complying, it often causes a divide. For many teenagers, it results in rebellion. Forget the peripherals and focus on the issues of the heart that really matter.

## Shaping Our Children's View of Taking Correction

Much has already been said in the sections on connection and acceptance and reasonable limits about how to give correction in a way that doesn't exasperate. It is important for parents to teach their children that they are expected to receive correction with humility and obedience. This may sound difficult but the teen years will be much easier if children were trained in this area during the growing up years! Husbands and wives should get united on expectations for the way they want their children to view correction and be consistent.

Parents should teach their children it is normal to make mistakes, but children and adults alike should own up to our mistakes and make amends for what we did wrong. Having a remorseful and contrite attitude about what we did that has hurt others is a crucial value we need to inculcate in our children. Children should see parents modeling that admitting wrongs and apologizing brings joy to the heart. Kids also need to be taught that when they choose to hide their mistakes and wrongdoings they will end up feeling guilty and miserable.

When children do find the courage to confess their struggles, parents should in turn respond with forgiveness, acceptance and reconciliation. We should refrain from being judgmental, negative and punitive. The "I told you so" and "How many times have I told you and you have not listened?" all convey our disbelief in them and will only turn them away from confiding in us further.

From the time they begin to speak their first words, children should be taught to take responsibility for their disobedience. They should learn to say "I'm sorry" from the heart, which should be followed by forgiveness from parents and assurance of our love for them with hugs and kisses.

How humble are the parents towards each other in managing their conflicts or conflicts with others? How ready are parents to apologize sincerely when they have done something wrong to the children, e.g., yelling at them or being punitive? How open are parents to feedback and input from their own children or from others? These are all noted by the watchful eyes of our little ones who will only learn from what they see in our lives, not from what we teach them.

**Shaping Our Children's View of Conflict, Forgiveness and Reconciliation**
When we forgive, bitterness, resentment, and anger are swept away. The negative emotional energy is gone and is replaced by feelings of light-heartedness, freedom, and peace. Indeed, forgiveness *is* the cornerstone for healing in relationships.

When defining forgiveness, researchers make a distinction between the genuine and the superficial. Dr. Everett Worthington and Dr. Robert Enright are among the foremost experts on forgiveness in North America. Dr. Worthington says, "In genuine forgiveness, one who has suffered an unjust injury chooses to abandon his or her right to resentment and retaliation, and instead offers mercy to the offender."[9] And

Dr. Enright writes, "People, upon rationally determining that they have been unfairly treated, forgive when they willfully abandon resentment and related responses (to which they have a right), and endeavor to respond to the wrongdoer based on the moral principle of beneficence, which may include compassion, unconditional worth, generosity, and moral love (to which the wrongdoer, by nature of the hurtful act or acts, has no right)."[10]

We would say forgiveness is made up of several components: we are aware the offense was unfair, we acknowledge we have the right to respond with anger, *we give up the right to revenge and retaliation that may cause injury to the offender*, and we replace the feelings of resentment with compassion, benevolence and love.

(We also believe that parents should teach children that while they have rights, their rights do not trump others' rights, so they do not have the right to hurt someone just because they feel like getting revenge (see italicized phrase above; also see Chapter Fourteen's discussion of bottlenecks). At any rate, we acknowledge that when people are hurt, they may *feel* like retaliating. Stephen Covey, the Seven Habits guru, says one of the differences between humans and other animals is that we have a pause button;[11] we believe that parents should teach their children to press the pause button when they feel they have been wronged.)

Back to forgiveness…Dr. Enright goes on to say that when people have successfully forgiven someone, they have reduced or eliminated negative feelings, thoughts and behaviors toward the offender. Instead those who forgive have developed:

- Positive *feelings or affect* toward the offender
- Positive *behavior* toward the offender
- Positive *thoughts or cognitions* toward the offender.[12]

(By substituting the counseling words "affect" for feelings and "cognition" for thoughts, we get Affect, Behavior, Cognition: The ABC's of Forgiveness).

According to Enright, forgiveness is *not* condoning the offender's actions, excusing the offender's actions, justifying the offender's actions, or just calming down.[13] Forgiveness does not necessarily equal reconciliation. As Dr. Enright puts it, "Reconciliation is the act of two people coming together following separation. Forgiving, on the other hand, is the moral action of one individual that starts as a private act, an unseen decision within the human heart."[14]

Reconciliation involves both parties coming together, both rendering forgiveness and asking for forgiveness. Both parties are willing to continue in a relationship with each other. However if one party feels unsafe being in a relationship with the other party who is not remorseful over his/her actions, then the injured party, after forgiving, may decide to not be reconciled, but have only a limited relationship with the other party. (For example, if bullies at school beat up your eight year old, you will hopefully want him to forgive them, but you will probably not expect him to become best friends right away.)

Research has shown convincingly that lack of forgiveness can be detrimental to health; all the more reason we should teach our children about forgiveness. Scientists have found that forgiveness impacts marriage: The higher the level of forgiveness between husband and wife, the higher the marital quality. Other studies show that people who forgive easily have less cardiovascular reactivity and better recovery patterns than those who do not forgive easily. Those who forgive easily also experience less anxiety, depression and anger. When we do not forgive the party that has hurt us, we are not "punishing" them; rather, we are putting ourselves in harm's way (RR19.2).

Most instances of children bringing the pain of childhood into adulthood relate to areas that were never brought to a proper closure through reconciliation and/or forgiveness. Most people do not know the proper meaning of forgiveness. For many, it is about "pushing things under the carpet", trying to "forget about it," or simply saying "sorry". Why let our children ruminate on unresolved issues when we know these will negatively affect their mental and emotional health?

Dr. Enright and his colleagues conducted two studies on forgiveness with children and came to the conclusion that younger children think about forgiveness differently than older children.[15] They found:

- Children ages 9-10 equate forgiveness with revenge ("if I haven't forgiven you yet, I deserve to take revenge.")
- Young children desire an apology *before* they are able to forgive; this should not be a requirement for adults, but for young children, this matters. (Even for adults, this goes a long way to helping people get reconciled.)
- Parents who apologize for mistakes that were their fault, both in front of, and to their children, are not only getting reconciled, but also being good role models for their children. We have heard many adults say their parents have *never* apologized to them!
- Children whose parents modeled forgiveness ended up practicing it themselves.

- Many adolescents listen to authorities on this matter, such as their teachers at school. When there is a clear, consistent message from teachers and parents, children will likely internalize it and make it part of their belief system.
- Older adolescents focus on the outcome after forgiveness is extended, such as whether or not it leads to a restored relationship afterwards.
- Some adults took a loving and unconditional view of forgiveness—they separated the behavior of the offender from the offender himself. When we do this, forgiveness becomes easier. The goal is to be able to see the behavior of the offender as wrong but not the person himself (RR19.3).

Other points to note when teaching children forgiveness:

- All people, regardless of color, religion, race, etc., have feelings and they all deserve respect. Some in society teach that only "important" people need to be respected. Whether our children are rude to their school principal or to a parking attendant at a grocery store, we must teach our children to extend apologies. In Singapore, we sometimes see children being very disrespectful to foreign domestic helpers employed by their parents, and parents simply ignore this; but when it comes to disrespect towards parents, the children get punished. This sends a very strong message that respect is only for certain people. It is sad to see anyone thinking they are "one-up" on domestic helpers from neighboring countries.
- Not all the people in our children's lives will apologize, respond to apologies, or agree to reconciliation; all the more reason why forgiving and getting reconciled should be a habit in the family. Children will then appreciate the family even more and understand that giving and receiving mercy and grace exists in the family but not necessarily everywhere else, and they will appreciate the family even more.
- When parents repeatedly model forgiveness as they encounter rude drivers, waiters, and salesmen, it becomes part of the family culture. For young children especially, using books (such as Dr. Seuss's *Horton Hears a Who*)[16] can be very helpful in teaching this concept. For older children, seeing movies and then discussing them together (rather than lecturing) with the parent is another great way.
- Resolve conflicts quickly in the family and between siblings. When conflicts go unresolved they cause a lot of anger, bitterness and resentment. These

layers of emotions become barriers that make it difficult for future acts of love and kindness to penetrate and heal. Family members can become numb and lose empathy for the person they are in conflict with—they become less concerned even if the other party is still in pain over the tension. However, when issues are sorted out quickly it teaches our children sensitivity to the feelings of others; that they should take into account what others are concerned about and not just focus on their own emotions. When tension is allowed to linger, our children will become immune to the pain and feelings of others. When children lose their ability to empathize, they then become adults who are not able to empathize. This will affect their own marriage and relationships with others.

## Healthy Community

Experts have long extoled the virtues of healthy community. When people connect with one another and each person has the interest of others at heart, something supernatural happens. Through that emotional connection, our deepest hurts get healed. We rejoice together, we mourn together. We love together, we laugh together, and we cry together. We are all weak at some points in our lives. In a healthy community, love, connection, care and acceptance flow from the healthy to the more needy individuals, and that is when healing takes place. Not instantly, but through a steady, slow and consistent process, people do get better. No wonder it is better for people to live in "community".

Unfortunately we live in a day and age when the responsibility for this kind of connection rests on counselors, educators and therapists. A *New York Times* article from May 2012 spoke of how we are losing the ability to connect and be intimate as we feel the need to outsource our private lives to specialists and no longer seek help from friends and family.[17] Research shows that, more than the *skill* of the therapist, the most helpful and healing ingredient when seeing a therapist is the *connection* between counselor and client.[18] Close friends should be able to provide that essential, most important emotional healing ingredient.

In the fast-paced world where couples have to schedule in love-making, and friends have to plan a month in advance to meet for coffee, people feel too awkward to show this kind of love and connection. Many times they do not even know how to go about it. Sometimes they feel ill-equipped and out of place. Sometimes it is because of a lack of trust. There exists a lot of hype about the global village and social networks keeping people connected, but for the most part, people in the world seem shallower and have fewer deep relationships than ever before. People rarely talk about their emotional pain with one another, and if they do, it's not unusual for their circle of friends to advise them to see a counselor or a therapist. We are professional counselors, so obviously we believe in these professions. We respect those skilled, trained and gifted professionals who pour themselves out in trying to bring emotional healing to others, and we do not want to play down the need to be adequately trained, but we wonder if people understand and appreciate the healing power that can come when people just connect with one another? We can surround ourselves with good, healthy and caring people, who want to take an interest in our lives, but if we refuse to let them in, we will not be healed—and it will be to our detriment. We are the ones who will get lonely and feel isolated as a result. This means each of us has the ingredient to heal someone else by giving of ourselves and by pouring out our hearts to one another.

When we feel truly connected, we feel accepted for who we are. Even though we have different gifts and limitations, we feel peaceful, knowing we are forgiven. These friendships add spiritual depth and blessings to our lives. Imagine what all these qualities can do for our well-being? Contemporary research points to the health and mental well-being benefits of a closely, connected community.

In today's world there are many valuable institutions that offer community: places of worship, universities, schools, child-care centers, Boy Scouts, sports teams, and others, not to mention the family. We believe that if we are going to meet the last "plus one" core need of our children, we cannot do it alone. We can only do it if we are part of a healthy community, and if we get our children immersed in that healthy community.

We have already seen statistics that show how much influence parents have on their children. Make no mistake about it—parents are the *primary influence* of their children. However, because we are all dysfunctional to a degree, we can only go so far. This is why the most we are able to be is "good enough".

When our children are weak physically, we take them to a doctor. When they want to improve in a sport, we get them a coach. When they are not doing well in their relationships with us as parents, what do we do? Normally, we just let time pass by and usually relationships and conflicts come to a standstill, and no progress is made. Whom do we call for help? Talking to our spouse, attending parenting seminars, and reading books are all helpful, however do we tap into the power of healthy communities? (RR19.4)

The use of the word "community" for many people carries a range of meanings. It can imply being part of a social club where people come together primarily for social reasons. Their friends are there, and so they feel comfortable there. In his book entitled, *Community: The Structure of Belonging*, Peter Block describes well what community is:

> *Community* as used here is about the experience of belonging. We are in community each time we find a place where we belong. The word belong has two meanings. First and foremost, to belong is to be related to and a part of something. It is membership, the experience of being at home in the broadest sense of the phrase. It is the opposite of thinking that wherever I am, I would be better off somewhere else. Or that I am still forever wandering, looking for that place where I belong. The opposite of belonging is to feel isolated and always (all ways) on the margin, an outsider. To belong is to know, even in the middle of the night, that I am among friends.
>
> The second meaning of the word belong has to do with being an owner: Something belongs to me. To belong to a community is to act as a creator and co-owner of that community. What I consider mine I will build and nurture. The work, then is to seek in our communities a wider and deeper sense of emotional ownership; it means fostering among all of a community's citizens a sense of ownership and accountability.[19]

This idea of belonging and of emotional ownership is really an accurate way to see our respective communities. Having a sense of ownership means caring about the community, playing a role in it, and constantly looking for ways to improve the practice of the values they hold dear. This includes giving feedback and attending meetings. Both of these concepts, the sense of belonging and emotional ownership, need to be grasped by all members, and to the extent that this is understood and practiced will be the extent of the health of that community.

We believe that we are never too young to begin experiencing community. But for children, this has to be balanced with safety. Whenever couples are allowing their children to be with others, they must ensure that the people are trustworthy. We hope this does not sound mean, but we have seen the damage done when parents were not vigilant.

Having said that, we are all for having great vacations with other families from your trusted communities. Combine family holidays and get together regularly, host sleepovers/slumber parties and outings and facilitate sports activities with others. Help your children to develop relationships with the children of other parents that you also know well—that is where community begins. It is not just about children knowing other children, but parents also knowing and having relationships with other parents and their children. Many parents do not know the parents of their children's friends and this is a mistake. Friendships must take place at both levels, children with children and parents with parents. This constant interaction, sharing, and giving, is what will help develop the sense of community.

● ● ● ● ● ● ● ● ● ● ● ● ● ● ● ● ● ● ● ● ● ● ● ● ● ● ● ● ● ● ● ● ● ● ● ● ● ● ● ● ● ● ● ● ● ● ● ● ● ● ● ● ● ● ● ● ●

### *Louis Lowdown*

When our children were young, we got priceless input on their behavior whenever we would hang out with more experienced parents—we felt a burning desire to ask for advice whenever we travelled or had guests over. We telephoned friends in the USA for advice about breastfeeding or how to put our children to sleep—usually at 3am Singapore time! We learned from our friends in India; they also helped us with discipline, scheduling, and taught us the importance of not allowing our children to moan and whine. We got input from older couples in England and Australia about making sure we did not back down from limits for our children or foster entitlement. We will be forever grateful for this feedback. However, we notice that in the 21st century, the Googling generation does not necessarily have this same sense of community and propensity to learn from older couples. It seems that young couples today are more likely to search the Internet rather than telephone a friend or drop by the home of mature friends who live down the street. We would like to encourage young married couples to seek out help from older folks (those worthy of respect) in their families and neighborhoods who can give real-time advice and feedback for and about their children.

● ● ● ● ● ● ● ● ● ● ● ● ● ● ● ● ● ● ● ● ● ● ● ● ● ● ● ● ● ● ● ● ● ● ● ● ● ● ● ● ● ● ● ● ● ● ● ● ● ● ● ● ● ● ● ● ●

## Service for Others

One of the activities young people really look forward to is being able to participate in acts of service that benefit other people. We have seen teenagers completely turn their lives around after getting involved in something bigger than themselves. It is exciting to see how acts of service could have a huge impact in people's lives. (By the way, have you ever noticed how children do not seem to learn gratitude by being told how grateful they should be? That doesn't seem to work!)

## Peer Relationships

It is important for parents to encourage teens to spend a lot of time together. Parents need to make the sacrifices necessary to get the children to hang out with other teens from trusted families. This helps like-minded teens have the chance to become close to one another and build community. If you're worried about your children being gone too much, make your home the center of activity.

## Involvement of Other Non-Family Adults to Mentor Your Child

In addition to great peer relationships, the value of having other non-family adults involved in the lives of our children cannot be overstated. Part of why community needs to be fostered at a young age is that this will help your children have relationships with safe adults they can trust when they get to the age where your words do not carry as much weight. Once this happens, you will be glad that they get along with trusted older friends.

In 2005, a nationwide sample of USA adolescents were surveyed and those who were involved in positive mentoring relationships were more likely to complete high school, attend university, be employed afterwards, have positive mental health in the areas of self esteem and life satisfaction, avoid problem behavior (gang membership, physical fighting, risk taking), enjoy good health, and have good relationships with their parents, peers, and other adults such as teachers.[20] Wow! Parents, let's make sure we tap into this positive by-product of mentorship and make things happen for our children as we meet the core emotional need of spiritual, and community values. (See the research in this next RR to discover proven traits of a great mentoring relationship!) (RR19.5)

## Partnership Between Parents and Mentors

We think it is particularly helpful for parents and mentors to be on the same page and not work at cross-purposes, working together for the benefit of the youth in question. We encourage parents to ensure that a healthy relationship is built between their teenagers and their mentors. Ideally, we think parents should invite their children's mentors over for dinner from time to time. Parents and mentors can exchange information on how the teens are doing, using the four plus one core needs as the basis for conversation, which helps ensure a consistency throughout. Mentors should experience our gratitude, not just a verbal thank-you. Think about it: Someone cares enough to invest in the well-being of your child! It is helpful for the teen to see both parents and mentors get along. A functional community calls for this kind of a relationship.

One of the issues in this relationship is confidentiality. Teens need to feel safe with their mentor; i.e., what they share in confidence with a mentor will not make its way back to their parents. *There are only two conditions upon which confidentiality should be broken, as in the counseling profession: When the teen is potentially causing harm to themselves or others or to another's property.*

When relationships are solid on all fronts, the bond becomes strong and the community is functional.

It is exciting to think that by meeting the plus one core emotional need of spiritual values and community, you will be able to influence the way your children view themselves, others, right and wrong, taking correction, and the huge area of dealing with conflict, and forgiveness! These essential values that define and shape our children are further entrenched into their hearts when they are part of a loving, connected community that continues to bring out the best in them as they grow up to be loving, healthy adults.

·····················································

### *Louis Lowdown*

When David was in first grade, or Primary One (P1) as it is known in Singapore, he had a nice circle of friends, including a boy named Jonathan who had a permanent disability and needed a walker. During the school's annual Sports' Day, of which I (Karen) was a volunteer organizer, the P1 kids took part in simple relay races and were allowed to choose their own team, six to a team. One of the relays was a beanbag race: the kids had to walk to a marked spot and back while balancing a small bean bag on their head, then place it on the next chap's head without dropping it. David ended up being on a team with all of his buddies, except for Jonathan, who had not been allowed to participate in any relay. For whatever reason, David's team had supersonic speed and was a person ahead of all the other teams by the time the sixth boy took off—victory was eminent! However, right at that moment, Jonathan's mother, holding the disabled child in her arms, asked David if he would allow Jonathan to race for their team, since he had not been allowed to participate in any other race all morning. I saw the conflict on David's face—they were seconds away from first place... If he said "No" to his friend, he would feel lousy; if he said "Yes", Jonathan would be happy, but they would surely come in last and his teammates might be angry. In that split second, he decided. *"Yes, Jonathan, you can join."* Seeing the look of absolute joy on Jonathan's face probably helped David to feel a little bit better as they came in last place. When Jonathan's mom carried him across the finish line, he was beaming, so glad to be a part of a team. I was holding back tears, proud of my son, and suffering for him, too, because I knew it was killing him to give up the trophy. After the hoo hah died down and the kids were getting refreshments, David walked over to me and said, *"Well, Mom, we may have come in last in the bean bag race, but I bet in heaven, we came in first place."* I hugged him and told him that he had made me the happiest mom on the planet.

•••••••••••••••••••••••••••••••••••••••••••••••••••••••••••••

# Chapter Twenty

## REPAIR AND RECONNECT

····················································

As we start the closing chapter of the book (to borrow Churchill's phrase, "the end of the beginning"),[1] we remind parents that we are advocating "*good enough* parenting", not *perfect* parenting. No one is perfect; we will all need to repair and reconnect at some point. Parents will sometimes feel frustrated when their children act out even after many reminders; moms and dads will rightfully take issue with their children for talking back, mistreating others, lying, overspending, not taking schoolwork seriously, staying up too late, and the list goes on. Even when trying really hard to be good enough parents, moms and dads will occasionally become frustrated and slip into exasperation interaction mode and stay there for a while...when this happens, the parent-child connection will be damaged and repair will be needed. If you find yourself at this stage, or if things are worse and there has been no connection for a while, *and you have already read the rest of this book,* then you are ready for this chapter, called "Repair and Reconnect".

Don't be deceived by the philosophy of "let's just cool down" or "let's forget the whole episode"; it is doubtful that things will get back to normal by accident or that you will experience connection after some time has passed. When heated arguments take place, with unhelpful words being spoken by one or both parties, the result is hurt feelings that need to be dealt with. If the relationship is repaired quickly, all will be forgotten—by nature, children are resilient and forgiving. If these hurts are not processed well, however, children or parents (or both) will ruminate, replaying the hurtful words over and over, and getting increasingly negative. When we ruminate, our thoughts get distorted and our pain gets worse, causing us to lose concentration. We could be driving, doing something for our boss at work, or even speaking with someone, but our mind will be preoccupied with the unresolved issue. How many times have we heard parents say, "If only I had talked with my child earlier, I would have spared him/her/the family a lot of pain and suffering."

Repair and reconnection are important skills for parents to learn. If children do not get reconnected with their parents quickly, they can feel abandoned, alone, unloved or misunderstood. Young children especially look at hurts and pain differently than adults. For example, the parent may feel angry, but the child may feel humiliated and shamed, or a child may feel hopeless, while parents may feel that things will get better. These emotions, if felt repeatedly, lead to exasperation and discouragement, which affects not only the way the child feels about the parent but also the child's physical and mental health. It is in the interest of every parent to know how to effectively repair the relationship with his child. Repairing and reconnecting will bring the relationship between the parent and child to a new level of intimacy.

If connection was good before the disruption, both sides will usually want to come back to the state of connection again; however, if the practice of one or both parties was to deny any hurtful feelings, and to simply avoid, reconnecting will be more difficult. Here's a rule of thumb—the longer you've gone without connection, the longer repair and reconnection will take. Still, it is never too late.

The process of getting reconnected involves both parent and child being vulnerable. The child will have to be old enough to talk about her feelings to be able to understand and do this effectively. If need be, the other parent or a safe adult can help to coach the child. Before describing how to be vulnerable, let us spend some time explaining this concept even further.

## Healing Comes from Being Vulnerable

When we are vulnerable, we allow ourselves to be known in an intimate way. We move toward healing as we vulnerably discuss our lifetraps, our coping styles, and their origins. We are assuming most of you feel safe enough to do this with at least one person—ideally with your spouse; alternatively, find someone else to talk to with whom you can feel safe. When we get to this point, we may discover a deep inner feeling of hurt, disappointment or fear, which we did not realize was there. When this happens, we are getting into the deep recesses of our soul. This is what experts call the "child side". This doesn't mean acting "childish", rather it is the side of us that is transparent with what we feel and need. (Children let you know when they are hungry, when they're scared, etc., without feeling embarrassed.)

Dr. Alice Miller, Dr. Donald Winnicott, and Dr. Emmet Fox, early experts in the field of child development, taught that we should experience the child side of ourselves, or our true self.[2] Dr. Charles Whitfield defines the child side as "who we are when we feel most authentic, genuine or spirited."[3]

Our child side experiences the feelings of joy and pain. It wants and needs to express these feelings without fear or judgment. This child side is who we *truly* are. It is the side that expresses what we need, when we are weak, when we are happy and contented, when we are sad, and when we are afraid. It is the side that cries at happy endings, the side that gets romantically soppy during the infatuation stage, the side that says, "I'm afraid", "I'm lonely", "I'm happy", and so forth. As adults we do not completely lose our child side; we only become good at hiding it.

When children experience unhealthy guilt or shame or fear at a young age, they are usually at a loss, and don't know how to cope with these emotions. Sadly, the people who induce such feelings are often the parents. As a result, these children, whose core emotional needs are probably not being met, develop a false sense of who they are. After all, children rely on their parents to meet their core needs. When they don't feel loved and accepted by their parents, or when the messages they receive are negative, they are powerless to know that these messages are false. When the negative messages get repeated over and over, the children believe them. When children accept these repeated distorted messages as the truth about themselves, lifetraps develop. In order to manage the pain and fear the lifetraps cause, children develop a false front in the form of unhealthy coping styles that hide their real needs and desires. They grow into adults who so habitually use their coping style, they no longer know they are shutting themselves off from their innermost thoughts and feelings. Eventually, with repetition, the child side gets completely hidden and comes out only intermittently, and the false side has now become a very natural part of their makeup and personality.

The more these adults rely on their coping styles, the less they are in touch with their child side. Moreover, the adult vocabulary is more extensive so, subconsciously, they know what to say to deter others from getting to their child side. The child side is not nurtured; the false unhealthy coping style takes over. This coping style is not the true inner self. The goal is to bring out the child side, which is genuine, sincere and teachable. It takes humility to expose the child side. When it does come out, *that* is being "vulnerable". Believing the false truths from lifetraps and masking the real self with coping styles only prolongs the pain and keeps people from healing. For example, when a parent loses his temper and quarrels with his child, he might act tough rather than be vulnerable. He might pretend that he does not need anyone and that he is fine, which is the avoidance coping style. He might cope by being busy, but in doing so would be keeping himself detached from his true child side. The coping style of avoidance may even put him on the path of addiction or being a workaholic. Whatever it is, it will prevent him from being in touch with his real self. When feelings of guilt or shame arise, he may overcompensate or counterattack in order to protect himself. Since he is not being vulnerable, the child side is hidden; a false angry side comes out instead by way of the overcompensation coping style. Then there are those who surrender because they hear a critical parent voice and give in, thinking that everything is their fault. While this may not lead to a volatile quarrel, they are still not being vulnerable, so the child side stays tucked away. Whatever the coping style, when parents respond to triggers by hiding their inner selves/child side, they will eventually become accustomed to the façade.

Speaking from personal experience, when we start being vulnerable, we will suddenly feel confusion, fear, excitement, sadness and even anger. When this happens, it is actually good news. However, many people will give up at this point because they feel awkward and hurt. It is easier to stay in touch with their old, false self and the coping style to which they have been accustomed for so long. They would rather stay with the *familiar* than move towards what's *healthier*.

As we practice being vulnerable, we should not let the awkward feelings dissuade us from pressing on. It is such a wonderful place to be, but it takes humility and courage. We may need to have a "do over" now and again, but with each attempt, we will get closer and closer to being healed. When we say "being healed", we mean getting healed emotionally, mentally, and spiritually, and as a result, attaining a sense of peace. The alternative is holding in our unhealthy feelings until they become unbearable. Our feelings have a way of coming out, whether we like it or not through our unhealthy coping styles. This may lead to all sorts of self-destructive behavior, including dependence on alcohol, smoking, over-eating, sexual promiscuity, or through counterattacking others, which damages relationships around us. While this is happening, we may numbly go about our routine.

Men are notorious for frowning at the thought of being vulnerable with anyone, let alone their children. They laugh at the idea of sharing emotions, but truthfully, it is their avoidant side that is reacting. Little do they realize that suppressed feelings lead to stress and illness; they end up experiencing less personal growth, and miss out on the benefits of getting in touch with their child side. As comfortable as we may be with our false self (coping style), our false self cannot help us get healed. Only the child side, the true self, can take us to a healthier place. So, let us get our child side out and be vulnerable! Whitfield says that most of us expose our child side for only about 15 minutes a day![4] Whether with our spouse, or children, or with other safe friends, it is time to get started.

We should be patient with each other and help each other go through this process. This is what love for each other is all about: making the effort to help ourselves and others change. As Dr. M. Scott Peck defines love in his book *The Road Less Travelled*, "[Love is] the will to extend one's self for the purpose of nurturing one's own or another's spiritual growth."[5]

## How To Be Vulnerable

When it comes to communicating in a vulnerable way, we like to think of being vulnerable as having four components:

- Weakness – Usually related to your unhealthy coping styles or lifetraps
- Feelings – What you are feeling but not in an accusing way, such as fears, worries, pain
- Needs – Core emotional needs for children and other needs and expectations for parents
- Apologizing if necessary – Taking responsibility, stating how you got triggered, how you responded in an inappropriate manner, if this was indeed the case, and apologizing for it.

Being vulnerable with each other helps a parent to know what the child is feeling when he says, "Mom, I am really angry at you for saying this", or "Dad, you just don't understand what I am thinking and feeling", or, "I don't agree with you". These are all common statements and with vulnerability something very powerful takes place—both the parent and the child will be able to truly understand and connect, which of course will greatly improve the parent-child relationship. There is something about exposing our weaknesses, feeling understood and voicing out our needs that draws us closer to one another. Usually these messages are hidden deep within us, and what comes out is our coping style, which is not helpful, and often leads us into the vortex of conflict escalation. Instead, when we are vulnerable, our hidden child side comes out, and healing takes place at an emotional level, which can be very powerful for reconciliation and connection.

Parents must learn how to put their finger on the emotions behind the coping styles (or identify how the child side is feeling), and that is what being vulnerable is all about—bringing our child side out into the open.

At www.gep.sg, we have presented different scenarios between a parent and an adolescent, and there are exercises on how both parties can practice being vulnerable. Bear in mind that after the child has been vulnerable, a lecture should not take place. What better way to shut down anyone's child side? Remember, the listening party should validate the other's feelings, summarize them back, identifying all the emotions of the other person, and say them back in a gentle tone—not lecturing (see Chapter Seven on Empathy).

Follow the steps outlined on how to validate and listen to your children. If the listening party disagrees with anything stated, this should also come from a vulnerable point of view. In this way both sides are entering into a state where they are attempting to understand and know each other's weaknesses and needs.

In all the examples on our website, we treat the components of being vulnerable separately. Please take time to do these exercises; the four components are essential and need to be memorized.

## Principles to Consider

When an argument ensues, do you as a parent take the time to reflect and gain awareness of your own issues? The following are some questions you can ask:

- What triggered me? Parents need to gain awareness of their own issues.
- Why did this trigger me? Did I get angry because my own agenda was not met, or did I get angry because I really want what is best for my child?
- Was there a sudden change in rules? If parents have been allowing children to get away with things and all of a sudden come to the realization that their kids need healthy limits, they must discuss the changes. If parents make changes abruptly, it may cause a huge reaction on the part of the children and inevitably result in a fight. Parents might try saying "Honey we realize that we have made mistakes in our parenting. We need to take responsibility for that. This part is not your fault. We have a new awareness of ourselves as parents. Especially after seeing this pattern in your behavior, we would like to discuss

with you some changes that we are going to implement. We know this is not going to be easy for you, and it is also not easy for us, but we have talked about it and we want to go over it with you." Then implement the boundaries, and this time stick to your convictions. When your children see your new stance, they will eventually come to respect it though initially they may be upset.

- Did I listen to my child empathically or did I jump to conclusions and start making judgments?
- Discuss with the other parent, if he or she was not involved in the argument. Ask them objectively and let them give you their feedback. Avoid turning this interaction into another fight, as this can make resolving the other previous one with the child even more difficult. Be vulnerable with each other.
- After reflecting on the above, be calm and be ready to be vulnerable with the child. When children are young, parents especially need to initiate. Children process tension in a very negative way and this can be detrimental to their mental health over the long haul if issues are not resolved quickly.
- Usually, if resolving conflicts quickly is a habit in the family then as the children get older they will also initiate to resolve issues. This is a good sign. If parents are still initiating this with adolescents, then this can also be an issue that parents bring up with the child, but do so after the argument is resolved. Both sides need to be in the practice of initiating. There should not be such an imbalance that only one side initiates most of the time.

## Forgiveness

Understanding forgiveness and knowing how to extend it to each other is a crucial component of a healthy family. Yet we have noticed how little emphasis forgiveness is given in major approaches to therapy. Experts and writers come up with all kinds of attending, assessment and intervention skills, but only in rare cases is forgiveness given the attention it deserves. We strongly believe that unless it is properly understood and rendered, the possibility of relapse will be high and families will not grow and change as part of their journey together. It is no doubt difficult, but it is still essential. When we forgive, all the bitterness, resentment, and anger are swept away. The negative emotional energy is gone and is replaced by feelings of light-heartedness, freedom, and peace. Indeed, forgiveness *is* the cornerstone for healing in our family relationships.

For more help on repairing and reconnecting, please review the teaching on forgiveness in the discussion of shaping our children's values (see Chapter Nineteen).

And make sure you review the huge section on meeting the core emotional need of connection and acceptance one more time (see Chapters Four to Seven).

# EPILOGUE

......................

We hope you have enjoyed the journey of *Good Enough Parenting*. You have been introduced to "lifetraps" and "coping styles", and learned how to avoid "exasperation interactions". You have become extremely familiar with the four plus one core emotional needs, and you have gotten up close and personal with our family through the Louis Lowdowns. You have read more research than you knew was out there, and you have learned how to be vulnerable, and how to repair and reconnect when the need arises.

Our dream is for parents everywhere to grow in their self-awareness, break the cycle of dysfunction, and raise loving families. We want to help moms and dads meet their children's core emotional needs, and create a legacy that leads to every successive generation becoming healthier. Hopefully you will be able to come back to these pages for reminders—"What was that second core emotional need again?" "Which one of the exasperation interactions did I do this time?" "How can I avoid the Vortex?!" Perhaps some of you will form *Good Enough Parenting* support groups in your neighborhoods and work with other parents, or organize workshops for communities, or schools. Remember that your children are not science projects, they are more like works of art…So hopefully, whether you are working on a Van Gogh, a Rembrandt or a Picasso, your masterpieces will be unique and beautiful, and will one day turn around to you and say, "Thanks for being Good Enough Parents!"

# Appendix 1

# EXASPERATION
# INTERACTIONS
# WORKSHEET

..............................

Identify the exasperation interaction(s) based on the cartoon illustration of each lifetrap. (For a larger, printable version, visit www.gep.sg)

| Lifetraps | Exasperation Interactions | | | | | | | | |
|---|---|---|---|---|---|---|---|---|---|
| | Belittling | Perfectionistic & Conditional | Controlling | Punitive | Emotionally Depriving & Inhibiting | Dependent & Selfish | Overprotective | Pessimistic | Overly Permissive |
| **Disconnection and Rejection** | | | | | | | | | |
| Mistrust | | | | | | | | | |
| Defectiveness | | | | | | | | | |
| Emotional Deprivation | | | | | | | | | |
| Social Isolation | | | | | | | | | |
| Emotional Inhibition | | | | | | | | | |
| Failure | | | | | | | | | |
| **Impaired Autonomy and Performance** | | | | | | | | | |
| Vulnerability to Harm or Illness | | | | | | | | | |
| Dependence | | | | | | | | | |
| Enmeshment | | | | | | | | | |
| Abandonment | | | | | | | | | |
| Subjugation | | | | | | | | | |
| Negativity | | | | | | | | | |
| **Impaired Limits** | | | | | | | | | |
| Entitlement | | | | | | | | | |
| Insufficient Self-Control | | | | | | | | | |
| Approval-Seeking | | | | | | | | | |
| **Exaggerated Expectations** | | | | | | | | | |
| Unrelenting Standards | | | | | | | | | |
| Punitiveness | | | | | | | | | |
| Self-Sacrifice | | | | | | | | | |

# Appendix 2

## EXERCISE ON PROCESSING EMOTIONS

••••••••••••••••••••••••••••••••••••••••••••••••••••••••••••••••••••••••••

Answering the following questions will help you to gain insight into the way you react and respond to your children's feelings:

1.  Think of some of the common types of emotions—joy, excitement, happiness, contentment, longing, anger, loneliness, embarrassment, fear, shame, sadness; feelings of betrayal, helplessness, depression; feeling unwanted or rejected. When you see any of these in your children, which ones make you feel uncomfortable?

2.  What is it about these feelings that make you uncomfortable?

3.  Which of the three broad coping styles (surrender, avoidance and overcompensation/counterattacking) are triggered when you see these emotions in your children?

4.  How does your coping style manifest when you see these feelings in your children? For example, do you blame yourself, avoid talking and leave, or get short-tempered with your children? Or let your spouse deal with these

uncomfortable emotions, or you blame yourself, or retreat by yourself and feel sad?

5. Do you behave in a similar way each time your children experience these feelings?

6. Can you remember specific incidents involving these feelings from *your* childhood? (Maybe you experienced these emotions or someone around you did.)

7. Did your parents welcome these feelings?

8. In general, how did your parents deal with *your* emotions?

9. When your parents dealt with you this way, how did that make you feel?

10. Is there anything you wish your parents had said or done instead?

11. What did you want from them?

12. In the end, how did you cope with these feelings when you were a child? What do you remember doing specifically?

13. Is this similar or different to how you deal with your children when they experience the same feelings?

14. What do you think your children wish you would do or say instead?

15. If you were to do that, how would *you* be feeling now?

16. Do you see that not talking about feelings with your children can be harmful?

# INDEX

·············

Page numbers in *italics* refer to illustrations

# ENDNOTES

·····················

**Chapter One**

1 Moore, K. A., & Zaff, J. F. (2002, November). Building a better teenager: A summary of "what works" in adolescent development, research brief. *Child Trends*, 1–5.

2 Whitfield, C. L. (2004). *The truth about mental illness: Choices for healing.* FL: Health Communications, Inc. 4–7, 253; Whitfield, C. L. (2001). *Not crazy: You may not be mentally ill.* Pennington: Muse House Press; Johnson, J. G., Cohen, P., Kasen, S., Smailes, E., & Brook, J. S. (2001). The association of maladaptive parental behavior with psychiatric disorder among parents and their offspring. *Archives of General Psychiatry, 58,* 453–460.

3 Winnicott, D. (1953). Transitional objects and transitional phenomena. *International Journal of Psychoanalysis, 34,* 89–97.

**Chapter Two**

1 Young, J. E., Klosko, J. S., & Weishaar, M. E. (2003). *Schema therapy: A practitioner's guide.* NY: The Guilford Press.

2 *Stress: The fight or flight response.* (n.d.). Retrieved May 30, 2012, from Psychologist World: http://www.psychologistworld.com

3 Maslow, A. H. (1987). *Motivation and personality, Third Edition*. New York: Harper & Row, Publishers, Inc. 27-28.

4 Ibid., 18.

5 Ibid., 31.

6 Lockwood, G., & Perris, P. (2012). A new look at core emotional needs. In M. B. van Vreeswijk, *Handbook of schema therapy: Theory, research and science* (pp. 41–66). West Sussex, UK: Wiley-Blackwell.

7 Young, Klosko & Weishaar (2003), *Schema therapy*, 10.

8 Cummings, E. M., & Davies, P. T. (2010). *Marital conflict and children: An emotional security perspective*. New York: The Guilford Press. 8

9 Ibid., 10.

10 Ibid., 28.

11 Ibid., 31.

12 Ibid., 31, 81.

13 Ibid., 102.

14 Ibid., 128.

15 Ibid., 75–76.

16 Ibid., 82.

17 Ibid., 87, 89, 157.

18 El-Sheikh, M., Buckhalt, J. A., Mize, J., & Acebo, C. (2006). Marital conflict and disruption of children's sleep. *Child Development, 77*(1), 31-43; Cummings & Davies (2010), *Marital conflict and children,* 157.

19 Hetherington, E. M. (1992). Coping with marital transitions: A family systems perspective. *Monographs of the Society for Research in Child Development, 57*(2-3), 1–14; Gottman, J., & Declaire, J. (1998). Raising an emotionally intelligent child—The heart of parenting. New York: Simon & Schuster. 141.

20 Cummings & Davies (2010), *Marital conflict and children,* 35.

21 Louis, J. P., & Louis, K. M. (2010). *I choose us: A Christian perspective on building love connection in your marriage by breaking harmful cycles.* Singapore: Louis Counselling & Training Services.

**Chapter Three**

1 Baumrind, D., Berkowitz, M. W., Lickona, T., Nucci, L. P., & Watson, M. (2008). *Parenting for character: Five experts, five practices.* (D. Streight, Ed.) Oregon: CSEE. 11.

**Chapter Four**

1 Young, J. E. (2003). *Young Parenting Inventory.* (Cognitive Therapy Center of New York) Retrieved October 4, 2011 from Schema Therapy: http://www. schematherapy.com/id205.htm

2 Teicher, M. H., Samson, J. A., Polcari, A., & McGreenery, C. E. (2006). Sticks, stones, and hurtful words: Relative effects of various forms of childhood maltreatment. *The American Journal of Psychiatry, 163*(6), 993–1000.

3 Hartt, J., & Waller, G. (2002). Child abuse, dissociation, and core beliefs in bulimic disorders. *Child Abuse and Neglect, 26*, 923–938.


**Chapter Five**

1 Perris, P., Young, J., Lockwood, G., Arntz, A., & Farrell, J. (2008). *Healthy schema inventory.* Swedish Institute for CBT/Schema Therapy, info@cbti.se

2 Mehrabian, A. (1971). *Silent messages* (1st ed.). Belmont, CA: Wadsworth.

3 Kindlon, D. (2001). *Too much of a good thing: Raising children of character in an indulgent age.* New York: Hyperion. 84.

4 Rosemond, J. (2001). *Teen-Proofing: Fostering responsible decision making in your teenager.* Kansas City: Andres McMeel Publishing.

5 Gottman, J., & Declaire, J. (1998). *Raising an emotionally intelligent child—The heart of parenting.* New York: Simon & Schuster.

6 Russek, L. G., & Schwartz, G. E. (1997). Perceptions of parental caring predict health status in midlife: a 35-year follow-up of the Harvard Mastery of Stress Study. *Psychosomatic Medicine, 59*(2), 144-149.

7 Ginott, H. G. (2003). *Between parent and child: The bestselling classic that revolutionized parent-child communication.* New York: Three Rivers Press.

8 Dreikurs, R., & Soltz, V. (1990). *Children: The challenge: The classic work on improving parent-child relationships—Intelligent, humane & eminently practical.* New York: Plume. 36–37.

9 Ibid., 57-67.

10 Elkind, D. (2006). *The hurried child: Growing up too fast too soon.* MA: Da Capo Press. 205.

11 Ibid., 211.

12 Faber, A., & Mazlish, E. (1980). *How to talk so kids will listen and listen so kids will talk.* New York: Avon Books, Inc. 18.

13 Gottman & Declaire (1998), *Raising an emotionally intelligent child*, 25.

14 Ibid., 67.

**Chapter Six**

1 U.S. Department of Health and Human Services, Administration for Children and Families, Administration on Children, Youth and Families, Children's Bureau. (2010). *Child Maltreatment 2009*. Available from http://www.acf.hhs.gov/programs/cb/stats_research/index.htm#can

2 Wong, M. L., Chan, K. W., Koh, D., Tan, H. H., Lim, F. S., Emmanuel, S., & Bishop, G. (2009). Premarital sexual intercourse among adolescents in an Asian country: Multilevel ecological factors. *Pediatrics.*

3 *How to prevent sexual abuse of your child?* (2009, February 19). Retrieved May 30, 2012, from The Parents Zone: http://www.TheParentsZone.com

4 National Center for Victims of Crime. (1997). *Child sexual abuse.* Retrieved August 31, 2012, from Network of Victim Assistance - NOVA: http://www.novabucks.org/childsexualabuse.html

**Chapter Seven**

1 Forthofer, M. S., Markman, H. J., Cox, M., Stanley, S., & Kessler, R. C. (1996). Associations between marital distress and work loss in a national sample. *Journal of Marriage and Family, 58,* 597–605; Muella, R. (2005). The effect of marital dissolution on the labour supply of males and females: Evidence from Canada. *Journal of Socio-Economics, 34,* 787–809; Turvey, M. D., & Olson, D. H. (2006). *Marriage & family wellness: Corporate America's business?* MN: Life Innovation, Inc. 11 12; Louis, J. P., & Louis, K. M. (2010). *I choose us: A Christian perspective on building love connection in your marriage by breaking harmful cycles.* Singapore: Louis Counselling & Training Services. 4.

2 Beals, D. E. (2001). Eating and reading: Links between family conversations with preschoolers and later language and literacy. In D. K. Dickinson & P. O. Tabors (Eds.), *Beginning literacy with language: Young children at home and school.* (pp. 75-92). Baltimore, MD: Paul H. Brookes Publishing; Fivush, R., Bohanke, J., Robertson, R., & Duke, M. (2004). Family narratives and the development of children's emotional well-being. In M. W. Pratt & B. H. Fiese (Eds.), *Family stories and the life course across time and generations* (pp. 55-76). Mahwah, NJ: Erlbaum.

3 YMCA. (2000). *Talking with teens: The YMCA parent and teen survey final report.* New York: The Global Strategy Group, Inc.; Doherty, W., & Carlson, B. (n.d.). *Overscheduled kids, underconnected families: The research evidence.*

Retrieved May 21, 2012, from Putting Family First: www.puttingfamilyfirst. org

4  Hersey, J. C., & Jordan, A. (2007). *Reducing Children's TV Time to Reduce the Risk of Childhood Overweight: The Children's Media Use Study.* Final report. Prepared for the Centers for Disease Control and Prevention and The Association of Preventive Medicine Teaching and Research. Washington, DC: Research Triangle Institute International.

5  Halford, J. C. G., Boyland, E. J., Hughes, G., Oliveira, L. P., & Dovey, T. M. (2007). Beyond-brand effect of television (TV) food advertisements/ commercials on caloric intake and food choice of 5-7-year-old children. *Appetite, 49,* 263–267; Harris, J. L. (2008). *Priming obesity: Direct effects of television food advertising on eating behavior and food preferences.* PhD thesis, Yale University, New Haven, CT.

6  Bowlby, J. (1988). *A secure base: Parent-child attachment and healthy human development. Tavistock professional book.* London: Routledge. 24.

7  Ibid.

8  Menehan, K. (2006). *Tiffany Field on massage research.* Retrieved May 20, 2012, from Massage Magazine exploring today's touch therapies: http://www. massagemag.com/News/2006/January/125/Tiffany.php

9  Anderson, S. (2000). *The journey from abandonment to healing: Surviving through— and recovering from—the five stages that accompany the loss of love.* New York: Berkley Books.

10  Winnicott, D. W. (1965). *Ego distortion in terms of true and false self. In The maturational process and the facilitating environment: Studies in the theory of emotional development* (pp. 140–152). New York: International UP Inc.

11  Elkind, D. (2006). *The hurried child: Growing up too fast too soon.* MA: Da Capo Press. 122.

12  Elkind, D. (2007). *The power of play: How spontaneous, imaginative activities lead to happier, healthier children.* Cambridge, MA: Da Capo Press. 3.

13  Ibid., 3–13.

14  Barber, N. (2000). *Why parents matter: Parental investment and child outcomes.* New York: Bergin & Garvey. 18.

15  Gottman, J., & Declaire, J. (1998). *Raising an emotionally intelligent child—The heart of parenting.* New York: Simon & Schuster. 143.

16  Louis & Louis (2010), *I choose us,* 17–30.

17  Ibid.

18  Elkind (2006), *The hurried child*, 124; Erikson, E. H. (1950). *Childhood and society*. New York: Norton.

19  Tan (2011, October 19), No enrichment classes? Good parenting works too.

20  Tan, H. Y. (2011, October 19). No enrichment classes? Good parenting works too. *The Straits Times*, A14.

21  Koestner, R., Franz, C. E., Weinberger, J. (1990). The family origins of empathic concern: A 26 year longitudinal study. *Journal of Personality and Social Psychology, 58*, 709–717.

22  MacDonald, K., & Parke, R. D. (1986). Parent-child physical play: The effects of sex and age of children and parents. *Sex Roles, 7–8*, 367–379.

23  Gottman & Declaire (1998), *Raising an emotionally intelligent child*, 170-171.

24  Toh, K., Chia, Y. M., & Lua, J. M. (August 28, 2012). 'Without extra lessons, our kids may lose out'. *The Straits Times*, A7.

25  Parker-Pope, T. (2012, August 23). Simon says don't use flashcards. *The New York Times*. Retrieved September 14, 2012, from http://well.blogs.nytimes.com/2012/08/23/simon-says-dont-use-flashcards/

26  Gottman & Declaire (1998), *Raising an emotionally intelligent child*, 199.

27  Christie, A. (1977). *An autobiography*. New York: HarperCollins Publishers.

28  Hartup, W., & Moore, S. (1990). Early peer relations: Developmental significance and prognostic implications. *Early Childhood Research Quarterly, 5*, 1–7.

29  Elkind (2006), *The hurried child*, 131

30  Bennett, W. J. (Ed.). (1995). *The children's book of virtues*. New York: Simon & Schuster.

31  Kohn, A. (1986). *No contest: The case against competition*. Boston: Houghton Mifflin.

32  *HealthyChildren.org - Stages of Adolescence*. (2011, May 10). (American Academy of Pediatrics) Retrieved May 20, 2012, from healthychildren.org: http://www.healthychildren.org

33  Baumrind, D., Berkowitz, M. W., Lickona, T., Nucci, L. P., & Watson, M. (2008). *Parenting for character: Five experts, five practices*. (D. Streight, Ed.) Oregon: CSEE. 11.

34  YMCA. (2000). *Talking with teens: The YMCA parent and teen survey final report*. New York: The Global Strategy Group, Inc.; Doherty, W., & Carlson, B. (n.d.). *Overscheduled kids, underconnected families: The research evidence*.

Retrieved May 21, 2012, from Putting Family First: www.puttingfamilyfirst. org

## Chapter Eight

1 Gottman, J., & Declaire, J. (1998). *Raising an emotionally intelligent child—The heart of parenting*. New York: Simon & Schuster. 20.

2 Ibid., 16, 38.

3 Baron-Cohen, S. (2011). *Zero degrees of empathy: A new theory of human cruelty*. London: Allen Lane.

4 Ibid., 4, 5.

5 Ibid., 16, 29.

6 Baron-Cohen (2011), *Zero degrees of empathy*, 42, 160; Bryer, J. B., Nelson, B. A., Miller, J. B., & Krol, P. A. (1987). Childhood sexual and physical abuse as factors in adult psychiatric illness. *American Journal of Psychiatry, 144*, 1426–1430.

7 Ginott, H. G. (2003). *Between parent and child: The bestselling classic that revolutionized parent-child communication*. New York: Three Rivers Press; Gottman & Declaire (1998), *Raising an emotionally intelligent child*; Faber, A., & Mazlish, E. (1980). *How to talk so kids will listen and listen so kids will talk*. New York: Avon Books, Inc.

8 Faber, A., & Mazlish, E. (1980). *How to talk so kids will listen and listen so kids will talk*. New York: Avon Books, Inc.

9 Ginott (2003), *Between parent and child*, 118; Gottman & Declaire (1998), *Raising an emotionally intelligent child*, 128–134

## Chapter Nine

1 Perris, P., Young, J., Lockwood, G., Arntz, A., & Farrell, J. (2008). *Healthy schema inventory*. Swedish Institute for CBT/Schema Therapy, info@cbti.se

2 Miserandino, M. (1996). Children who do well in school: Individual differences in perceived competence and autonomy in above-average children. *Journal of Education Psychology, 88*(2), 203–214.

3 Deci, E. L., & Flaste, R. (1996). *Why we do what we do: Understanding self-motivation*. New York: Penguin Books. 30.

4 *Self-determination theory: An approach to human motivation & personality*. Retrieved September 14, 2012 from http://www.selfdeterminationtheory.org/

5 Deci & Flaste (1996), *Why we do what we do*, 220; Lepper, M. R., & Greene, D. (1975). Turning play into work: Effects of adult surveillance and extrinsic reward on children's intrinsic motivation. *Journal of Personality and Social Psychology, 31*, 479–486; Lepper, M. R., Greene, D., & Nisbett, R. E. (1973). Undermining children's intrinsic interest with extrinsic reward: A test of the 'overjustification' hypothesis. *Journal of Personality and Social Psychology, 28*(1), 129–137.

6 Deci & Flaste (1996), *Why we do what we do*, 66.

## Chapter Ten

1 Lum, S. (2008, January 16). Paedophile jailed 22 yrs for sex acts on 2 boys. *The Straits Times*. Retrieved September 14, 2012, from asiaone news: http://www.asiaone.com/News/AsiaOne%2BNews/Crime/Story/A1Story20080116-45304.html

## Chapter Eleven

1 Deci, E. L., & Flaste, R. (1996). *Why we do what we do: Understanding self-motivation*. New York: Penguin Books. 33.

2 Ibid., 149.

3 *ParentFurther*. (n.d.). (Search Institute) Retrieved April 23, 2012, from ParentFurther: A Search Institute resource for families: http://www.parentfurther.com

4 Ibid.

5 Rosemond, J. (2001). *Teen-proofing: Fostering responsible decision making in your teenager*. Kansas City: Andres McMeel Publishing.

6 Popkin, M. H. (1998). *Active parenting of teens*. Georgia: Active Parenting.

7 Bryce, I., Ziskin, L. (Producers), Lee, S., Ditko, S., Koepp, D. (Writers), & Raimi, S. (Director). (2002). *Spiderman* [Motion Picture]. United States: Columbia Pictures.

8 Louis, J. P., & Louis, K. M. (2010). *I choose us: A Christian perspective on building love connection in your marriage by breaking harmful cycles*. Singapore: Louis Counselling & Training Services.

## Chapter Twelve

1 Perris, P., Young, J., Lockwood, G., Arntz, A., & Farrell, J. (2008). *Healthy schema inventory*. Swedish Institute for CBT/Schema Therapy, info@cbti.se

2 *Dr.Phil.com – advice – parenting.* Retrieved September 14, 2012, from http://Dr.phil.com/articles/category/4/

3 Henner, M., & Sharon, R. V. (1999). *I refuse to raise a brat: Straightforward advice on parenting in an age of overindulgence.* New York: HarperCollins. xvii.

4 Szalavitz, M. (2011, January 24). *The key to health, wealth and success: Self-control.* Retrieved May 20, 2012, from Time.com Healthland: http://healthland.time.com; Moffitt, T. E., Arseneault, L., Belsky, D., Dickson, N., Hancox, R. J., Harrington, H., et al. (2010, December 21). A gradient of childhood self-control predicts health, wealth, and public safety. *Proceedings of the National Academy of Sciences of the United States of America.*

5 Duckworth, A. L., & Seligman, M. E. P. (2005). Self-discipline outdoes IQ in predicting academic performance of adolescents. *Psychological Science, 16*(12), 939–944.

6 Solomon, G. *Cinemaparenting.* http://www.cinemaparenting.com

7 Hotchkiss, S. (2002). *Why is it always about you? The seven deadly sins of narcissism.* New York: Free Press.

## Chapter Thirteen

1 Behary, W. T. (2013).*Disarming the narcissist: Surviving and thriving with the self-absorbed.* Oakland, CA: New Harbinger Publications, Inc. 18.

2 Douglas, G. (2009). Pathological video game use among youth 8–18: A national study. *Psychological Science, 20*(5), 594-602; Huesmann, L. R. (1982). Television violence and aggressive behavior. In: D. Perl, L. Bouthilet, & J. Lazar (Eds.), *Television and behavior: Ten years of programs and implications for the 80's* (pp. 126-137). Washington, DC: U.S. Government Printing Office.

3 Doherty, W. J. (2000). *Take back your kids: Confident parenting in turbulent times.* Notre Dame, Indiana: Sorin Books. 138–142; *Television & Health.* (n.d.). Retrieved May 30, 2012, from California State University Northridge: http://www.csun.edu/science/health/docs/tv&health.html

4 Steyer, J. P., & Clinton, C. (2002). *The other parent: The inside story of the media's effect on our children.* New York: Atria Books.

5 *Kids-in-mind: Movie ratings that actually work.* (n.d.). Retrieved May 29, 2012, from Kids in mind: http://www.kids-in-mind.com

6 Rideout, V. J., Foehr, U. G., & Roberts, D. F. (2010). *Generation M²: Media in the lives of 8- to 18-year olds—A Kaiser Family Foundation study.* The Henry J. Kaiser Family Foundation, California.

7  Ibid.
8  Wong, M. L., Chan, K. W., Koh, D., Tan, H. H., Lim, F. S., Emmanuel, S., & Bishop, G. (2009). Premarital sexual intercourse among adolescents in an Asian country: Multilevel ecological factors. *Pediatrics*; Haggstrom-Nordin, E., Hanson, U., & Tyden, T. (2005). Associations between pornography consumption and sexual practices among adolescents in Sweden. *International Journal of STD and AIDS, 16*(2), 102-107.
9  Williams, T. M. (Ed.). (1986). *The impact of television: A natural experiment in three communities.* New York: Praeger.
10  Singer, M. I., Slovak, K., Frierson, T., & York, P. (1998). Viewing preferences, symptoms of psychological trauma, and violent behaviors among children who watch television. *Journal of the American Academy of Child and Adolescent Psychiatry, 37*, 1041–1048.

**Chapter Fourteen**

1  *Dictionary and Thesaurus—Merriam-Webster Online.* (n.d.). Retrieved July 17, 2014, from http://www.merriam-webster.com/dictionary/need
2  *Dictionary and Thesaurus—Merriam-Webster Online.* (n.d.). Retrieved July 17, 2014, from http://www.merriam-webster.com/dictionary/right

**Chapter Fifteen**

1  Cynaumon, G. (2003). *Discover your child's D.Q. factor: The discipline quotient system.* Brentwood, TN: Integrity Publishers. 20–22.
2  Suzuki, S. (1983). *Nurtured by love: The classical approach to talent education.* Miami, FL: Warner Broz. Publication Inc.
3  *Pretend play: The magical benefits of role play.* (n.d.). Retrieved May 29, 2012, from One Step Ahead: http://www.onestepahead.com
4  Faber, A., & Mazlish, E. (1980). *How to talk so kids will listen and listen so kids will talk.* New York: Avon Books, Inc.
5  Gottman & Declaire (1998), *Raising an emotionally intelligent child*, 132
6  Dreikurs, R., & Soltz, V. (1990). *Children: The challenge: The classic work on improving parent-child relationships—Intelligent, humane & eminently practical.* New York: Plume.

## Chapter Sixteen

1 Perris, P., Young, J., Lockwood, G., Arntz, A., & Farrell, J. (2008). *Healthy schema inventory*. Swedish Institute for CBT/Schema Therapy, info@cbti.se

2 Chua, A. (2011, January 8). Why Chinese mothers are superior - WSJ.com. Retrieved April 23, 2012, from *The Wall Street Journal*: http://www.online.wjs.com

3 Hofferth, S. L. (1999). *Changes in America children's time, 1981-1997*. University of Michigan's Institute for Social Research, Center Survey.

4 Maggio, R. (Ed.). (1998). *The new beacon book of quotations by women*. Beacon Press.

5 *Socrates quotes*. (n.d.). Retrieved May 28, 2012, from Goodreads: http://www.goodreads.com/author/quotes/275648.Socrates


## Chapter Seventeen

1 Goh, C. L. (2012, April 26). Singapore 'has lowest youth death rate' among rich nations. *The Straits Times*; Patton, G. C., Coffey, C., Cappa, C., Currie, D., Riley, L., Gore, F., … Ferguson, J. (2012). Health of the world's adolescents: A synthesis of internationally comparable data. *The Lancet, 379*(9826), 1665–1675.

2 Petersen, A. (2011, January 18). *How much sleep do children and teenagers need? Grown-up problems start at bedtime*. Retrieved February 10, 2012, from The Wall Street Journal: http://online.wsj.com

3 Khalik, S. (2012, April 20). Not enough sleep? Kids in S'pore sleep less than those in Switzerland: Study. *The Straits Times, C1*.

4 Cohen, D. A., Wang, W., Wyatt, J. K., Kronauer, R. E., Dijk, D.-J., Czeisler, C. A., & Klerman, E. B. (2010). Uncovering residual effects of chronic sleep loss on human performance. *Science Translational Medicine, 2*(14), 14ra3.

5 Negrini, S., & Carabalona, R. (2002). Backpacks on! Schoolchildren's perceptions of load, associations with back pain and factors determining the load. *Spine, 27*(2), 187–195; Lai, J. P., & Jones, A. Y. (2001). The effect of shoulder-girdle loading by a school bag on lung volumes in Chinese primary school children. *Early Human Development, 62*(1), 79–86; Iyer, S. R. (2001). An ergonomic study of chronic musculoskeletal pain in schoolchildren. *Indian Journal of Pediatrics, 68*(10), 937–941.

6 Morgan, I. G., Ohno-Matsui, K., & Saw, S. M. (2012). Myopia. *The Lancet, 379*(9827), 1739–1748.

## Chapter Eighteen

1  Zhan, M. (2006). Assets, parental expectations and involvement, and children's educational performance. *Children and Youth Services Review, 28*, 961–975

2  Kim, C. C. (2008). Academic success begins at home: How children can succeed in school. *Backgrounder (Published by The Heritage Foundation), 2185*, 1–12; Wimer, C., Simpkins, S. D., & Dearing, E., et al. (2008). Predicting youth out-of-school time participation: Multiple risks and developmental differences. *Merrill-Palmer Quarterly, 54*(2), 179–207.

3  Ibid.

4  Biblarz, T. J. (2000). Family structure and children's success: A comparison of widowed and divorced single-mother families. *Journal of Marriage and the Family, 62*(2), 533–548; Louis, J. P., & Louis, K. M. (2010). *I choose us: A Christian perspective on building love connection in your marriage by breaking harmful cycles.* Singapore: Louis Counselling & Training Services. 11.

5  Ely, M., West, P., Sweeting, H., & Richards, M. (2000). Teenage family life, life chances, lifestyles and health: A comparison of two contemporary cohorts. *International Journal of Law, Policy and the Family, 14*, 1–30; Ross, C. E., & Mirowsky, J. (1999). Parental divorce, life course disruption, and adult depression. *Journal of Marriage and the Family, 61*, 1034–1045; Amato, P. R., & Booth, A. (1997). *A generation at risk: Growing up in an era of family upheaval.* Cambridge, MA: Harvard University Press. 173–175; Louis & Louis (2010), *I choose us*, 11.

6  Dweck, C. S., & Leggett, E. L. (1988). A social-cognitive approach to motivation and personality. *Psychological Review, 95*, 256-273; Ablard, K. E., & Parker, W. D. (1997). Parents' achievement goals and perfectionism in their academically talented children. *Journal of Youth and Adolescence, 26*(6), 651-667.

7  Hills, T. W. (1987). Children in the fast lane: Implications for early childhood policy and practice. *Early Childhood Research Quarterly, 2*, 265-273.

8  Parker, W. D. (1997). An empiracal typology of perfectionism in academically talented 6th graders. *American Educational Research Journal, 34*, 545-562

9  Ibid.

10  Ablard & Parker (1997), Parents' achievement goals and perfectionism.

11  Ibid.

12  Deci, E. L., & Flaste, R. (1996). *Why we do what we do: Understanding self-motivation.* New York: Penguin Books. 21.

13  Ibid., 22

14 Deci & Flaste (1996), *Why we do what we do*, 38.

15 McKergow, M., & Clarke, J. (2007). *Solutions Focus Working: 80 real life lessons for successful organisational change.* Glasgow: SolutionsBooks. 54.

16 Assor, A., Roth, G., Israeli, M., Freed., & Deci, E. (2007). *Parental conditional positive regard: Another harmful type of parental control.* Paper presented at the Society for Research in Child Development (SRCD), (Boston USA).

17 Roth, G., Assor, A., Niemiec, C. P., Ryan, R. M., & Deci, E. L. (2009). The emotional and academic consequences of parental conditional regard: comparing conditional positive regard, conditional negative regard, and autonomy support as parenting practices. *Developmental Psychology, 45,* 1119–1142.

18 Rimm, S. (2006). *When gifted students underachieve: What to do about it.* Waco, TX: Prufrock Press Inc. 3.

19 Gardner, H. (1993). *Frames of Mind: The Theory of Multiple Intelligences.* New York: Basic Books.

## Chapter Nineteen

1 Levine, P. (2006, February 8). *What do parents want.* Retrieved May 30, 2012, from Peter Levine: A blog for civic renewal: http://www.peterlevine.ws

2 Tan, H. Y. (2012, March 3). What matters most? *The Straits Times*, D2.

3 Baumrind, D., Berkowitz, M. W., Lickona, T., Nucci, L. P., & Watson, M. (2008). *Parenting for character: Five experts, five practices.* (D. Streight, Ed.) Oregon: CSEE. 18.

4 Popkin, M. H. (1998). *Active parenting of teens.* Georgia: Active Parenting.

5 Baumrind, Berkowitz, Lickona, Nucci & Watson (2008), *Parenting for character.*

6 Popkin (1998), *Active parenting of teens*, 83.

7 Baumrind, Berkowitz, Lickona, Nucci & Watson (2008), *Parenting for character*, 47.

8 Ibid., 84.

9 Worthington, E. L., Jr. (1998). *Dimensions of forgiveness: Psychological research & theological perspectives.* Radnor, PA: Templeton Foundation Press. 140.

10 Enright, R. D., & Fitzgibbons, R. P. (2000). *Helping clients forgive.* Washington, DC: American Psychological Association. 29.

11 Covey, S. (1997). *The 7 habits of highly effective families.* New York: Golden Books Publishing Co., Inc. 29.

12 Enright, R. D. (2001). *Forgiveness is a choice: A step-by-step process for resolving anger and restoring hope*. Washington: APA LifeTools. 34.

13 Ibid., 28–30.

14 Ibid., 31.

15 Ibid., 218–224.

16 Seuss. (1982). *Horton hears a who!* New York: Random House.

17 Hochschild, A. R. (2012, May 5). The outsourced life. Retrieved May 31, 2012, from *The New York Times*. Sunday Review: http://www.nytimes.com

18 Clients, not practitioners, make therapy work - British Association for Counselling & Psychotherapy. (2008, October 17). *Medical News Today*. Retrieved May 28, 2010, from http://www.medicalnewstoday.com; Crabb, L. (1997). *Connecting: Healing for ourselves and our relationships, a radical new vision*. Nashville, Tenessee: Word Publishing; Lambert, M. J., & Barley, D. E. (2001). Research summary on the therapeutic relationship and psychotherapy outcome. *Psychotherapy: Theory, Research, Practice, Training, 38*(4), 357–361.

19 Block, P. (2008). *Community: The structure of belonging*. San Francisco: Berrett-Koehler Publishing, Inc. xii.

20 Rhodes, J. E., & DuBois, D. L. (2006). Understanding and facilitating the youth mentoring movement. *Social Policy Report: Giving Child and Youth Development Knowledge Away, 20*(3), 1–19.

**Chapter Twenty**

1 Toye, R. (2013). *The roar of the lion: the untold story of Churchill's World War II speeches*. Oxford, UK: Oxford University Press.

2 Whitfield, C. L. (2006). *Healing the child within*. FL: Health Communications, Inc. 1.

3 Ibid., 9.

4 Ibid., 11.

5 Scott Peck, M. (1978). *The road less travelled*. NY: Touchstone. 81.

Lightning Source UK Ltd.
Milton Keynes UK
UKOW02f0003200115

244718UK00003B/149/P